DESERT
HUMANITIES

Series Editors: Francisco Robles and Celina Osuna

Also in this series:

The Belly of the Whale:
Bilingual Edition
by Claudia Prado; translated by Rebecca Gayle Howell

Sand, Water, Salt:
Managing the Elements in Literature of the American West, 1880–1925
by Jada Ach

Wild, Weird, West:
Essays on Arid America
by Gary Reger

DESERT DISTORTION

REVEALING THE ABUNDANCE OF CONTEMPORARY BORDERLANDS ECOLOGIES

CELINA OSUNA

TEXAS TECH UNIVERSITY PRESS

Copyright © 2025 by Celina Osuna

All rights reserved. No portion of this book may be reproduced in any form or by any means, including electronic storage and retrieval systems, except by explicit prior written permission of the publisher. Brief passages excerpted for review and critical purposes are excepted.

This book is typeset in Adobe Caslon Pro. The paper used in this book meets the minimum requirements of ANSI/NISO Z39.48-1992 (R1997). ♾

Designed by Hannah Gaskamp
Cover design by Hannah Gaskamp

Library of Congress Cataloging-in-Publication Data

Names: Osuna, Celina author. Title: Desert Distortion: Revealing the Abundance of Contemporary Borderlands Ecologies / Celina Osuna. Description: Lubbock: Texas Tech University Press, 2025. | Series: Desert Humanities | Includes bibliographical references and index. | Summary: "Re-centers the deserts of the American Southwest as places of vibrant abundance"—Provided by publisher.
Identifiers: LCCN 2025025648 (print) | LCCN 2025025649 (ebook) |
ISBN 978-1-68283-262-2 paperback | ISBN 978-1-68283-263-9 ebook
Subjects: LCSH: Deserts in literature | Deserts—Southwestern States—In literature | Deserts—Southwest, New—In literature | Ecocriticism
Classification: LCC PN53.D477 O88 2025 (print) | LCC PN53.D477 (ebook) |
DDC 809.9332154—dc23/eng/20250616
LC record available at https://lccn.loc.gov/2025025648
LC ebook record available at https://lccn.loc.gov/2025025649

Texas Tech University Press
Box 41037
Lubbock, Texas 79409-1037 USA
800.832.4042
ttup@ttu.edu
www.ttupress.org

To those who call deserts home.

CONTENTS

	ILLUSTRATIONS	ix
	ACKNOWLEDGMENTS	xi
	About	3
Chapter 1:	From	21
Chapter 2:	Through	39
Chapter 3:	Above	71
Chapter 4:	Against	101
Chapter 5:	With(out)	131
	Beyond	159
	NOTES	165
	BIBLIOGRAPHY	203
	INDEX	219

ILLUSTRATIONS

5	Fig. 1: Roden Crater at sunset
73	Fig. 2: Still from *Sicario*, directly above the mountains
74	Fig. 3: Still from *Sicario*, bottleneck of traffic into US at Bridge of the Americas
74	Fig. 4: Still from *Sicario*, aerial view of bottleneck traffic
75	Fig. 5: Still from *Sicario*, overhead view of gridded neighborhood
75	Fig. 6: Still from *Sicario*, aerial view of suburban neighborhood toward desert land
78	Fig. 7: Still from *Sicario*, view with the border wall
78	Fig. 8: Still from *Sicario*, aerial view with road and border wall
79	Fig. 9: Still from *Sicario*, aerial view with border wall
79	Fig. 10: Still from *Sicario*, helicopter flying along border fence above El Paso / Juárez
81	Fig. 11: Still from *Sicario*, conversation at the base after a shootout on the bridge
83	Fig. 12: Still from *Sicario*, interagency task force walk toward the horizon at dusk
92	Fig. 13: Still from *Sicario*, cartel members moving drugs into police car trunk
94	Fig. 14: Still from *Sicario*, Kate Macer approaching busloads of migrants
134	Fig. 15: Celestial vaulting at the top of the eye of Roden Crater
152	Fig. 16: Adobe panel and portrait of bracero workers being sprayed with DDT at the Hidalgo Processing Center, 1950s
153	Fig. 17: Adobe panel by rafa esparza with portrait of San Cha
154	Fig. 18: Adobe panel by rafa esparza with portrait of Sebastián Hernández
155	Fig. 19: Adobe panels by rafa esparza with portrait of someone grabbing chain-link fence
157	Fig. 20: Standing on adobe bricks at rafa esparza's *Staring at the Sun*

ACKNOWLEDGMENTS

Writing this book has been a practice of reflection and growth. It took nearly a decade to build my vocabulary and find frameworks that would help elucidate the concept of desert distortion, and it would not have been possible without countless conversations and convenings along the way. Of course, I would not have found this direction for my scholarship as early as I did were it not for Rune Graulund's class at the University of Strathclyde. Truly, it changed everything for me, and I've been dedicated to learning more about the world's desert places ever since.

To those who mentored me and worked with me at Arizona State University, I am appreciative of the encouragement I received towards this project. It was in preparation for a conference that I first discussed distortion as a tactic, a notion spurred on by a discussion with Emiddio Vasquez. I'll never forget the ease with which he suggested I continue exploring the idea in my presentation, even if it didn't initially include desert aesthetics. Meeting with my friend Fredrick Brown at the library or a café to study and talk shop helped remind me of the endless ways that arts and humanities are meaningful. Doubt would creep in, and Fredrick would always say something brilliant to reassure me that the work we do does matter. I also want to thank Roberto Ortiz Manzanilla (Beto), who first showed me rafa esparza's work—a computer lab chat session that has influenced the trajectory of this project and my teaching ever since. To Joni Adamson, Matt Bell, Ron Broglio, Dan Gilfillan, Kevin McHugh, Adam Nocek, Sha Xin Wei, I am grateful for your questions and guidance throughout the earliest stages of this work. They have trained me to think carefully and intentionally about

ACKNOWLEDGMENTS

what critical theory and practice can do in the world. To Ruben Espinosa, thank you for your mentorship, support, and for holding the door open. You were the first professor I had who was from El Paso, and from that undergrad class until serendipitously attending your talk nearly ten years later as I was set to defend for my PhD you remained an example of what is possible despite the odds. My thanks to the Faculty Woman of Color writing group, whose consistency not just in meeting daily but also in encouragement and support helped me complete this manuscript. To Mako Fitts Ward, Vanessa Fonseca-Chávez, and Liz Grumbach I extend my gratitude for your advocacy and for the ways you created space for me and my scholarship when I didn't always know how to do that for myself.

Thanks to Travis Snyder and the team at Texas Tech University Press, who have created a wonderful home for this book. This would have been an inferior project without Travis's vision and support navigating all things press related. To Christie Perlmutter and Hannah Gaskamp, it has been an absolute pleasure working with you.

I've been fortunate in my nonlinear journey to have crossed paths with some incredible people, inside and outside of the academy. For thinking with me, hearing out my obstacles at various stages in this process, and offering support I'd like to thank Steve Abell, Jada Ach, Victoria Baugh, Kerry Banazek, Angie Bautista-Chavez, Elise Boxer, Jonathan Bratt, Grant Cameron, Jerome Clark, Lauren Alexandra Copley, Pamela Rodríguez Díaz, Joshua Filer, Travis Franks, Alice Gibson, Joshua Grant-Young, Gia and Nosrat Heidarian, Kelly Jackson, Garrett Laroy Johnson, Brian Keen, Kimberly Koerth, Diana J. López, Chawa Magaña, Kyoko Matsunaga, Emily Melser, Nat Mengist, Chris Muniz, Justin Noga, Carlos and Aida Osuna, Carlos Palacios, Gary Reger, Justin Rodier, Jesus Sabas, Asa Sakrison, Mathew Sandoval, Zach Thomas, Aidan Tynan, Lydia Zulema Martínez Vega, and Sondra Washington. I would especially like to give my appreciation to Marinela Golemi, whose friendship and moral support have been unwavering at the peaks and valleys of my scholarly life so far. Thank you for celebrating each new step with me, and for your thoughtfulness.

I'm grateful for my colleagues, students, and community members who have welcomed me at the University of Texas at El Paso and in the El Paso–Juárez and Las Cruces areas more broadly. I hope this book honors our desert home.

DESERT DISTORTION

ABOUT

/// This book is a process of convocation—a calling together of texts, experiences, ways of thought, and embodied practices. \\\

•

Halfway through the tunnel, I face a faraway circle of light. My eyes are fixed on what's ahead while my body begins leaning forward, adjusting to the steep upward incline, feeling what I can't see. With each step forward I feel smaller and the tunnel seems longer. In this near darkness, curious and disoriented, I become Alice in the liminal space of the rabbit hole—not yet in Wonderland though definitely beyond the limits of the familiar.

I realize I don't know how long this journey is going to be. As with any walking trek, I look back to gauge the distance I've come, but it's indiscernible. I'm suspended between obscurity and clarity as I turn again toward the light. It holds my gaze, drawing me forth in search of sense. I know I'm looking at sunlight, but the faraway ball of white light I saw upon entering the tunnel has since transmuted into an elongated though still round shape the color of a late afternoon blue sky. I'm trying not to blink because I want to process these changes as they happen. Moment to moment. When did the white light turn to blue atmosphere? When did the circle become an ellipse?

When I reach the top, the light at the end of the tunnel is actually the light above the end of the tunnel, and the end of the tunnel is just the start of a path to another tunnel. It's not an endless parade of tunnels, but it does make me stop and think about interconnectedness. Once I emerge, I feel like somehow I better understand how the sky meets the ground and how my focus on the light at the end of the tunnel distracted me from the fact that as the light changed throughout the journey, so have I.

The sun is setting and I'm standing at the rim of a volcanic cinder cone known as Roden Crater. From this elevation, I watch my shadow stretch to the east, from my shoes below to the horizon across (fig. 1). There is a deep redness of the dirt here in the high desert of Arizona just north of Flagstaff; it's so different from the dusty brown valleys of Phoenix or El Paso that I'm familiar with. I'm trying to be present, to soak in the dusk, but I'm also searching for the words that I'll use to describe this singular experience once I get back to my desk. I'm thinking about what elements I'll remember to describe and which will fade. I don't know if I should tell readers how windy and cold it was or if it matters that I wasn't standing there alone. The circle became an ellipse through both my movement toward it and a perceptual shift; this is an embodied version of the work I've cut out for myself with this book—the work of desert distortion.

Rather than solve the wicked problem of collapsing felt experience into text, I've decided to try and make allies with words, accepting that there are always limitations. I've especially befriended prepositions, which teach me the power of situating things within language. We work well together; they encourage engagement with *how* something is situated, and I encourage engagement with *why*. One of my favorite characteristics of prepositional phrases is you can have as many as you like in a sentence and it will still be syntactically sound. Eventually, the sentence semantically may not make much sense, but it can still radically perform the act of infinity. I won't belabor the grammar lesson, but I want to highlight the work that prepositions do connecting thoughts, keeping language in motion, and illuminating the possible. For all of these reasons, this book is structurally centered around prepositions as chapter titles and the diversity of perspectives they provide for thinking from, through, above, against, with, and beyond desert places. If you get disoriented, look to the chapter titles for guidance; they are the bright stars of this book's constellation.

THE DESERT

I had to leave "the desert" in order to know it better. In the fall of 2012, on the fifth floor of Livingstone Tower at Strathclyde University, a class convened

ABOUT

Figure 1: From the rim of Roden Crater at sunset, where its shadow and mine reach toward the horizon. (Photo credit: Celina Osuna.)

in a room where a giant window invited the thick gray clouds to think with us. The class was called *Writing the Void: Desert Literature*, designed and taught by Rune Graulund. Up to this point, I had spent the last year and a half in Scotland, adapting the best I could to the grays, greens, damp and cold. I can attest that the people in Glasgow more than make up for the dreary weather, but the lack of sunshine, heat, and aridity created incredibly difficult environmental conditions for me.

Reading over the syllabus, I was almost giddy. Not only was the discussion of deserts easing my homesickness, this was the first time I'd ever seen deserts centered as a subject of serious critical study. On our first day in session, Professor Graulund asked each of us what we expected from the class. My response, as cheeky as it was earnest: "everything." Throughout the course, the framework for my approach to literature shifted, and as the semester progressed, we engaged with deserts in world literature. I started to care deeply about how desert places were represented, taking special offense to the damage caused by the aesthetics of wilderness and wasteland, which often celebrated vastness and isolation and erased or inaccurately portrayed desert places and communities in order to valorize a protagonist or so-called nature writer in search of himself.

By the time I was applying for my doctorate, the chip on my shoulder loomed large, and it had become my mission to challenge the desert as void.

But it wasn't enough.

To say, "no, that's not right," is, on its own, not a generative method of discourse and practice. What really began to fuel my thinking and the ambitions of this book was a desire to engage, reveal, and produce generative alternatives to those portrayals of emptiness—to make the shift from lack to abundance. If deserts aren't empty or void, what are they? This has been my preferred approach of encouraging people to build more complex and robust relationships with desert places and beginning to unpack the uniqueness and importance of the earth's deserts. Sure, I had of course grown tired of stereotypical representations of desolate landscapes lined with saguaros and solitary male figures, but beyond this my interests became increasingly invested in how stale images of a generic desert void have harmful impacts on real desert places and peoples.

American literature and popular culture of the twentieth century have consistently emptied deserts of their complex histories and cultural diversity in favor of exoticism and aesthetics, enabling both erasure and extraction to occur unabated. The result of homogenizing desert places into "the desert" in human imaginations and representations has truly impacted both human and nonhuman populations. American deserts are infamously full of problematic

ABOUT

and fatal experiments like uranium mining, oil drilling, nuclear bombing, border surveillance, and militarization—it's no wonder that so many near-future postapocalyptic tales take place in deserts. For a while I was most interested in which came first: the wasteland aesthetic[1] or the colonization of land and resources? Eventually I stopped trying to figure out whether it was lived realities or desert aesthetics that started the feedback loop between the two. Instead, I seek now to interrupt it with the intervention of desert distortion, which illuminates the many ways its perpetuation has caused harm to land and people into contemporary times with no signs of slowing down.

It is clear to me that changes in perspectives and relationships to desert places are overdue, especially in the wake of the Anthropocene. Setting the stage for such changes is the purpose of this project. This book moves toward understandings of desert places as agential, full of human and nonhuman histories, complexities, cultures, and possibilities. To study deserts in this way is to practice polyphony, to embrace the palimpsest.

To this end, French philosophers Gilles Deleuze and Félix Guattari's discussion of multiplicity provides rich contexts for why adopting an approach of "both/and" instead of "either/or" could help break contemporary Western thought from centuries-old problematic binaries like mind/body and nature/culture. However, you don't have to read *A Thousand Plateaus* to understand multiplicity; you live multiplicity every day through your many roles as community member, family member, friend, plant parent, coffee drinker, etc. In order to keep the conditions of multiplicity present in language, I pluralize singular nouns wherever possible.

This is especially deliberate in my aversion to the generic phrase "the desert." It's very likely that, as a phrase, "the desert" conjures an affectively intense image of a hot, dry landscape in which, if there is a person or people present, they are in motion, in search of something, whether it's a source of water, other people, or spiritual awakening. This is the archetype of "the desert" as a harmful abstraction. In numerous presentations over the years, I have asked audiences to share their ready associations with the phrase and, though the answers do vary depending on who's present (students, colleagues, community members), invariably the elemental makes up a majority of the answers. Sand, sun, heat/hot, sky, mountains, cactus are usually offered. Then there are people who say things like home, beautiful, sunsets, family, and community, and others who name very specific phenomena (like haboob or monsoon season) or flora or fauna (like creosote, ocotillo, or coatimundi).

After I ask for these associations, I share a screenshot of a search engine image search for "the desert" and then another, more regionalized, one for "Desert Southwest." Though the technology behind the algorithms has changed over time, especially with the rise of artificial intelligence, the spread of images still conveys depictions of environments composed primarily of sand dunes, blue sky, beautiful geologic formations like Monument Valley or Arches National Park, and flora like saguaro or Joshua trees. Upon my last check, only two of the images of the first thirty show people, and in them, they are facing away, towards a distant horizon across dunes or mountains. I often wonder, and use this exercise to do so, how much of the elemental imagery (devoid of human and even animal) is algorithmically reinforced through such an online search.

I know, "the desert" just sounds cool. I can't tell you how many times I've used it or heard it used to mean "a place away from the city and/or people." But over time its use has begun to hit a raw nerve that pangs with the act of erasure. It is a phrase that obscures the diversity of the world's deserts in favor of a singular, colonial view—one that centers barrenness, void, and wasteland. As this book and much contemporary desert research attests, the longer we hold this view, the more the land is at risk to be exploited by governments and industries in ways that have had and will continue to produce detrimental effects. Taking into account that environmental racism and its injustices are not reserved for any one particular biome, Traci Brynne Voyles writes:

> wastelanding—a racial and spatial signifier that renders landscapes pollutable—is only *incidentally* about deserts. The wasteland, I argue, is a floating signifier in the Western environmental imagination: it does not always have a specific somatic or material referent, but rather it flexibly (floatingly) marks different objects, landscapes, and bodies. Deserts, thus, are not the reason for wastelanding. They are, rather, its frequent but not exclusive target.[2]

With this in mind, I urge readers to consider the ways in which "the desert" lives and performs in their vocabularies and imaginations, and to what degree it may be possible to interrogate its function as such. It may at first seem a small gesture, but replacing "the desert" with the pluralized "deserts" or "desert places" or especially mentioning the specific desert location by name immediately obscures any monolithic desert image, diffracting it into an awareness of difference and requiring a more specific attention. Pluralizing invokes the multiplicity necessary for thinking-with desert places and creates opportunities to engage with local knowledge as opposed to perpetuating an abstraction. In previous work, I've taken up cultural geographer Doreen Massey's definition of place as "a constellation of processes rather than a thing. This is place as open and as internally multiple."[3] My alignment with this perspective has only strengthened, as it is the perspective from which I can appreciate countless other perspectives.

DESERT DISTORTION

It's very unlikely that anyone in Mesa, Arizona, would *stroll* from their car to a storefront across a giant parking lot in the middle of a summer day. It's much more likely that the walk would become a journey in the 118-degree heat that makes even the closest parking spaces seem too far away. The tar, sidewalk, and vehicles all radiate visible, suffocating heat, though it's probably being seen through squinting eyes on account of unrelenting brightness. This scene is a phenomenological example of what I term "desert distortion," or the dynamic processes by which one can know deserts differently, in terms of abundance as opposed to lack. These kinds of examples are easy to find throughout well-known desert texts like Edward Abbey's *Desert Solitaire* (1968) and Reyner Banham's *Scenes in America Deserta* (1982). For Abbey and Banham alike, desert vastness, geology, and light contribute to prosodic musings of being human in a desert world. While I of course acknowledge that such elements as heat and light are pertinent to desert thinking, so-called nature writing has largely emphasized the individual (often white, male, outsider) experiences with these forces and eclipsed human and nonhuman communities of desert places as a result. It is time to decenter the well-worn narrative of the individual (hu)man taking on the fierce desert environment and its often racialized inhabitants and to pay attention to who and what the agential entanglements and communities of desert places are.

In the tunnel at Roden Crater, the circle becomes an ellipse because the circle and ellipse exist simultaneously and because I move toward or away from the end of the tunnel. Multiplicity is fundamental to the concept of distortion, which is foundationally defined by the relationality of what is or can be and that which once was and is no longer. Though there is a rich, centuries-long discourse discussing the relationships between model and copy, simulacra and simulation, original and replica, I have decided to forge ahead and embrace what Timothy Morton in *Being Ecological* (2018) calls the "distortion of distortion."[4] In other words, rather than view distortion as a singular warping or ruining of an original, pristine, or normal state, distortion can be thought of as *in medias res*, or as always-already taking place. The prior and forthcoming states are just part of what Deleuze and Guattari call assemblages, which create the conditions for their own possibilities.

The distortion of *desert distortion* is productive and takes after the distortive conditions and felt intensities of desert places. Experiencing the heat, light, and distance on a midday trek across a parking lot in the summer is entirely different from a nighttime walk in the winter, but they both allow for different ways of knowing or sensing place.[5] The theoretical work of desert distortion is to provide an inexhaustive set of lenses for engaging with histories, borders, bodies, cultures, and languages that reveal the abundance of desert places. This book, through its use of prepositions, offers desert distortion as a generative mode of engaging desert agency in texts to unsettle old understandings and allow for experiencing dynamic deserts anew. In a similar way to Anna Tsing, who invites readers to learn from the fungal flushing of matsutake mushrooms, or Jeffrey Jerome Cohen, who looks for inhuman wisdom in the lithic, I've extended my invitation to readers through what I've learned and am still learning from and with desert places.[6] Tsing affirms how the chapters that make up *The Mushroom at the End of the World* (2015) "gesture to the so-much-more out there."[7] I hope that the ever-incomplete work of this project does the same. As such, desert distortion is an invitation to inhabit the storied deserts[8] of literature and other cultural productions in order to create new collaborations of thought and practice in times of ecological emergency.

Embracing this notion and recognizing the limits for any one project, the texts examined within each chapter were carefully chosen for the important work they do in employing various modes of desert distortion. What follows are juxtapositions of literary texts, including film and visual arts, as well as theoretical frameworks from environmental humanities, Latinx Studies, Indigenous Studies, literary theory, critical theory, new materialisms,

ABOUT

posthumanism, and cultural geography. To discuss desert entanglement requires so many knots and more. These curated assemblages offer readers modes of understanding the palimpsestic realities of desert places, including their multiethnic, multicultural, and more-than-human assemblages.

In "From," my readings of three contemporary Indigenous women poets, Ofelia Zepeda (Tohono O'odham), Leslie Marmon Silko (Laguna Pueblo, Mexican, and Anglo-American heritage), and Natalie Diaz (Mojave and enrolled member of the Akimel O'odham, or Gila River Indian community), take into account their distinct desert places—the Sonoran Desert, the Arizona/New Mexico Plateau and Chihuahuan Desert, and the Mojave Desert respectively. This chapter is interested in how Indigenous cosmologies and epistemologies often rely on embodied relationships with land as relative and story as meaningful and restorative. The notion of storied deserts here is an intersection between non-Indigenous and Indigenous scholarship: ecocritics have been working towards the significance of stories, place, and nonhuman agency, and Indigenous cosmologies emerge from it. Though this book, and certainly this chapter, has a regional focus, the possible applications of thinking with storied deserts reach far beyond the geographic regions concerned, inviting readers to understand all deserts "as sites of narrative production, places where signs and imaginaries are born from the materialities of space and entanglement."[9]

In "Through," a spatiotemporal analysis of Cormac McCarthy's *Blood Meridian* (1985) explores the co-constitutions of time and place, investigating how its characters move through both during the mid-1800s, experiencing the original implementation of the contemporary US-Mexico border in the wake of the Mexican Cession and the Treaty of Guadalupe Hidalgo. Additionally, this chapter provides an ecocritical reading of McCarthy's novel in order to establish the concept of elemental immediacy, which is a fundamental contribution of this book, due to its ever-expanding applications to present-day "natural disasters" whose conditions and consequences are intensified by global climate change. Thinking about the land or climate as invariably stable or slow, for example through the framework of geological time, is interesting but far from the whole spectrum with which we should be considering desert places. Deserts are especially prone to droughts, extremes of heat or cold, and anthropogenic activities affecting climate that include nuclear testing, natural resource extraction, and waste disposal. Elemental immediacy names the quick and intense effects of natural phenomena and the land on people, places, and infrastructures. It includes events such as flash floods, forest fires, and wind or lightning storms. Their speed and immensity is overwhelming, yet they provide a legible glimpse of the hyperobject of climate change which can be otherwise amorphous or too gradual, too vast, or too complex to make sense of. These eruptions, though often devastating, can bring necessary and urgent attention to better, more sustainable and reciprocal practices of dwelling and stewardship.

Titled "Above," chapter 3 demonstrates verticality through the hierarchy of power present in Denis Villeneuve's *Sicario* (2015), where the US federal agencies, cartels, local law enforcement on both sides of the border, and migrants are shown to have very distinct relationships with the law and a malleable concept of justice. I argue that the film's cinematography, specifically its use of aerial shots via helicopters or surveillance technologies like satellites and drones, presents a desert aesthetics that challenges the "Wild West" trope of the horizon by visually emphasizing the geopolitical importance of verticality as a position of power above the law. A physical distance from the US-Mexico border maintained by the heads of federal agencies and even top cartel members throughout the film keeps those without that privilege in situations affected by governmental actions—sanctioned or otherwise.

An attempt to reflect the positionality of those who are stuck or struggling in the thick friction of the horizontal, chapter 4 is titled "Against." With a focus on bodies and borders, this chapter pivots from aesthetics to the real consequences of border policies, like Prevention Through Deterrence, which was created to alleviate culpability surrounding migrant deaths in bordered desert places of the US, and the implementation of the North American Free Trade Agreement (NAFTA), which saw both drastic increases of *maquiladoras* (factories) for making cheap goods with cheap labor and the rise of femicides in Ciudad Juárez. Luis Alberto Urrea's *The Devil's Highway* (2004) enables a discussion about the many borders—cultural, geographical, psychological, and phenomenological—that a group of migrants from tropical Veracruz encounter during their walk into the US through one of the Sonoran Desert's harshest areas. Alicia Gaspar de Alba's *Desert Blood: The Juárez Murders* (2005) depicts dangers of gendered violence in the El Paso-Juárez area for women who work in deplorable conditions at the maquiladoras. The two texts contribute to a desert hauntology of the US-Mexico borderlands, which recognizes centuries of racialized, gendered, and colonial violences and their lasting influences through trauma and place and concerns spectral connections with land, individual and collective memories, and embodied experiences.

The book's final chapter, "With(out)," takes interest in two very different contemporary artists, James Turrell and rafa esparza, and their collaborative practices with the celestial and terrestrial. While both invite strong attention to our relationships with the more-than-human, the question begged by the inclusion of two prepositions in the chapter's title is one centered around the importance of community and relationship-building in desert places. To investigate, I focus on Turrell's decades-long Roden Crater Project in Arizona and esparza's early installations producing and using adobe bricks and panels. Both have works that contribute to what I term a desert phenomenology, or embodied experiences that explore and reveal the relationships between humans and the more-than-human desert elements, where one can attune/detune/reattune to desert places or their conditions in order to know them differently, even intimately. But esparza's work with adobe also understands a lineage of colonial arts practices that have historically marginalized, erased, or excluded the work of queer people, and especially queer people of color. Working with friends and family to make the adobe bricks, what he calls "brown matter," makes inclusion and relationship-building an essential part of his practice. This is, I argue, an encouraging way to demonstrate the intrinsic values of desert placemaking, which must always include attention and engagement with community.

POLYCHROMATIC PRECEDENTS

It was pretty easy being green for ecocriticism and the environmental humanities at the end of the twentieth century. As Stephanie LeMenager and Teresa Shewry write, "green shares affective space with ideas about nature, the countryside, fertility and life. . . . Its multitude of vital referents have lifted the word 'green' toward ecology and global alternatives to supercapitalism."[10] At the start of the twenty-first century, the equation of the color green with aesthetic, pastoral beauty included the promise of sustainability in the face of global warming and climate crises, cementing the term "going green" into popular vocabulary. Additionally, as climate changes continue to raise ecological concern for resource management and ethical practices, corporations have increasingly employed "green marketing strategies to help gain competitive advantage and appeal to ecologically conscious consumers."[11] However, they also often participate in the phenomenon of "greenwashing," where "not all green marketing claims accurately reflect firms' environmental conduct" and which "may not only affect a company's profitability, but more importantly, result in ethical harm."[12] And though greenwashing has come under some scrutiny, for the most part, modifying things with green to make them sound productive or environmentally friendly has ultimately continued to reinforce green as the color of nature and vitality for newer generations. Offering some pushback, ecocritic Lawrence Buell takes the stance that "ecology as green . . . understates the potential for self-intoxicated fetishization of greenery as such, especially when channeled into out-of-control feats of bioengineering."[13]

In 2001, Scott Slovic edited an anthology titled *Getting Over the Color Green: Contemporary Environmental Literature of the Southwest*, which celebrates "the abundance of outstanding women writers and writers of diverse cultural backgrounds [that] is the hallmark of today's environmental writing from the desert Southwest."[14] The collection is great in its array of perspectives, and it contributes appreciably to the understanding of the multiplicity and value of desert places. As can be inferred from the title, Slovic also takes Americanist literature to task for its delay in recognizing "the value of vast sprawls of land devoid of human forms and lacking in the verdant, accommodating color green," demonstrating the problematic color scheme of Nature.[15] Slovic's anthology is one of several key desert scholarship texts from the turn of the twenty-first century, including David W. Teague's *The Southwest in American Literature and Art: The Rise of a Desert Aesthetic* (1997), Peter Wild's *The Desert Reader* (1991) and *The New Desert Reader* (2006), and Gregory McNamee's *The Desert Reader: A Literary Companion* (2003). With the exception of Teague's, these texts are primarily anthologies of work from and about desert places. The shift to ecocritical scholarship about deserts was most influentially established by Tom Lynch's *Xerophilia: Ecocritical Explorations in Southwestern Literature* (2008), which intentionally joins ecocriticism, literature, and an appreciation for the multiethnic, multicultural Desert Southwest. Lynch's book has set a precedent for writing about the abundance and multiplicity of desert places that my work advances.

A pause to state that as a Latina person from a desert place, it can be a point of shame and struggle that the scholars who have done this work so far are not as diverse in background as the writers that they engage—but I remain grateful for their critical contributions to the field. This lack of diversity reveals a couple of things about what one might call early work in desert humanities: first, the broader, more well-known problem of "the whiteness of mainstream environmentalism" that Wald et al. explain is "working on behalf of nonhuman nature for the preservation of wilderness or the conservation of species,"[16] and second, that the loudest voices in academic discussions about "the desert" have primarily been from people who aren't from desert places, but who fall in love with them once they spend time there. It just so happens that this is also true outside of academia; director John Ford, who pioneered the Western film genre, was from Maine, artist Georgia O'Keeffe, whose watercolors have imprinted the mountains of New Mexico into our national imagination, was from Wisconsin, and author Edward Abbey, whose call to arms to conserve what was left of his beloved desert wilderness, was from Pennsylvania. I don't point this out to insist you must be born in a desert to make films or paintings or books about desert places, but instead to highlight the absence and erasure of certain desert place–based experiences and representations in favor of others in both academia and pop culture. Perhaps, more than anything else, my intervention about the multiplicity of desert places stems from loneliness.

And so, we arrive at the blues.

Slovic wasn't the only critic to grow tired of the prominence of green: environmental humanities took a turn toward the aquatic to engage with what's often called the blue humanities. At the helm of this shift, one can find scholars like Steve Mentz and Stacy Alaimo. *Ocean* (2020), Mentz's contribution to the Object Lessons series, leaves landscape for seascape and professes that "the blue humanities name an ocean-infused way to reframe our shared cultural history."[17] In 2019 Alaimo edited a special volume of the journal *Configurations* dedicated to "Science Studies and the Blue Humanities." From the perspective of someone interested in deserts, I think that studying oceans in tandem with arid environments can be incredibly fruitful for addressing planetary concerns. Mentz has seemingly forsaken Aldo Leopold's mountain-centric "land ethic" for Rachel Carson's blue environmentalism, but, as someone professing multiplicity as an imperative mode of forming deeper connections and understandings of human and more-than-human naturecultures, I'd like to keep both and more.

Enter the volume *Prismatic Ecologies: Ecotheory Beyond Green* (2013). This collection also stems from reactions against "green exclusivism" with the hope of engaging an entire spectrum of colorful environments.[18] Each chapter is an ecological exploration of a different hue. When I first picked it up during my dissertation research, I had just spent an entire year trying to convey the relationships of color, place, and memory in Leslie Marmon Silko's *Gardens in the Dunes*. Opening the book to the table of contents, I got excited at the experiment of centering environmental thinking around specific colors. The volume has no shortage: the range is indeed prismatic, from red and pink to blue and ultraviolet. But there were also entries on chartreuse, violet-black, and x-ray, which provoked my very notion of color.

Despite the long list and the temptation to start at the beginning, I went first to the chapter "Brown," hoping to find something to fuel my own rejection of green exceptionalism. Part of me thought that surely when I got to the chapter, it would have something to do with mountains or dirt or deserts. It began: "Smelly, rancid, and impure, it is no one's favorite color. We need brown but do not like looking at it."[19] My heart sank. Only one of my assumptions was close. The author, who happens to be the same Steve Mentz of the aforementioned blue humanities, was going to talk about brown ecologies in terms of dry sand, wet swamp, and shit.[20] As someone who loves what some might call the "impurity" of brown, I was disappointed but somehow not surprised that the brown ecology put forth was not going to be one in which I could see myself. To this end Mentz addresses the awkwardness:

> This racialized brown stains my metaphors, so that it is difficult to argue that brown is the color of shit, excess, and revulsion without courting racist codes. This chapter wants to bracket race and explore brown as an organic–inorganic borderlands, a swampy terrain of hybridity and exchange. But brown logic proclaims that all things mix together, the ones you want and the ones you try to reject, living bodies and dead matter and pernicious cultural fantasies.[21]

This passage made me wonder what it must be like to be able to "bracket race" or even proclaim the want to do so in an ecological or social context.

ABOUT

All of this to say, regardless of my own fondness for the browns that for me evoke kinship with arid environments and my communities alike, I intend to steer clear of relegating the work herein to a Brown Humanities/Ecologies—which for this project would only ever be an inadequate container because in truth there are infinite amounts of vibrant colors to be found in the spectacular lights of desert atmospheres or in the skin tones of its inhabitants. I will note, however, that were this a field of interest for someone to explore further, I highly recommend the research and practice being done through Black Ecologies as a highly effective model. According to J. T. Roane and Justin Hosbey,

> On the one hand, this idea [Black ecologies] provides a way of historicizing and analyzing the ongoing reality that Black communities in the US South and in the wider African Diaspora are most susceptible to the effects of climate change, including rising sea levels, subsidence, sinking land, as well as the ongoing effects of toxic stewardship. On the other hand, Black ecologies names the corpus of insurgent knowledge produced by these same communities, which we hold to have bearing on how we should historicize the current crisis and how we conceive of futures outside of destruction.[22]

This is an approach that invites scholars and community members alike to engage with how the environmental intersects with racial, sociopolitical, and cultural identity on individual and collective levels. As Roane explains, "alongside environmental justice movements more broadly, Black Ecologies also names the ways of knowing that emerge when engaging communities at the ecological margins, taking seriously their visions for futurity and survivability in the face of disaster, and examining how this is reflected through Black expressive cultures and everyday social life."[23] A Brown Humanities/Ecologies would also necessarily engage with Black Ecologies to address centuries of Afro-Latinx erasure. Further, as with this book, it would be interested in the nuances and even the harmful legacies of mestizaje towards Indigenous peoples across North America and it would need to recognize and explore the multicultural, multiracial histories of the US-Mexico borderlands.

ABOUT

DESERT HUMANITIES

To begin to define a field is a daunting task fueled by prediction and hope. Definitions, like sand, shift with time. Though this book may be one of the first to engage the field as such, the work of Desert Humanities in the forms of art, storytelling (written and oral), and performance has been a practice of Indigenous peoples since Time Immemorial. Indigenous care, creativity, and land stewardship of the region popularly known as the Desert Southwest is vital not only for its histories but for its futures. And though the scope of my analyses in this book are firmly tied to this region, the Desert Humanities more broadly defined are interested in the flourishings of cultural thoughts and practices in the arid environments across the globe; are concerned with multiethnic human, nonhuman, and more-than-human interrelationships of desert places and the urgent care necessary for deserts and their inhabitants in the time of climate crises; and, at their core, are dedicated to the creative practices of imagination and storytelling centered from and about desert places.

Two texts published in 2020 assured me at the start of writing this book that critical conversations about desert places, both real and imagined, are evolving and increasingly necessary. *Reading Aridity in Western American Literature* is exemplary in its engagement with desert places as dynamic, and it sets its sights on provoking polyvocal discussions about the deserts of the Southwest. Editors Gary Reger and Jada Ach have produced a volume interested in "reexamining the diverse ways that arid landscapes have shaped both American and global imaginaries from the nineteenth century to today" with an intent to "cultivate new environmental modes of human-environmental engagement and activism."[24] In his book *The Desert in Modern Literature and Philosophy*, Aidan Tynan notes that "an exploration of the desert in modern literature and philosophy is able to speak in important ways to our contemporary environmental condition," and thus maps out a myriad of literary deserts in order to push critical thought about what a desert is or can be, and how their representations can teach us during unprecedented ecological crisis.[25]

Another source of reassurance that there is plenty of interest in Desert Humanities stems from the years that Aidan and I spent collaborating on the edited volume *Storied Deserts: Reimagining Global Arid Lands* (2024), which highlights how the storied matter of the Earth's deserts informs lived realities, environmental histories, cinematic and literary imaginaries, political conflicts, and even intellectual categories such as "the human" and "the elemental." During the process of working on the volume, we started to discover that there are many people producing exciting and insightful research on the world's desert places, which was a welcome change from feeling otherwise isolated in our interests.

There is also plenty of scholarship that may not consider itself to be under the umbrella of Desert Humanities but that can be read for its attention to relevant, arid place-based themes. For example, a book like Myrriah Gómez's *Nuclear Nuevo México* (2022) is undoubtedly a powerful text that I would suggest to anyone seeking a critical look at the impacts that the Manhattan Project, mining, and nuclear testing have had on the area's communities. Gómez's intention to write about nuclear colonialism and its origins in New Mexico is strengthened by her perspective as someone impacted by the very histories she's examining.

In the years I've held on to—I mean, revised—this manuscript, ever more scholarship and popular culture with clear interests in desert places and peoples has been produced. A few edited collections like *The Invention of the American Desert: Art, Land, and the Politics of Environment* (2021), *Deserts Are Not Empty* (2022), and *Desertscapes in the Global South and Beyond* (2023) have been published; a group known as the Desert Futures Collective, hosted by Yale, has held workshops and symposia; and another interdisciplinary group based in Mexico, ALTAR Centro de Investigación, has hosted a series of virtual discussions about life in arid lands around the world. And these are just the projects that I'm currently aware of, though more emerge all the time. Outside of academic spaces, television and cinema have seen a resurgence for deserts through the undertakings of Denis Villeneuve's *Dune: Part One* (2021) and *Part Two* (2024), *Nope* (2022), *Dark Winds* (2022), *Asteroid City* (2023), *Furiosa: A Mad Max Saga* (2024), *Oppenheimer* (2023), *High Desert* (2023), and many others. Even *Barbie* (2023) has a desert scene.

My entire life I've known the abundance that deserts hold, though I haven't always had the vocabulary or access to discourses or a platform to affirm this sentiment. The work of *Desert Distortion* is of building a lexicon and hopefully an audience who will recognize that this book brims with wonder and possibilities as much as it relays felt and intense realities of desert existences. In coming to understand desert distortion as a tool for engaging desert humanities, I hope that readers will be challenged to think through varying perspectives. Where

ABOUT

does wonder intersect with fear? With justice? How do identity and place transform one another? When does the circle become an ellipse?

CHAPTER 1

FROM

"The four (or more) cardinal directions generally serve as allegories for sacred orientations to places in Indigenous traditions. Each has associated plants, animals, and natural phenomena. And each of the plants and animals represents a perspective, a way of looking at something in the center that humans are trying to know. The idea of moving around to look from a different perspective, from the north, the south, the east, and the west, and sometimes from above, below, or from within, is contained in the creative process. Everything is like a hologram; you have to look from different vantage points to understand it. In the Indigenous causational paradigm, movement is relational, or back and forth in a field of relationships, in contrast to Western science's linearity (A to B to C and so on). Indigenous logic moves between relationships, revisiting, moving to where it is necessary to learn or to bring understandings together. Eventually this process, a synthesis, leads to a higher reflective level of thinking."
—Gregory Cajete, *Native Science*, 210

CLARITY

As a step toward unsettling the desert-as-void thinking that arrived with European colonizers at the turn of the fifteenth century and has transformed and intensified in scope and scale ever since, this book begins with

CHAPTER 1

deliberate attention to Indigenous writers whose lived experiences, stories, and imagined futures carry their long-lasting ties to desert places as home. To this end, I aim to establish a firm understanding that "the importance Native Americans traditionally place on 'connecting' with their place is not a romantic notion that is out of step with the times. Instead, it is the quintessential ecological mandate of our time."[1] This is notably felt in the region commonly known as the Desert Southwest, where, in the wake of the Anthropocene, hyper-industrialization during the past century has intensified widespread socio-environmental injustices and climate change while increasingly threatening all human futures on this planet.[2] Throughout my research, I've repeatedly found that the tendency of Western humanities scholarship to overlook the biodiversity of desert places includes similarly glossing over the Indigenous peoples who inhabit them.

To someone not from a desert place, the landscape—real or imaginary—is vulnerable to becoming a background object upon which action occurs instead of a vibrant environment in which the elemental forces and other than human persons have agency. Flattening the land means flattening life from the land, and flattening Indigenous cultures is a practice consistent with the colonial project. European colonizers degraded, enslaved, and committed acts of genocide against multiple Indigenous communities across the arid American West long before it was claimed as American territory, and they brought their perceptions of desert places as wasteland with them as a justification for doing so. As settlers wrote about their experiences encountering and exploring present-day Mexico and the Southwest, they created a narrative of peoples and places that were inhospitable. Famously, Spanish conquistadors arriving in the late fifteenth century searched for gold and silver to plunder, and by the eighteenth century, various additional metallic and mineral resources were sought and extracted by various additional European empires—regardless of the destruction to and disruption of various ecosystems and communities. When the US War with Mexico ended in 1848, Northern California became a magnet for anyone in the nascent nation hoping to strike it rich by prospecting for gold. Less well known than the Gold Rush is that the first governor of California, Peter Hardeman Burnett, armed and supported militias across the state with the overt purpose of murdering Indigenous people, arguing in his 1851 Governor's Message "that a war of extermination will continue to be waged between the races until the Indian race becomes extinct, must be expected."[3] Bounties, encouraged by the state though not the nation, were being provided at local levels for the exchange of Indigenous scalps.[4] And so, many Anglo-Americans in California "advocated and carried out a program of genocide that was popularly called 'extermination,' and in the process thousands of California Indians were killed."[5] I discuss the California Gold Rush's impact on Indigenous people of the area in further detail in the next chapter but bring it up here to demonstrate how violence across the land and towards its people continued as droves of settlers traveled west with little or no regard for either.

Settler colonial depictions of land and people evolved over the course of the twentieth century, as literature and other mediated pop culture breathed new life into harmful representations of Indigenous North Americans in films, novels, television shows, and even product advertisements. These depictions cultivated and reinforced centuries-long misbeliefs of Indigenous peoples as either "noble savages" belonging to an ossified past in which all lived in some primitive harmony or the last of their people, a portrayal perpetuating the "vanishing Indian" myth—false narratives that proliferated alongside settler colonialism.[6] Chippewa scholar Gail Guthrie Valaskakis posits, "neither representation allows newcomers to identify Native peoples as equals, or to recognize Native North Americans as 'real inhabitants of a land.'"[7] Indeed, these misrepresentations eclipse the rich intergenerational experiences and distinctive worldviews of Indigenous communities whose various creation stories tell how they emerged from and live with the land.

A prism, when held up to a white light, will refract that light into a whole spectrum of colors. Each hue travels a different speed as it passes through the glass. Homogenizing individual and collective Indigenous experiences is a perspective that cannot discern the beam of light from the rainbow; it sees one but not the many, and fails to see the multiplicity in either the one or the many.[8] For example, a single color on the spectrum contains various intensities within itself; navy and cerulean coexist as different shades of blue, only slightly varying in wavelength and frequency. Understanding the scope of colonial violence inflicted upon Indigenous peoples means acknowledging the range of intensities within it. Immediate and "slow violence" exist simultaneously.[9] Governor Burnett's aforementioned orders to kill Indigenous people in the mid-nineteenth century and the act of kidnapping children from their families for the purpose of slavery and acculturation are examples of immediate violence, while slow violence includes the resulting intergenerational trauma and loss thrust upon and inherited by Native peoples on account of federal governments displacing, exploiting, and killing entire populations. Yet there is also a slow violence to the notion of a unified Indigenous experience as something that must be centered around loss and trauma. Steadily, it contributes to a dangerously abstract idea, ignoring all other aspects of Indigenous existence like creativity and joy. Valaskakis attests that, "like other peoples of colour who are positioned outside the perimeters of dominant continental cultures, Indians battle historical projections of invisibility and exclusion that absorb the realities and specificities of their cultures."[10] Over time, this abstraction erases complex understandings about Indigenous histories, cultures, and places—learned *from* Indigenous peoples—and produces a whitewashed narrative to maintain the ultimate goals of settler colonialism, which seeks to destroy, assimilate, and abuse. It is the white light turned to blue, preventing the possibility needed for a rainbow.

Historically, this mode of abstraction applied to Indigenous communities from desert places demands defining Native communities by the losses they have suffered instead of by their joy, presence, and *survivance*, and it echoes the mode of abstraction that helps sustain representations of deserts as barren, lifeless spaces and vice versa—absence amplified.[11] It is the reason that familiar portrayals of deserts in literature, film, and visual art often lack people and most other forms of life. These are particular kinds of stories told about deserts, really *the* desert, as either an exotic or empty space of extreme possibilities that Aidan Tynan investigates in terms of "wasteland aesthetics" in *The Desert in Modern Literature and Philosophy*—which he traces from a lack of representation of or engagement with deserts through silence and omission to a rise in disgust for deserts in seventeenth and eighteenth century travel writing, through to the British Romantic writers who "came to be inspired by the new possibilities offered by waste spaces of various kinds" and thus influenced modernist, postmodernist, and contemporary authors like T. S. Eliot, William Burroughs, Cormac McCarthy, Octavia Butler, and Margaret Atwood in their conceptions of deserts and wastelands.[12] The shift from disgust to fascination with wasteland aesthetics over the past few centuries, Tynan argues, "was made possible by a new imaginary of landscape in which affect and environment came to reflect one another" and has impacted not only literature but the philosophy of Nietzsche, Heidegger, Derrida, and

Deleuze and Guattari as well.[13] Tynan admits that his work offers "*not* a view of the desert as a natural wilderness, nor does it pursue an ecocritical reading of the desert in any kind of traditional sense" but instead it holds "that the desert in literature and philosophy can tell us some important things about the experience of being modern."[14] He elaborates: "modernity finds, and indeed must find, ways to aestheticise and thus absorb its limits, its uncertain borders and cutting edges. This, I claim, is what gives rise to an aesthetic fascination with the desert as a site from which modern experience comprehends the spatial alterity through which it must inevitably pass."[15] Tynan's wasteland aesthetics is a foundational concept to critical thought about deserts, confronting readers with the tensions between space and place, local and global, and realities and imaginaries, and has informed my own approach to exploring both tensions and aesthetic fascinations with deserts.

While Tynan deliberately steers clear of a traditional ecocritical reading of literary and local deserts in order to think through a global lens and "widen the parameters of what constitutes the desert as a critical object," in this chapter I wish to engage ecocriticism most directly.[16] The field's attention to the simultaneous exchanges between arid environments, affect, and especially narrative, as a result of the materialist turn—a development in Western scholarship that provides a vocabulary with which to think about nonhuman agency—has been generative for my thinking through desert distortion and emplacing it locally in the texts and environments of the so-called Desert Southwest.[17] Italian scholars Serenella Iovino and Serpil Oppermann are well known in environmental humanities for their work on material ecocriticism, which as a field "shed[s] lights not only on the way agentic matter is narrated and represented in literary texts, but on matter's 'narrative' power itself. Matter, in all its forms . . . becomes a site of narrativity, a storied matter, embodying its own narratives in the minds of human agents and in the very structure of its own self-constructive forces"[18] This has been a vital contribution to environmental humanities and beyond, resulting in more thoughtful discussions about entanglements of human and more-than-human assemblages. Attention to stone, water, animals, and the vegetal are important in this urgent time of climate crises.[19] As storied matter, I argue geographic and imaginary deserts are such "sites of narrativity," from which a plethora of stories continually emerge.

CHAPTER 1

Indigenous peoples have always defined their existences by listening to and creating stories from the land, though perhaps one of the biggest disconnects between traditional Indigenous lifeways and traditional Western epistemologies is how each regards the significance of Indigenous stories.[20] While the former has centered stories as vital to community, cosmology, and future-making, the latter has typically relegated Native stories to "folklore, not history, construct[ing] Indians as historyless vagrants without an authenticated written past."[21] In truth, all history is storytelling, and stories, written, verbal or otherwise, are always subject to interpretation, adaptation, and eradication—and they matter. In her book *Braiding Sweetgrass*, biologist and writer Robin Wall Kimmerer (Potawatomi) writes, "The traditional ecological knowledge of indigenous harvesters is rich in prescriptions for sustainability. They are found in Native science and philosophy, in lifeways and practices, but most of all in stories, the ones that are told to help restore balance, to locate ourselves once again in the circle."[22] Fortunately, material ecocriticism seems to buck the trend of considering story as ineffectual or esoteric and aligns much more closely with the idea that stories construct more robust, complex relationships with place—that stories are restorative. For me, this is an incredibly interesting intersection between non-Indigenous and Indigenous scholarship: ecocritics have been working *towards* the significance of stories, place, and nonhuman agency, and Indigenous cosmologies emerge *from* it.

Gregory Cajete writes, "Native cultures describe their place as a living presence in the context of its mythic and spiritual meaning. The storied and living homeland[s] of Native cultures provide a holistic foundational context for Native life and participation with the universe and illustrates the primacy of space and place in Native cosmology."[23] Ergo, land and stories co-constitute one another. To explore desert distortion, the rest of this chapter engages with the meaning of land from Indigenous perspectives and poetry, but in the parlance of critical theory and environmental humanities, "land" henceforth encapsulates nonhuman, more-than-human, other than human, and inhuman agencies; it is the storied matter which should be encountered "*in* texts and *as* a text, trying to shed light on the way bodily natures and discursive forces express their interaction whether in representations or in their concrete reality."[24]

FROM

DISTORTION AS TECHNIQUE

In 1958, rock and roll guitarist Link Wray released his most famous song, "Rumble." Though it's not particularly fast and despite a lack of lyrics, its sound had an unprecedented affective quality that feels eruptive. Wray's tune was banned from radio stations in some cities "for fear it might actually incite gang violence—the first and only instrumental song to be banned from the air."[25] The provocative tone was not accidental. Initially, the song was a product of improvisation during a show, but when it came time to record in the studio they couldn't quite capture the show's live essence. In a search to mimic the sound of the first performance's wild atmosphere, Wray grabbed a pencil and made history. He took the writing utensil and "punched holes in the speaker of his guitar amp and turned it into a fuzzbox, the first of its kind."[26] Link Wray's experiment helped pave the way for the astounding array of music genres popular today, most of which employ distortion as a technique explored through things like guitar pedals, tube amplifiers, and even auto-tune. With its roots in the material conditions of an amplifier, a guitar, and a microphone, distortion became an endless source of play and possibility in the world of music.

Poetry similarly uses distortion, playing with line breaks, word meanings, and page layout to explore possibilities of form and language. In this chapter, I bring together the poetry and writing of three Indigenous women from three different tribes and three different deserts across the US-Mexico borderlands: Ofelia Zepeda, a Tohono O'odham poet and professor of linguistics; Leslie Marmon Silko, a poet and author of Laguna Pueblo, Mexican, and Anglo-American descent; and Natalie Diaz, a Mojave poet and enrolled member of the Akimel O'odham (Gila River Indian Tribe). Bundled together here, their poetry provides distinctive Indigenous perspectives about desert places and helps illustrate that "Native cultural differences are braided in a web of narratives and practices from the tribalized past that are intertwined with the disordered experiences of the present; and this 'difference' explodes into millions of differences, tiny or huge, that one picks up by living their culture."[27] Each poet provides readers with insights to what it's like to be from a desert, to call a desert home not just in terms of dwelling but in a true sense of belonging to and having been created by the land.

I encourage readers to think about desert distortion in the same way I've just discussed distortion in poetry and music: as a desirable technique emerging from entanglements with desert places—their stories, their material conditions and felt intensities, and their representations—through which the human "we" can become better kin to our other than human relatives.[28] To expound upon what I mean by being better kin, I turn to Kim TallBear (Sisseton-Wahpeton Oyate), who writes:

> Making or creating kin can call non-Indigenous people (including those who do not fit well into the "settler" category) to be more accountable to Indigenous lifeways long constituted in intimate relation with this place. Kinship might inspire change, new ways of organizing and standing together in the face of state violence against both humans and the land.[29]

Desert distortion is a step towards this kind of making and creating kin, especially for non-Indigenous people. It's my deepest hope that such kinship with desert communities and places will indeed inspire change beyond thinking differently and will result in more ethical, just, and creative practices—towards healing and better environmental futures for all.

In *Braiding Sweetgrass*, Kimmerer describes what Indigenous communities in the Great Lakes refer to as "the Original Instructions": "These are not 'instructions' like commandments, though, or rules; rather they are like a compass: they provide an orientation but not a map. The work of living is creating that map for yourself. How to follow the Original Instructions will be different for each of us and different for every era."[30] Desert distortion is an unending process of orientation, reorientation, and even disorientation through which I hope readers will learn to appreciate desert places. Using Kimmerer's analogy, I consider Zepeda, Silko, and Diaz as cartographers with their own unique ways of using orienting arrows, lines, and language respective to their communities' cosmologies and their individual experiences; their words are tools with which to navigate being-with and from desert places that centralize Indigenous relationships to land and decentralize harmful representations of land and people outlined earlier. By bringing together these three poets, I invite readers to embrace the processes of (re-/dis)orientations and know that "the idea of moving around to look from a different perspective . . . is contained in the creative process. Everything is like a hologram; you have to look from different vantage points to understand it."³¹ The rest of this chapter examines desert distortion through the concept of storied deserts, "moving to where it is necessary to learn or to bring understandings together."³²

STORIED DESERTS

> He begins, "The first time I saw the place
> where clouds are formed was from
> the window of a train . . ."
> Another time was in a mirage
> in the heat outside Tucson.
> Once he thought he saw it in the dry light of stars.
> The place he remembers best
> was when he saw it in the eyes
> of a woman he spoke to.³³

The poem that opens Ofelia Zepeda's *Where Clouds Are Formed* echoes the collection's title with its own: "The Place Where Clouds Are Formed." In its first part, the poem's speaker describes a relationship between a man and a woman where the woman asks the man to tell a story she doesn't want to hear; in truth, she only tells him she wants to hear the story because his breath creates cool condensation on a "dry June day" and "each aspirated sound" provides her with some respite.³⁴ The atmosphere of oppressive desert heat established, the above lines introduce readers to the man's story. It quickly becomes clear that the place where clouds are formed has no one fixed location but many emergent ones—it exists in the starlight, in another's eyes, in a mirage, and in the poem through his memories and storytelling. Where mirages tend to be disorienting, the one recalled in the poem is a way for the man to reorient his relationship to this specific place. Most common in deserts, a mirage is a phenomenon co-constituted by heat, light, and perceiver where the bending of light and the difference in air temperatures create optical illusions that confront what one sees with what one knows. Desert distortion teaches that both are real; it's a difference of feeling and thinking, a difference that produces the multiple. The place where clouds are formed transforms with each memory, and Zepeda conveys these memories through an elemental sense of desert place—using

CHAPTER 1

heat, light, and aridity—revealing a stratified understanding of multiplicity, a record of the possible.

The second part of the poem switches seasons and subjects, and instead of an emphasis on human stories in the heat of summer, readers bear witness to nonhuman relationships near the peak of winter:

> clouds, mist find solace in the canyons of the Santa Catalina
> Mountains.
> White moisture quietly moving amid the cactus.
> Truly, clouds, wind, and rain are the few elements
> that can touch the saguaro from head to foot.
> Oblivious of spines, needles.[35]

Rather than a static scene of an exotic landscape, the speaker observes the more-than-human elements with deep familiarity as they actively engage one another. Much like the first part of the poem, the imagery Zepeda uses here has specific, emplaced referents to her Tohono O'odham community's desert homelands. And, something more than a landscape description is going on; the nonhumans of the poem are active, the clouds and mist are not just being, they are *doing*, searching for a place to rest between the mountains. The desert place of this part of the poem is full of movement and possibility—of "elements that *can* touch the saguaro from head to foot"—and operates according to "the Native cosmological assumption that we live in an interrelated living world in perpetual creative motion."[36] In the poem as much as in life, the clouds, wind, rain, and moisture are never still. Zepeda here gives readers a glimpse at what critical theorists might term nonhuman phenomenology, rooted in her Tohono O'odham lifeways that recognize land as relative, extending personhood to the saguaro cactus as something to be caressed, *en totale*, by the elements—an embrace that no human can perform. Such intimate interactions between cacti and cloud, "oblivious of spines, needles," perpetuate the possibility of desert place beyond the human.

Most often, if someone asks you where you live, you'll answer differently depending on where that person is asking from. If they're in a different country, they might be asking for the name your country; if they're in a different state or province, they may want the name of your state or province and even your city; and if they're in your city, they may want the name of a neighborhood or cross streets. Each of these examples holds place names as the common factor for orientation while adjusting to scalar differences. In "The Place Where Clouds Are Formed," the speaker uses specific place names like Tucson and the Santa Catalina Mountains to situate readers within the Sonoran Desert. The sense of place is amplified by mention of the saguaro cactus, which is a way of naming the region through its native flora. In another of Zepeda's poems, "Proclamation," the speaker explores the value of place names in O'odham, English, and "forgotten languages / heard even before the people arrived."[37] It begins by naming a place in three different ways:

> Cuk Ṣon is a story.
> Tucson is a linguistic alternative.
> The story is in the many languages
> still heard in this place of
> Black Mountains.[38]

Opening with the O'odham word for the place that many non-O'odham people recognize through the signifier Tucson, Zepeda demonstrates how her native language engages with naming—beyond representation—as a practice of story. The iteration of different names for what could be considered the same place invites readers to take into account the multiple perspectives and possibilities of place(making), which is built upon individual and collective interrelationships to a place and its many stories. In this case, the story of Cuk Ṣon tells readers that long ago the land shaped the O'odham people and how they have shaped it since and are shaping it still. As the poem continues, the speaker makes reference to a single "true story of this place," but this one story contains infinite others. It "recalls people walking / deserts all their lives and / continuing today, if only / in their dreams."[39] The vastness of deserts lends them well to such imagery, filled with memories, bodies, dreams, and spatiotemporal distances. Zepeda conveys the constant convening of time and space by describing her people's perpetual motion; for them the place's true story is "ringing / in their footsteps," and is many stories over many lifetimes as they continue connecting themselves to the land and "give shape to the / mountains."[40] These practices affirm relationships between language, place, and possibility from a Tohono O'odham perspective, influencing perception and lived realities with the land of the Sonoran Desert.

CHAPTER 1

Like "The Place Where Clouds Are Formed," "Proclamation" contains examples of place as multiple. Both of Zepeda's poems recognize the Sonoran Desert as it is—storied. Keeping in mind Iovino and Oppermann's definition of storied matter, as discussed earlier, and centering Indigenous approaches to stories as vital to community histories and futurities, I suggest storied deserts as a way to acknowledge and engage desert places as agential, biodiverse, and full of memory and wonder while also interrogating depictions of deserts as wastelands. As demonstrated throughout this chapter, such a concept is not new to Indigenous peoples from desert places, but it is important now more than ever for non-Indigenous people to look to Native worldviews of land, place, and environment and learn to be better relatives. As Gregory Cajete reminds us, "Native people were the first ecologists, as the mythologies, understandings, and technical knowledge were always directly tied to specific ecologies, or specific regions, plants, and animals."[41] Perceptions of deserts will only change when peoples from desert places are centered as specialists, when everyone understands that deserts, like all places, are richly and uniquely storied. The theoretical work of desert distortion, for which storied deserts is an imperative, provides an inexhaustive set of lenses for examining the reciprocal binds between place, stories, and animacies that reveal the multiplicity and possibility of desert places.

From a Laguna Pueblo perspective, Leslie Marmon Silko describes that these binds can be so tight that sometimes "it is impossible to determine which came first, the incident or the geographical feature that begs to be brought alive in a story."[42] Silko explains that because Pueblo people, whose homelands are located in the eastern half of the Arizona/New Mexico Plateau, were not displaced from their land "like so many Native American groups who were torn away from their ancestral land . . . [Pueblo] stories are so much a part of these places that it is almost impossible for future generations to lose them—there is a story connected with every place, every object in the landscape."[43] To be from the land, for Silko, means that her people can still point to almost anywhere and feel connections to their creation stories, community histories, and lived realities. The differences illuminated here not just between Pueblo and other Native peoples, but especially between Indigenous and settler colonial relationships to and perceptions of desert places, are drastic. Where Indigenous peoples encounter their histories, their emergences, their connections with desert land as relative, settler colonizers have historically seen exotic, mysterious, or threatening territory. Further, the perceived lack, the narrative of emptiness, wasteland, and void imposed onto deserts, is a reflection of the real lack of deep relationships settler colonizers have maintained with desert places. As Voyles writes, "Remaking Native land as settler home involves the exploitation of environmental resources, to be sure, but it also involves a deeply complex construction of that land as either always already belonging to the settler—his manifest destiny—or as undesirable, unproductive, or unappealing: in short, as wasteland."[44]

In her collection *Storyteller*, originally published in 1981, Silko brings together her community's oral histories as told, remembered, and written. It includes poetry, short stories, recollections, and photographs of her family and community, providing a depth of experiences to readers beyond the written word. Among these is an unnamed poem recollecting and retelling a story Silko's Aunt Alice told her when she was a child. Like many of the pieces in *Storyteller*, it is about Kochininako, or Yellow-Woman, who "represents all women in the old stories."[45] In this piece, Kochininako is a young girl and good hunter who comes across a giant animal called Estrucuyu. When the animal asks Kochininako to give him the rabbits she's just hunted, she does so until there are none left. When there are no more animals, Estrucuyu keeps demanding she give him everything she has, including her bow and arrows and the clothes off her back. After realizing there will be no appeasing his unending desire and that she is in danger, Kochininako tricks Estrucuyu and hides in a nearby cave too small for him to enter. She calls for the Twin Brothers, or Hero Brothers, to help her. They quickly show up to rescue Kochininako from peril, severing Estrucuyu's head and cutting him open. They take his heart out of his chest and throw it:

> *those things could happen*
> *in those days—*
> and it landed right over here
> near the river
> between Laguna and Paguate
> where the road turns to go
> by the railroad tracks
> right around
> from John Paisano's place—

> that big rock there
> looks just like a heart,
> and so his heart rested there
> and that's why
> it is called
> *Yash'ka*
> which means "heart."[46]

This is how the piece ends, with a journey through time that recounts how Estrucuyu's heart became part of the land, became rock, became storied desert. As a being of the days when such things could happen, the giant animal's heart-as-rock has borne witness to its own geologic formation in a time only land can remember. Since then, as the story indicates, roads, railroad tracks, and houses have been built, contributing new elements to the storied desert of the Laguna Pueblo people. Each line, with the help of prepositions, reveals another way to orient the heart's location and the stanza thus stratifies time so that one can better understand its plasticity—a beautiful distortion of time which emplaces past and present alongside one another. This stratification includes the italics at the beginning of the excerpt, which express Silko's own reflections of the story and offer an additional layer to her retelling of her Aunt Alice's retelling. In this way, Silko's italics inform readers of her story within the story, a "perspective on narrative . . . [that] represents an important contribution of Native American cultures to the English language" as it holds that "one story is only the beginning of many stories and the sense that stories never truly end."[47] Yash'ka is at once the giant rock, the giant's heart, and the word for heart; the rock itself both resembles and is Estrucuyu's heart. Multiplicity tells countless stories through desert distortions, through orienting and reorienting, through iterations, and through space-time.

Zepeda and Silko's poems engaged here illustrate the unique relationships of their respective Indigenous communities to their desert places. And just as their stories about place provide multiple layers of meaning and endless opportunities for possibility, place itself creates those same conditions. In my work on color, place, and memory in Silko's *Gardens in the Dunes*, I employ the following definition of "place as event" from geographer Doreen Massey: "a constellation of processes rather than a thing. This is place as open and as internally multiple."⁴⁸ This definition remains one of the most salient for my work with desert distortion, which requires place to be internally multiple. In this context, thinking of place as event intersects with Indigenous perspectives of place dating back to Time Immemorial. If you are not from a culture that already appreciates this view, place as event is a great way to remember the dynamism of storied deserts.

And while this understanding of place is and should be accessible to all, Indigenous cosmologies are primarily rooted in stories and specific places that connect them to how their people came from the land. From this connection comes a depth of understanding that spans every generation since their creation. As another demonstration of the importance of names as stories, Indigenous names for their own people often reflect relationships between people and place: Tohono O'odham translates to "Desert People," Laguna Pueblo means "lake people," and Mojave means "beside the water," and each of these communities is built upon intimate understandings of their storied deserts.⁴⁹ As a tool for non-Indigenous people who might be unfamiliar with the complexities of desert places, the concept of storied deserts creates and encourages deepening connections with these environments. Sometimes this tool is helpful for parsing scalar phenomenological encounters of geologic time, vast distances, and extreme heat and sometimes because it challenges antiquated and harmful notions of empty deserts and vanished cultures.

And more than using story as a narrative methodology, this approach takes up storytelling as an epistemology. In Michi Saagiig Nishnaabeg scholar and activist Leanne Simpson's words: "Storytelling then becomes a lens through which we can envision our way out of cognitive imperialism, where we can create models and mirrors where none existed, and where we can experience the spaces of freedom and justice."⁵⁰ Storied deserts, as an idea "that works not only to overturn long-established figures of the desert as empty wasteland, [but] is also meant to move traditions, histories, and cultures that have been systematically subjugated or erased to the forefront of our environmental consciousness," begins the work of breaking the hyperobjective Desert⁵¹ apart in order to reveal desert places as they are and can be—through their varying but legible biomes, imaginations, realities, and possible futures.⁵²

It's in this way that Natalie Diaz's *Postcolonial Love Poem* (2020) experiments with making desert and body legible. The poem "Snake-Light" begins with a boast: "I can read a text in anything."⁵³ From here, Diaz centers the poem's storied desert around a practice of reading, transforming the land and all of its bodies into texts to be read *through* the speaker's desert. The speaker elaborates this process: "To read a body is to break that body a little. / When my desert reads a life out loud, / it takes the body down, back to caliche and clay, / one symbol at a time."[54] The distortion of bodies into pieces, texts-turned-symbols, is a deconstructive act of recognizing things through the desert's physicality, its storied matter of caliche and clay. This visceral depiction paces the desert's reading of a life out loud down to "one symbol at a time," creating space to digest every morsel.

But the symbols of an alphabet, once learned, are meant to be arranged and rearranged into endless possibilities of words and sentences. As quickly as the poem breaks bodies down into symbols, it invites readers to reverse the process—turning bodies, turning everything, into text: "Let's say it's all text—the animal, the dune, / the wind in the cottonwood, and the body. / Everything *book*: a form bound together."[55] The transformation of everything into text—"everything *book*"—is profound; dunes and the wind join bodies as things to be distorted so they can be read, parsed, and understood.[56] In other words, rendering everything into text, into book, can make complex interrelationships of humans and more-than-humans legible through the use of a familiar form. This is the same principle under which something like a pair of 3-D glasses operates to bring separate static imprints into one dynamic one. Legibility is especially key for orienting readers to the speaker's desert because the poem is place-specific. Much in the same way Zepeda's poetry examined earlier situates readers to her native Sonoran Desert, Diaz's poem demonstrates the possibilities of her native Mojave Desert.

Dunes, rattlesnakes, cottonwoods, the Colorado River, and Diaz's Mojave language convene to evoke this desert as text, but something more is happening here, and being "bound together" is less about becoming-book and more about finding a way to understand things as they already are: interconnected.[57] Diaz's writing in "Snake-Light" illuminates a storied desert through her extensive use of anatomical and literary nomenclature. The following passage is a striking example of how these two vocabularies work with each other throughout the poem:

> This is also *book:* the skeleton of a rattlesnake
>
> sheathed tightly in its unopened flesh.
> Apex of spine and spit, the wet-black
> curves of unlit bone, dark parentheses—letters
> flexed across a mica-lit gulley, a line.
> What is a page if not a lingering, an opaque
> Waiting—to be marked, and written?[58]

The words "flesh," "spine," "bone," and "gulley" entangle with "parentheses," "letters," "line," and "page" to create a world in which the snake's skeleton is both book and body, therefore the reader must perform a reading of book and body simultaneously.[59] To engage the poem this way enacts the multiplicity of all things bound together in its desert.

Towards exploring the realm of the possible, the poem's speaker approaches a snakeskin hanging from a tree and touches it "the way I touch a line while reading."[60] Readers can again note the meeting of book and body, and, in this moment of touch, the reverberations of the past encompass the present and create futures; the snakeskin is "trembling with the body of the snake before it left itself, / like leaving one word for the next—becoming and possible."[61] This is an intimate insight into the process of life and language as it is and could be. The poem continues, "I gave the skin to my love and said, *Now I am a story*— / *like the snake, I am my own future.*"[62] A lesson learned from attention to the snake's own conditions of becoming and possibility, the speaker understands and is empowered by the ways their becoming and possibility create their future. There are many other such revelations in the poem, notably Diaz's use of the rattlesnake's name in Mojave, *hikwiir*, for which the act of speaking it aloud feels "like making lightning" and is the only way to know the rattlesnake's power.[63] Each of these examples presents an explicitly storied desert in which memory is tangible and futures are felt, creating a sense of hope and wonder for what may come.

The poetry of Zepeda, Silko, and Diaz demonstrates connections between their respective communities and the places they're from, makes kinship between human and more than human visible, and thus provides ample understandings of storied deserts. While their words do not, cannot, apply to all people and all deserts, they each bring multiplicity and possibility to the fore, dwarfing misrepresentations of desert places as void. Their work centers and uplifts their lifeways, languages, and stories, and from their different vantage points an abundance unfolds—for it is difference that creates abundance, a key tenet of desert distortion. Most importantly, I want readers to understand that the stakes of storied deserts and desert distortion are grounded in very real experiences and hopes for just environmental futures. Scholar Candace Fujikane writes that "Indigenous ancestral knowledges are now providing a foundation for our work against climate change, one based on what [she] refer[s] to as Indigenous economies of abundance—as opposed to capitalist economies of scarcity."[64] Through these Indigenous economies of abundance, Fujikane posits, it's possible to see "that climate change is bringing about the demise of capital, making way for Indigenous lifeways that center familial relationships with the earth and elemental forms."[65] As used throughout this book, desert distortion is about experiencing and understanding differently, to whatever extent possible, our human relationships with one another and with the nonhuman and more-than-human kin with whom we share this planet.

Increasingly, I find myself looking to Indigenous scholarship and activism for ways of thinking and practicing otherwise. For most, deserts are not associated with abundance and even such a seemingly minor shift in thought can have significant impact. Recognizing a river, like the Colorado or the Salt, as kin means respecting it enough to eradicate pollution and nearby mining. It means protecting the water and respecting its ecosystem—its birds, bugs, fish, algae, trees, shrubs, and banks. Such shifts in thought, and especially action, are how Cajete explains "Indigenous logic moves between relationships, revisiting, moving to where it is necessary to learn or to bring understandings together. Eventually this process, a synthesis, leads to a higher reflective level of thinking."[66] By engaging these stories, or rather a notion of storied deserts, I set the intention of this book to embrace not just multiplicity but abundance of desert places. This book is my invitation to "bring understandings together" and explore this abundance through the many complexities of living, dying, and dreaming in deserts imposed upon by borders, bodies, and geopolitics—through desert distortion.

CHAPTER 2

THROUGH

"In any event the history of all is not the history of each nor indeed the sum of those histories."

—The Judge, *Blood Meridian*, 329

HISTORY → HISTORIES

It's a daunting task to understand how relationships to land, nation, and identity have changed through the past five centuries. There are so many variables—time, location, gender, ethnicity, class, culture, and technological advancements amongst them—and too many emergent conditions to ever hope to account for it all. Even so, History (with a capital H) provides opportunities and methodologies to parse and interpret the who-what-when-where-why of these relationships primarily based on documented information found in items like newspapers, personal diaries, letters, photographs, interviews, and more recently through online content. In some sense, then, History is the not-lost, the not-erased; it is the official record of events through time and place that lends a throughline to something like a national narrative.

Officially, the US War with Mexico began in 1846 and ended with the Treaty of Guadalupe Hidalgo in 1848, a so-called peace treaty between the United States (which at the time was a total of thirty states) and the newly independent Republic of Mexico. Of course, the conditions for the war began brewing many years earlier: at least as early as Mexico gaining its independence from Spain in 1821, certainly as more settlers headed south and west in search of valuable natural resources and land to call their own, and undoubtedly as the American government sought to acquire more land into which they could extend slavery. The terms of the Treaty of Guadalupe Hidalgo devastated the newly independent Republic of Mexico, forcing it to cede "55 percent of its territory, including the present-day states California, Nevada, Utah, New Mexico, most of Arizona and Colorado, and parts of Oklahoma, Kansas, and Wyoming. Mexico also relinquished all claims to Texas, and recognized the Rio Grande as the southern boundary with the United States."[1] The loss, termed the Mexican Cession, was just the most recent transference of land ownership, as all of these territories and states were previously claimed and demarcated as a result of the Spanish imperial conquest that dates back to the 1500s. And before it was Spanish, Mexican, or a part of the United States, the land was lived-with and named according to the relationships between its Indigenous peoples, whose diversity of lifeways as relatives to the land was explored in the previous chapter.

These layers of conflict, culture, and colonization make the US-Mexico borderlands a rich but complicated place to study through the perspective of History. Though settler colonizers in the 1800s are favored in popular accounts of the so-called Desert Southwest, they were far from the first group to interact with the Indigenous peoples there. In 1519, Hernán Cortés led a colonial expedition into what is now central Mexico, resulting in the Spanish Empire subsuming and supplanting that of the Aztecs. This kicked off the "Age of Discovery" and created a hub for Spanish colonial forces in Mexico City, resulting in expeditions further north into the continent. Conquistadors including Álvar Núñez Cabeza de Vaca, Francisco Vázquez de Coronado, and Juan de Oñate spent much of the sixteenth century in the regions we now know as the borderlands in search of riches and resources, often settling for the latter. These men and their troops subjugated the Native peoples of North America for hundreds of years, forcing them into horrific living conditions, including slavery and war. During that time, the Spanish missions became epicenters for spreading as much disease as religion, systematically killing and converting Indigenous peoples en masse. All of this was taking place well before the US War with Mexico, before there was even a United States to speak of, and contributes to the complexity of ownership, identity, and belonging for the people living in the region then and now.

This chapter's two parts are experiments for exploring the co-constitutive and reciprocal relationships of time and place, particularly focused on how they work *through* one another. Investigating *place through time*, I encourage readers to challenge History (capital H) and embrace pluralities and palimpsests like the so-called Desert Southwest. Taking this emphasis on the multiple into the ecocritical, the second part focuses on *time through place*, reflecting on the polytemporal perceptions required of us in the age of the Anthropocene and revealing a desert abundance that thwarts the void and consists of being better kin to our human and nonhuman relatives. Whereas the previous chapter centers Indigenous perspectives on the multiplicity and possibility of desert places as storied from Time Immemorial to the present, this chapter is interested in the many experiences of a more specific time and place—the middle of the nineteenth century in the deserts of the US-Mexico Borderlands. Through an analysis of Cormac McCarthy's *Blood Meridian or the Evening Redness in the West* (1985), this chapter encourages readers to think about relational variations in experience through time and place, or desert distortions, as interacting fractal reverberations. The storied deserts of the Southwest have borne witness to eons of sovereignty, centuries of imperial rule, the setting and resetting of national borders, and the emergence of diverse identities and relationships between the people living and dying by the colonial process. In *Blood Meridian* they are ever-present, vibrating throughout the novel, amplified by the heightened intimate encounters between its characters and the land. Elements such as heat, light, and wind—reckoned with from the vast scale of geologic time to the speed of what I call elemental immediacy—push the limits of the human mind and body to extremes, a desert distortion where "we find a contrast between the limited capacities of human sensation and something too great to sense."[2] They are reminders that we are entangled with the nonhuman agencies and more-than-human forces of a place.

HISTORIES AND BORDERLANDS: PLACE THROUGH TIME

Centered on the plight of a young protagonist simply referred to as the kid, McCarthy's novel situates readers in the US-Mexico borderlands, when the US War with Mexico's long-term effects are still unclear, and its immediate damages are still being felt. The war's aftermath provides a setting rife with clashing cultures, languages, and identities, calling attention to how history is told and by who, as well as the transformative power of borders. It is an unsettling environment that orients readers as much as it dis-/reorients readers, and I agree with Aidan Tynan's reading of it as an anti-Western that "shows how the myth of the West both realises *and* extinguishes itself in the bloodshed of settler colonial conquest."[3] From its opening imperative line, "See the child," we follow the kid as he travels swiftly westward, across the plains from his home in Tennessee and through St. Louis in a matter of a few pages, until "in the spring of the year eighteen and forty-nine he rides up through the latterday republic of Fredonia[4] into the town of Nacogdoches," where *Blood Meridian* settles into its present.[5] From there, the kid rides further west with some filibusters before joining a ruthless band of scalp hunters known as the Glanton Gang, a fictionalized version of a very real historical group, who have been hired by Mexican government officials to collect Apache scalps for money.[6]

Much of *Blood Meridian* scholarship addresses McCarthy's descriptions of its vast desert landscapes as a harsh emptiness, especially as a space of violence.[7] To be sure, the author uses a litany of modifiers like "cauterized," "incoordinate," and "purgatorial" to describe the desert as wasteland and "cratered," "shoreless," "hallucinatory," and "lonely" to depict it as void.[8] However, I argue that readers are not following the kid in a vacuum of desert space—"waste apposite"—as it might seem, but instead through the novel's many storied deserts, of which the "desolate mineral waste" is only one register.[9] We follow the kid into the thick atmosphere of the American West, through the fresh repercussions of the French and Indian War and the American Revolution; through the consequences of Lewis and Clark's journey to the Pacific and back; and through the aftereffects of the American Industrial Revolution, which brought with it technologies like steamboats, railroads, and the cotton gin, as they ripple across the region with varying intensity. If History is the concentric undulations around a single drop landing on water, histories are the fleeting, indiscernible waves of countless drops, crashing into one another as the rain hits a body of water during a storm. In this way *Blood Meridian* captures the cacophony of the storm, obscuring any one historical center in favor of multitudinous histories, a diversity of desert distortions, making it a compelling text precisely for its attempts at representing the unrepresentable—as in life, the histories compete with one another, each trying to override the other as new events occur.

Signed on February 2, 1848, the Treaty of Guadalupe Hidalgo went into effect at the end of May that same year. A year later, *Blood Meridian*'s the kid is riding through the Southwest Borderlands in the aftermath of the war, caught within its multiple histories, witnessing the reverberative effects of entanglement and encounter.[10] Though the hindsight of History often provides exact dates for past events, as with any event, everything does not change all at once for everyone the same way. There are spatial and temporal distances, lags, obstacles, disconnects, and reconnects that emerge and unfold until, by some homogenizing, power-influenced process, histories become History, become ossified. *Blood Meridian* emanates with these spatial and temporal distances, the times and places that attest to infinite simultaneous realities *before* they become History, when they still hold possibility.

When a band of filibusters headed to Mexico "to whip up on the Mexicans" tries to recruit the kid, the kid's response to them is: "the war's over."[11] A man replies to him confidently, referring to their leader Captain White: "he says it aint over."[12] Intent on taking land south of the newly minted US-Mexico border through violent means and despite federal orders, the Captain's choice to pursue vigilante justice illuminates how the effects of the Treaty of Guadalupe Hidalgo were not total and immediate. Against the notion of a single History, White and his followers demonstrate alternative, realistic outcomes of the time and provide readers with a window to deepen understandings of postwar complexities. Literary scholar Liana Andreasen attests that, though McCarthy's work is rooted in historical and cultural realities, "McCarthy is not interested in rewriting history. His west is not a succession of moments through time but a comprehensive view of the stories, rumors, and causes that history erases."[13] To Andreasen's point about historical erasure I add a few examples from the novel's primary villain, Judge Holden, who is also its most prominent historian. A seven-foot, 300-pound, bald albino man, the judge demonstrates his power through the deployment of his immense knowledge and his unflinching infliction of violence on anyone in his path. Indeed, McCarthy uses the judge to demonstrate most poignantly that History is told by the victors and that power over it can be wielded as a form of violence, a weapon of erasure, against other, more local histories.

CHAPTER 2

Several times the judge takes out a leather ledger into which he draws the places and things he encounters. In one instance, the judge, the kid, and the Glanton Gang are riding through a desert canyon, and after a long day of studying artifacts amidst what the narrator describes as "the ruins of an older culture deep in the stone mountains," the judge takes up "each piece, flint or potsherd or tool of bone, and deftly sketched it into the book."[14] Once he is pleased with his drawings, the judge destroys the actual items, so that only his copies exist. Thus, the judge becomes the ultimate harbinger of cultural erasure, stifling the effects of place through time—histories—by arresting the original objects into the realm of pure representation. When asked about his plans with the notebook, the judge "smiled and said that it was his intention to expunge them from the memory of man."[15] With such an explicitly terrifying agenda, McCarthy reminds readers that this is in fact the violent process of History. That all it takes is a person with the right position of power to control consequential narratives of collective memory. By this demonstration, also, the author alludes to the many histories that the judge is trying to destroy—they exist, persist because the reality is there are impossibly infinite histories, infinite Southwests.

In one of the most consequential occurrences in US, Mexican, and Native North American histories, and just months after California was ceded to the US by Mexico, settlers in the Maidu village Coloma, Alta California literally struck gold. What began in January 1848 as the construction of a sawmill for John Sutter carried out by his partner James Marshall and the Maidu people he employed swelled into the phenomenon now known as the California Gold Rush of 1849.[16] As local news from the American West made its way back east during 1848, President Polk included an "official announcement of the gold strike in his State of the Union message to Congress . . . [and] triggered a mass exodus to California. The 'Forty Niners' were on their way."[17] The national drive to fulfill Manifest Destiny was joined by the arrival of international migrants; tens of thousands of settlers headed to California, driven primarily by their quest for wealth and the unprecedented opportunities they were promised.[18] The California Gold Rush, like Manifest Destiny and the Spanish colonial empire, was the latest iteration of settler-colonialism to set its sights on today's American West.

To this day, History centers a single story of those who made it to California to some success before the rest arrived to great disappointment.

This narrative is etched firmly into collective memory and curricula—there's even a national football team dedicated to it. A crucially underrepresented consequence and one of the multiple histories of the Gold Rush is the displacement and violence it inflicted upon Indigenous communities whose land was being colonized by Americans through the tactics of prejudiced treaty and law. When the goldseekers moved west, they brought with them disease—literal plagues—that killed masses of Indigenous people as a result. Within the first two years of statehood and "the initial gold discovery, California's non-Native population increased from just 15,000 to over 165,000, and by 1860 it would reach nearly 400,000, devastating Native lives and resources."[19] The rapid increase of a non-Native population to California meant a severe decrease in Indigenous populations: "According to most estimates, before the Gold Rush, 150,000 Native Peoples lived within the state's boundaries; only 30,000 survived the following maelstrom."[20] Numbers like this are near impossible to comprehend. More than 100,000 people killed, all with their own individual stories, in the name of gold, of greed. What numbers like this do provide is a chance to think about the many histories that this place through time has accrued in its storied landscape.

As the largest mass migration in US history and the substrate for the novel's action (Glanton hunted people for scalps to fund his westward quest for gold), McCarthy explicitly includes the plight of the forty-niners only briefly, along the periphery of *Blood Meridian*'s scope. The author reorients readers away from familiar associations with the Gold Rush and toward the abject and far-reaching destruction of peoples and landscapes that their movement through the territory brought with them: "They saw patched argonauts from the states driving mules through the streets on their way south through the mountains to the coast. Goldseekers. Itinerant degenerates bleeding westward like some heliotropic plague."[21] Clearly, the phrase "heliotropic plague" dismisses the myth of national advancement and the success of Manifest Destiny. Rather than seeing the goldseekers directly, we instead see them through the filter of the riders' perception, seeing what "they saw." In this case, the group of riders, including the kid, focuses on the goldseekers long enough to acknowledge them from a distance, but they do not follow them into California, into the myths of the Gold Rush, thus nor do we. We move through space and time with the riders at their speed and scale, only getting a glimpse of the goldseeking journey. Still, we know the goldseekers are in motion, in their only direction of promise. *Blood Meridian* readers encounter complex histories like the above in much the same way the riders do—through rumor, perception, and experience—by staying with the riders, who never stay in any one place too long. The novel's key refrain, "they rode on," reinforces the felt passage of time and their movement through space, through various events and encounters. The phrase marks the pivot from one event to another and serves as a periodic reminder that to be moving in any one direction is to be moving away from others.

Histories take time to affect place. Toward the end of *Blood Meridian*, the kid has grown into middle age, traversing through the West alone, with no gang of outlaws, vigilantes, or companions. It's been nearly twenty years, and the US, having endured the Civil War, has begun to resemble what it is today. Of the kid's travels and disposition, McCarthy writes:

> They were remote places for news that he traveled in and in those uncertain times men toasted the ascension of rulers already deposed and hailed the coronation of kings murdered and in their graves. Of such corporal histories even as these he bore no tidings and although it was the custom in that wilderness to stop with any traveler and exchange the news he seemed to travel with no news at all, as if the doings of the world were too slanderous for him to truck with, or perhaps too trivial.[22]

The phrase "uncertain times" briefly adopts an official, historical narrative tone, implying present clarity and progress from the past. Yet it's most important as a way to understand that times are always already uncertain.[23] Here, temporal uncertainty is intensified by the remoteness of places that require extra time for news to reach them: a result of desert distortion. In other words, the landscape is too vast for information to blanket it all at once. What does make its way through is emplaced in and limited by human bodies, "corporal histories" which, compared to the vastness of the desert, are extremely minuscule despite being the most reliable way to keep track of events. The kid, whether through under- or overwhelm, disrupts the flow and exchange of information "in that wilderness" by *not* bringing news or tidings, by a refusal to engage with any person he encounters. This alleviates his responsibilities to anyone else and emphasizes the role of the wild environment of *the* desert, a wilderness that has a way of absorbing, disrupting, and making seem small the duties of man, including the construction and enforcement of national borders.

Border → Borderlands

For most of his life, the kid moves through the US-Mexico borderlands with the flow of air or water, neither giving nor carrying much information and afforded relative safety due to his positionality as a young white man. But *Blood Meridian* also reflects the increasingly rigid realities—*extra*-corporal histories—of how the US government established and enforced its new borders with Mexico in the 1840s and '50s, borders that it expected its patriots to uphold postwar. In his initial encounter with the kid, Captain White speaks at length about his belief that he and his crew of filibusters "are to be the instruments of liberation in a dark and troubled land. . . . We have the tacit support of Governor Burnett of California."[24] In the previous chapter, I mentioned Burnett's role in the government-sanctioned genocide of California's Indigenous peoples, including his encouragement of local government officials to pay for bounties for their scalps and his policy of extermination via a race war. Captain White's invocation of Burnett signals his alignment with the genocidal practices Burnett carried out as the first governor of California in the years following the US War with Mexico.

Further, White is speaking during a moment where now-familiar national outlines are still the border yet-to-be, not quite fixed or in focus. White pontificates, "right now they are forming in Washington a commission to come out here and draw up the boundary lines between our country and Mexico. . . . Americans will be able to get to California without having to pass through our benighted sister republic and our citizens will be protected at last from the notorious packs of cutthroats presently infesting the routes which they are obliged to travel."[25] The Captain's racist rhetoric exemplifies Gloria Anzaldúa's argument that "Borders are set up to define the places that are safe and unsafe, to distinguish *us* from *them*."[26] Captain White maintains a clear distinction between his Anglo-American "us" and the other primarily Mexican and/or Indigenous peoples of the area, "them," in the name of protection for other Anglo Americans.

Borders, as elements of human histories, manifest geopolitical events of time affecting place. They are used as biopolitical and necropolitical tools

CHAPTER 2

to sustain certain spatiotemporal distortions at the expense of all others. In her *Borderlands/La Frontera* (1987), Anzaldúa famously writes: "The US-Mexican border *es una herida abierta* [is an open wound] where the Third World grates against the first and bleeds. And before a scab forms it hemorrhages again, the lifeblood of two worlds merging to form a third country—a border culture."[27] Countless scholars, artists, and activists have engaged—vitally and creatively—with the concept of the border as an open wound, centering the colonial violences inflicted upon people who are from, in, and moving through the bifurcated space and the individual and collective traumas that we inherit.[28] This book's aim, however, is to find additional or alternative ways to define border experiences in the Desert Southwest that acknowledge our struggles but don't define us solely through the lived realities of pain. I encourage readers to set aside for a moment the idea of the open wound and instead imagine a flowing river. As you envision the river, a giant stick comes along that somehow gets lodged in the mud beneath the surface. Largely resistant to ebbs and flows, the stick causes the water, people, animals, and things to move around it—for a time. Now pretend this stick represents the current US-Mexico border. Prior to its getting stuck, there were other sticks that similarly disrupted the flow of people and things around them—these previous sticks could represent the borders of Mexican Texas and Spanish Texas, for example—all of which, to extend this metaphor, washed away by the end of the US War with Mexico in 1848. In addition to the wound metaphor, which encapsulates the day-to-day grind for all who are caught between two worlds, I offer the stick in the river metaphor to provide a different scale for which the coming and going of borders is well established. It's at this scale that there is ample room for hope that borders will eventually become obsolete as weapons to perpetuate, separate, and surveil any version of "us" and "them." In combining these perspectives, the wound and the sticks in the river, the complexity of borders as somewhat arbitrary social constructions that bring with them severe consequences is more fully understood.

Since the arrival of the conquistadors in the early sixteenth century, Texas, as such, has flown the flag of six nations—the Kingdom of Spain, the Kingdom of France, the Republic of Mexico, the Republic of Texas, the Confederate States of America, and the United States of America—making it an especially fruitful example for investigating the complexity of borders in both their arbitrariness and their harsh realities. By the start of the 1830s, American settlers in Mexico's province of Texas had outstayed their welcome.[29] As a result, Mexico began a "military occupation of Texas, encouraged colonization by Mexicans and Europeans, initiated stronger economic ties between Texas and the rest of Mexico, and made it illegal for Americans to enter the territory."[30] Contrary to today's fear-mongering narratives of illegal immigrants flooding the US border from the south, Mexican Texas had become the target of many illegal immigrants crossing from the *north*, illustrating how from one century to another the border politics of a place can shift dramatically. Also during this time, both Mexican- and American-born Texans were rallying against the Republic of Mexico as a response to the government's move towards centralism. By 1835, President Santa Anna's new congress "had established a new centralist state in Mexico, which dissolved the state legislatures and transformed the former states into military departments governed by presidential appointees."[31] That year, Texans fought for their independence from Mexico and in 1836, depending on who you asked, they had won it. The Republic of Texas's status as a sovereign nation, like the land itself, was stuck between the US and Mexico; "whereas Mexico viewed Texas as a province in revolt, the United States recognized it as an independent republic on March 3, 1837."[32] Thus there was a time when Texas was simultaneously a territory that Mexico couldn't afford to lose, land that the United States would benefit from gaining, and its own independent republic.

In much the same way, depending on which government one was loyal to, the Republic of Texas had simultaneous southern borders: the Nueces River and Rio Grande. Historian Ernesto Chávez writes, "Since the republic's founding, Texans had claimed that the Rio Grande formed the border with Mexico. With annexation [in 1845], the United States upheld that claim, despite countless Spanish and Mexican maps placing the boundary farther north, at the Nueces River."[33] It was the dispute over which border (really which river-made-border) was official that eventually incited the US War with Mexico—a string of events over the course of two years, 1846–1848, that demonstrated imperious changes to the US-Mexico border and created profound consequences for the people living in the region now known as the American Southwest. In 1854, when the Gadsden Purchase was finalized, the US-Mexico border took its present-day shape. Today the boundary has intensified and materialized the border, from the Pacific Ocean to the Gulf of Mexico, as a "dividing line" in the way Anzaldúa describes it, as the border wall nears completion and border enforcement prepares to make use of robot dogs to go after migrants and newly declared National Defense Areas (NDAs) bring further military presence.[34]

A borderland, as a place of paradox and possibility, of movement and multiplicity, rejects fixity and embraces the messy realities of entanglement. Borderlands for Anzaldúa are a place where one is simultaneously conflicted and comfortable, where "you are the battleground / where enemies are kin to each other; / you are at home, a stranger."[35] In the US-Mexico borderlands specifically, the ideas of mestizaje and Aztlán[36] have loomed large, stemming from Chicanx engagements with our mixed heritages of colonizer and colonized. Initially established as "a racialized identity based on the mixture of Spanish and Indian blood," the concept of mestizaje has gone through waves of use, critique, and evolution.[37] Most commonly in today's scholarship, it is understood as "the political performance that creates a nation out of colonial mythology," that serves as "a romanticized notion of racial and cultural hybridity . . . that, when expressed through utopian narratives such as Aztlán, often obscures the violent dispossession that Spanish and Mexican colonialism inflicted on indigenous peoples."[38] Like mestizaje, Aztlán became a vital concept to Chicanx people because it "embodied the multiple longings, the aspirations, and the poetic allure of the Chicano movement; it spoke to the desire for connection and unity, homeland, and the condition of diaspora, while contesting the notion of Chicanas/os as outsiders or foreigners."[39] What makes these two ideas simultaneously useful and problematic are their origins in very complex experiences of belonging and identity. María Josefina Saldaña-Portillo and Simón Ventura Trujillo attempt to name these complexities with their recent dossier for *Aztlán* titled "Revisiting Mestizaje Twenty Years Later." In their introduction they offer that time to reflect on the idea "suggests that mestizaje names many things in addition to this political performance of nationalism. It also names domains of political economy, loss, relationalities, resistance, solidarity, and knowledge production."[40] In other words, the term has taken on so many new meanings that it's beyond our abilities to name all the ways it works in the world. Similarly, to try and define ourselves through these concepts is like trying to parse the palimpsest of the US-Mexico borderlands itself—though they do provide new vocabularies, for better and worse, to navigate the "complex and often conflicting narratives of belonging to shared geographic landscapes."[41]

Blood Meridian deals with this complexity in interesting ways; while its primary focus seems to be the plight of white male figures of power and force like the kid, the judge, and John Glanton, the novel is also telling the stories of racialized Others and the land that many of them belong to. John Glanton and his gang are hired by Chihuahua Governor Angel Trías, whom I return to shortly, to hunt Apache people for their scalps in exchange for money. Their contract requires the Mexican government to pay "a hundred dollars a head for scalps and a thousand for Gómez's head."[42] At one point during their search for Apache leader Gómez, the judge and John Glanton raid a peaceful village of sleeping Gileños, "the partisans nineteen in number bearing down upon the encampment where there lay sleeping upward of a thousand souls," and after their subsequent taking of hundreds of scalps, the gang spots the remaining Apache warriors in the distance.[43] Glanton manages to shoot their apparent leader and, thinking it could be Gómez, parades the body's severed head around in victory.[44] The judge then tells Glanton:

> It's not him.
> What's not?
> The judge nodded. That.
> Glanton turned the shaft. The head with its long dark locks swung about to face him.
> Who do you think it is if it aint him?
> The judge shook his head. It's not Gómez. He nodded toward the thing. That gentleman is sangre puro. Gómez is Mexican.
> He aint all Mexican.
> You cant be all Mexican. It's like being all mongrel. But that's not Gómez because I've seen Gómez and it's not him.
> Will it **pass** for him?
> No.[45]

The scene is grotesque for reasons beyond the dead man's head on a stick. The racist equation of Mexican with mongrel sets up an ethnic, racial, and US-centric hierarchy and economy of violence between Indigenous people, Mexicans, and white people, resting cultural identity on appearance and shedding light on identity politics that many Latinx peoples with Indigenous descent in the US-Mexico borderlands still face and grapple with today. Additionally, Indigenous people from the area face a double discrimination. As a contemporary example, Lipan Apache author and activist Margo Tamez writes: "By virtue of being indigenous and intrinsically bound up in relations with Mexico and Spain—empires that the United States both races and classes in its past and present construction of the villainous, dark-skinned, non-English speaking individual/nation as both 'foreign' and 'enemy'—Lipan Apaches experience *multiple* oppressions."[46]

To determine Gómez's identity based on appearance engages the idea of racial "passing," one that hinges on the tensions between being of so-called pure or mixed blood and how one appears to others in terms of race and ethnicity. Discussions of passing in North American literature are often in the context of African Americans passing or not passing for white. One of the most prominent examples is author Nella Larsen's novel *Passing* (1929) which uses the act as both a title and premise and is a literary staple for thinking through race relations between Black and white people in the early twentieth century. The discussion around passing in the Southwest—whether Indigenous, Mexican, or Mexican American—is equally complex. To Glanton, the head he presents the judge could serve as Gómez's, but the judge deems that it belongs to someone "sangre puro," of pure blood. The fact that the judge doesn't approve is what stops them from taking the severed head back to Governor Trías for their reward. The head is not Gómez's, but more importantly it will not pass for him because Gómez is Mexican, and therefore mixed-race. That a brown body is subjected to passing, even in death, is indicative of the violent scrutiny inflicted upon people with certain ethnic features like dark hair, skin color, and particular facial structures that white people have used to oppress people of color for centuries—McCarthy is telling this history, too.

Additionally, this passage is one of many in the novel depicting what Jason De León terms necroviolence: "violence performed and produced through the specific treatment of corpses that is perceived to be offensive, sacrilegious, or inhumane by the perpetrator, the victim (and her or his cultural group), or both . . . [it] is specifically about corporeal mistreatment and its generative capacity for violence."[47] A person's head on a stick, the infamous passage of a tree of dead babies, and the idea of scalping itself are all examples of the politics of necroviolence between the different groups. What unfolds during the rest of the Glanton Gang's hunt, both historically and in the novel, is that they ultimately decide to take advantage of the common physical features that Indigenous people often share with Mexican people from the borderlands as a result of settler-colonizer occupation and violence, namely brown skin and dark, long hair. The gang begins scalping and killing Indigenous people and Mexican villagers alike, attempting to pass the scalps off for pay somewhat successfully. Though the gang initially returns to Chihuahua to be greeted with "a hero's welcome," the celebrations do not last.[48] Upon their second return to the city, "haggard and filthy and reeking with the blood of the citizenry for whose protection they had contracted," the Gang's ruse is eventually found out, and "within a week of their quitting the city there would be a price of eight thousand pesos posted for Glanton's head."[49] The fact remains that they killed people purely based on their shared physical traits to suit their own barbaric, monetary goals.

In addition to drawing attention to the injustices carried out by the Glanton Gang and countless other Anglo Americans who took to violence against Mexicans, Mexican Americans, and Indigenous people as an amalgamated "Other," *Blood Meridian* inverts the flawed perception that all Americans are civilized and all Mexicans are savages. When readers first meet Governor Trías, he is hosting a banquet to welcome the Glanton Gang back from their hunt in all their gory glory. McCarthy's portrayal of Trías incorporates the politician's background as a worldly man of power who was "sent abroad as a young man for his education and was widely read in the classics and was a student of languages. He was also a man among men and the rough warriors he'd hired for the protection of the state seemed to warm something in him."[50] In a novel made infamous by its numerous and meticulous descriptions of borderlands violence, this brief glimpse at a Mexican governor who is sophisticated, educated, and amused by the Americans he has hired to do his bloody bidding opposes the former equation of Mexican to "mongrel," a racial slur denoting mixed-race heritage and a word that suggests a subhuman being.

Further, the description of Trías's wealth and lifestyle challenges the dominant narrative found throughout American literature of Mexicans as uneducated and impoverished. Conversely, it is the Glanton Gang who are proven to lack education: "Patriotic toasts were drunk, the governor's aides raising their glasses to Washington and Franklin and the Americans responding with yet more of their own country's heroes, ignorant alike of diplomacy and any name at all from the pantheon of their sister republic."[51] Evidently, the Americans have no knowledge of or interest in Mexico's history, while the Mexicans are quite familiar with the lore of prominent figures in the United States. After the banquet, the Glanton Gang ravages the town for days on end with debauched antics like riding horses indoors, groping and assaulting women, and firing their guns so often that the sound "became general."[52] In response, the Mexican townspeople, who had previously cheered them on in their crusade, have a change of heart, and "charcoal scrawls appeared on the limewashed walls. Mejor los indios."[53] Through this example, the novel exhibits a paradigmatic cultural and historical shift on the part of the Mexican people, who now prefer their Indigenous neighbors to their American ones. It's in scenes like this that *Blood Meridian* showcases all parties in close proximity, illustrating the dynamic tensions between people living through the birth of a borderland.

Anzaldúa distinguishes a borderland from a border by asserting that the former is "a vague and undetermined place created by the emotional residue of an unnatural boundary. It is in a constant state of transition."[54] As discussed earlier, *Blood Meridian*'s refrain "they rode on" propels the events of the novel forward with the gang of riders. Literary scholar Lee Clark Mitchell observes that the phrase "repeated endlessly from scene to scene, [serves] as at once the most gently paratactic of narrative spurs and a suturing phrase stitching together otherwise disparate moments and modes."[55] Through its repetition, the phrase indicates the perpetual flux of the US-Mexico borderlands in the mid-nineteenth century while signaling that even amidst intense and widespread sociopolitical upheaval and violence, the characters ride on. This onward horizontal nature of the text mirrors the vast horizons of desert places and the infinite march and stretch of time. Places like towns and mountain ranges become temporal markers of change that display the storied deserts of the borderlands, holding traces, if not monuments, of their many histories. The rest of this chapter is interested in how we engage simultaneous human, nonhuman, and more-than-human temporalities, which enriches our relationships with nonhuman and elemental agencies of desert places, through desert abundance.

DESERT ABUNDANCE: TIME THROUGH PLACE
Simultaneous Temporalities

Desert distortion is a method for thinking differently about arid places. Its application has great potential to transform individual and collective perceptions towards better futures. With it, as examined in the first part of this chapter, one can view *place through time* in order to engage the consequential human concepts of History or of borders, but it is especially helpful for expanding thought to consider the multiple histories of the US-Mexico borderlands as well as present and future possibilities of borderlands cultures. The second half of this chapter makes a dedicated shift toward thinking about *time through place*, in hopes of building more robust relationships to deserts and their nonhuman and more-than-human inhabitants with an attention to temporality. Through the ongoing process of orientation, disorientation, and reorientation, desert distortion reveals the simultaneous temporalities of desert places as an aspect of desert abundance. Practicing a polytemporal perception is an exercise in thinking beyond human pasts and futures in order to move towards a thinking-with in our present, a thinking-with that is required in our times of unprecedented climate crises.

If one reads historically canonical desert literature—for example, Edward Abbey's *Desert Solitaire* (1968) and Reyner Banham's *Scenes of America Deserta* (1982), or, to get beyond the American Southwest, Percy Bysshe Shelley's poem "Ozymandias" or Wilfred Thesiger's *Arabian Sands* (1959)—deserts feature as sublime landscapes that present the awe of geologic time to individual men navigating the "alien" terrain.[56] Note that this perspective is profoundly different from the approaches to poetry and literature by the Indigenous women poets engaged in the previous chapter. Not one of these canonical nature or travel writers is from a desert place, so landscapes like those in Moab, Utah or the Mojave Desert in California are regarded as highly exotic or wild. Abbey joins the National Park Service in the 1950s and is interested in surrounding himself with anything-but-humans, enraged that tourists (a demographic that was, ironically, inspired to visit national parks because of his writing and the book's publication in the late 1960s) were increasingly pervading and changing the land; Baudrillard, in his *America* (1986), is incredibly impressed with the speed afforded by interstate highways; Banham, an architectural critic from England, is similarly enamored by the desert's expanse, but to his credit begins *Scenes* with a confession that "all it can claim to be is the view of the archetypical British tourist. . . . I view the Southwest through a vision that has been largely formed by the powerful British tradition of writing about quite other deserts"; and Shelley's poem has for centuries made the point that grand human endeavors are ultimately swallowed up by the sands of time.[57] While Shelley's "Ozymandias" does effectively illustrate the vast difference between geologic and human temporalities, we have at present reached a turning point where human impact—primarily through extraction of natural resources like oil, coal, precious metals, minerals, and water—is damaging desert places at unprecedented magnitudes that may well continue into a world-without-us.

Of course, terms like global warming make clear that these damages are not limited to deserts or any one particular biome but exist at a planetary scale. The collective actions of our species in the twenty-first century have become sedimentary. Geologist Marcia Bjornerud informs us that, "worldwide, humans now move more rock and sediment, both intentionally through activities, like mining, and unintentionally by accelerating erosion through agriculture and urbanization, than all of Earth's rivers combined. It can no longer be assumed that geographic features reflect the work of geologic processes."[58] The dawn of the Anthropocene is giving way to its morning, as increasing evidence mounts that humans "are now agents of geomorphic catastrophe" who are "incalculably transforming the earth's systems on every level - altering the hydrosphere, atmosphere, lithosphere and biosphere."[59] A term first used and defined by Dutch scientist Paul Crutzen in 2002, debates about the Anthropocene as an appropriate label for both a new geologic epoch and a concept for thinking through irrevocable anthropogenic climate changes have proliferated a number of new "-cenes," such as the Chthulucene, Capitalocene, Plantationocene, and Symbiocene.[60] Donna Haraway has argued that the "issues about naming . . . have to do with scale, rate/speed, synchronicity, and complexity" and that "more than one name is warranted."[61] Unsurprisingly, I agree that movement toward multiplicity is vital to apprehend the complexity of the times in which we find ourselves living on this planet.

Despite the popularity of Haraway's work on the Chthulucene, which "entangles myriad temporalities and spatialities and myriad intra-active entities-in-assemblages—including the more-than-human, other-than-human, inhuman, and human-as-humus," it seems for now that the

Anthropocene is the name that's sticking, sedimenting itself in applications across disciplines in the arts, humanities, and social and natural sciences with the most consistent impact.[62] The name is not without its complications, of course. As Jemma Deer notes in her book *Radical Animism* (2020), "the denomination of the Anthropocene has been criticized for figuring human agency as a unified—or unifiable—force."[63] However, Deer doesn't wish us to get rid of the term, stating:

> The naming of a geological epoch massively broadens the frame through which we view human history, thereby effecting temporally what the 1968 "Earthrise" image did spatially, imaginatively providing a radical new perspective from which to understand the contemporary moment—*including* the unequal distribution of culpability and power by which it is characterized.[64]

Expanding the frame of perception, through radical new perspectives with which to understand time and place—in this example by the Anthropocene and the first image of Earth—is the broader aim of distortion as put forth throughout this book. It's a process of perceptual shifts, of disorientation and reorientation, attunement and detunement, decentering and recentering, that allows us to better understand the value of life and death on this planet. Such transformations are key to Deer's radical animism, which "recognizes that the traits or characteristics of life are not restricted to what we usually think of as 'living things,' that non-human and non-living entities are also animated, alive."[65] We live in a moment that requires us to acknowledge our environmental impact upon and our responsibilities to all others with whom we share the earth; a time to do away with human exceptionalism.

Deserts are apt places for experiencing changes in perception—literal, embodied senses of distortion—because their often extreme conditions like heat or cold, light, distance, and aridity can push phenomenological limits to their thresholds. Their storied landscapes provide exposed geologic records that Westernized science uses to parse and think through deep time. Bjornerud makes clear the importance of this concept, taking into account the limits of human perception:

CHAPTER 2

> Fathoming deep time is arguably geology's single greatest contribution to humanity. Just as the microscope and telescope extended our vision into spatial realms once too miniscule or too immense for us to see, geology provides a lens through which we can witness time in a way that transcends the limits of our human experiences.[66]

Interestingly, Bjornerud's use of the microscope and telescope as examples for thinking through space and geology as a comparative tool through which we "witness time" parallels Deer's explanation of how the Anthropocene epoch and the Earthrise image establish new temporal and spatial parameters. In both Bjornerud and Deer's arguments, the importance of shifting temporal perceptions becomes clear: such shifts are important ways of informing and investigating our current moment, encouraging people to be better kin to human, nonhuman, and more-than-human relatives. "We need a new relationship with time," Bjornerud writes in her call for what she's termed timefulness, "an acute consciousness of how the world is made by—indeed, made of—time."[67] By revealing and engaging simultaneous temporalities, which require changes in perception, desert distortion, like Bjornerud's timefulness, Deer's radical animism, and Haraway's Chthulucene, provokes deeper understandings of our responsibility/response-ability[68] in these urgent times of climate crises. Its emphasis on multiplicity and (dis-/re-) orientation is especially resonant with Haraway's pleas to cultivate such response-ability through which "we are all responsible to and for shaping conditions for multispecies flourishing in the face of terrible histories, but not in the same ways. The differences matter—in ecologies, economies, species, lives."[69]

Geologic processes exposed and explored through deep time often occur imperceptibly to us because of their relative slowness—the fossilized logs scattered throughout Arizona's Petrified Forest have been decaying for over 200 million years—requiring perceptual shifts towards a much grander scale of time and space. Even so, Bjornerud points out, "the tempo of many geologic processes is not quite as *larghissimo* as once thought; mountains grow at rates that can now be measured in real time, and the quickening pace of the climate system is surprising even those who have studied it for decades."[70] While this finding provides some sense of lithic animation that humans can recognize as agential, slowness and stillness, common associations with vast, "open desert" places, are only one kind of desert temporality. It may have taken over 200 million years for water, sediment, and minerals to crystallize the wood into what it is today, but it was because the logs "washed into an ancient river system and were buried quick enough and deep enough by massive amounts of sediment and debris also carried in the water, that oxygen was cut off and decay slowed to a process that would now take centuries."[71] Suddenness and slowness here are complementary.

Opposite the crawl of geologic time, elemental conditions of deserts such as heat, light, aridity, and even distance operate through immediacy when intra-acting[72] with humans, providing a temporarily legible burst of our entanglement with the non- and more-than-human. Elemental immediacy in desert places is responsible for confronting us with our own finitude: What amount of wind or heat can our bodies withstand? Our cities and structures? How long can one last without food? Water? Shelter? How far can one walk in scathing daytime temperatures across rugged terrains? Across city streets? What about at night? How long will it take for help to find you or you to find help if you need it?

Here I return to *Blood Meridian* to illustrate the concept of elemental immediacy, showcased in the text by its qualities of eruption and emergence. In his reading of the novel, philosopher Steven Shaviro notes that *Blood Meridian* is "obsessed with open space," a book "with an open topography . . . in which the endless, unobstructed extension of the desert allows for the sudden, violent and fortuitous irruption of the most heterogeneous forces."[73] Indeed there are passages where the desert landscape is so vast that the riders "could count five separate storms spaced upon the shores of the round earth" or "can hear the drum of rain miles away on the prairie," stretching readers' imaginations to the horizon and revealing the nonhuman agencies at work.[74] I argue that the novel is equally obsessed with time, as the temporalities of its deserts are vast and acute: for example, the way the riders encounter irruptive "heterogeneous forces" like dust devils—entities created by the sudden interaction of the ground's surface heat, warm and cool air in the atmosphere, and particles of dirt or sand. While the kid and the filibusters ride west, they watch as

> dustspouts rose wobbling and augered the earth and some said they'd heard of pilgrims borne aloft like dervishes in those mindless coils to be dropped broken and bleeding upon the desert again and there

CHAPTER 2

> perhaps to watch the thing that had destroyed them lurch and land like some drunken djinn and resolve itself once more into the elements from which it sprang. Out of that whirlwind no voice spoke and the pilgrim lying in his broken bones may cry out and in his anguish he may rage, but rage at what? And if the dried and blackened shell of him is found among the sands by travelers to come yet who can discover the engine of his ruin?[75]

The dust devil comes into being as suddenly as it "resolve[s] itself once more into the elements from which it sprang," illustrating the eruptive nature of elemental immediacy. By the end of this passage, McCarthy's narrator muses about a pilgrim being maimed and left for dead by a dust devil, meditating on the idea that those who will pass his body will have no way to know how he died. This tale is a reminder that the more-than-human forces of place are active; they do not exist in the background because there is no background and they operate on their own timescales.

From lightning strikes and flash floods to the winds that carry seeds, sands, or storms, elemental immediacy entails movement, defined by Deer as "the action or play of forces that is not restricted to human beings or even to the living."[76] Over the course of several hot desert days, the kid and another survivor of an attack, Sproule, ride through "a terra damnata" and "kept watch for any green thing that might tell of water but there was no water."[77] Realizing they are too far out to head back, they ride on to find succor, even though "they were very small and they moved very slowly in the immensity of that landscape."[78] The elemental immediacy of heat, light, and distance take their toll. The riders witness how "the scalloped canyon walls rippled in the heat like drapery folds," and a few grueling days later "an immense lake lay below them with the distant blue mountains standing in the windless span of water and the shape of a soaring hawk and trees that shimmered in the heat and a distant city very white against the blue and shaded hills."[79] Of course, the next morning there is no lake; it was just the emergent effect of heat, light, and the color of the atmosphere upon weary travelers—"it is the sun that powers the book's hallucinatory images."[80] Whether transforming canyon rock to fabric or producing a mirage, the mutability and movement of deserts flourishes in this imagery—defying common portrayals of a desolate landscape even as this scene ironically follows the kid and Sproule who are somewhat helpless in its expanse. As their exposure to the elemental pushes the limits of their perception, the riders realize "the ground on which [they] stand is not stable, passive and unmoving, but that it too is a force, has agency, responds."[81]

While deep time and elemental immediacy are simultaneous temporalities that require us to pay attention to the range of various agencies and assemblages of desert places, the human histories discussed at the start of this chapter comprise yet another scale with which to think *time through place*, especially in the sense of intergenerational temporalities—what gets carried forward, what gets forgotten, what gets remembered, and by whom. This can be thought of in terms of the spectral, "a concept that discloses the fact that the experience of a space and place is always haunted by a noncoincident spatiotemporality in which past and future participate simultaneously and in unpredictable ways."[82] Like the storied deserts of the previous chapter—in which the past is fully present and informs all possible futures—the spectral here describes the "unsettling complication of the linear sequence of past, present and future."[83] Spectrality is created by a place's palimpsest of pasts, present, and futures, a way of thinking about time, in fact, that challenges us to understand these delegations as co-constitutive instead of in three separate parts.

The spectral in *Blood Meridian* saturates the novel, which is rife with bones, bodies, and ruins—all active reminders of what has been and what will be—creating a spectral geography of the US-Mexico borderlands. John Wylie defines spectral geographies as "geographies in which place appears, when it does, as a sudden and displacing punctum of pasts and presents."[84] This, like Bjornerud's timefulness, is a perspective which understands that place is constituted of time. And, like desert distortion, spectral geographies require "displacing" as a modality of place itself. At one point, in a montage of hauntology,[85] *Blood Meridian*'s riders pass through a terrain where the carcasses of animals like mules, horses, and cattle whose "ribbed frames . . . under their patches of dried hide lay like the ruins of primitive boats upturned upon that shoreless void" and objects like chains, packsaddles, and "saddletrees eaten bare of their rawhide coverings and weathered white as bone" are scattered across the desert landscape; they ride on, crossing "a vast dry lake with rows of dead volcanoes."[86] These bodies and objects wear the passage of time in this desert place, especially its elemental immediacy, demonstrating what Shaviro calls "the immanence of the landscape and the imminence of death."[87] But there is something about their not-quite-complete deterioration that haunts the land, serving as physical reminders that death is literally always near.

During the filibusters' ride, McCarthy writes that "death seemed the most prevalent feature of the landscape," and I argue that the looming threat of death due to extreme elemental conditions is matched in the novel by the threat of death from extreme human violence.[88] In yet another morbid scene, Glanton and his gang come across "a band of peaceful Tiguas camped on the river and slaughter them every soul."[89] As a Tigua woman returns from upriver, she is confronted with the aftermath:

> All about her the dead lay with their peeled skulls like polyps bluely wet or luminescent melons cooling on some mesa of the moon. In the days to come the frail black rebuses of blood in those sands would crack and break and drift away so that in the circuit of a few suns all trace of the destruction of these people would be erased. The desert wind would salt their ruins and there would be nothing, nor ghost nor scribe, to tell to any pilgrim in his passing how it was that people had lived in this place and in this place died.[90]

What begins as a vivid depiction of bodily violence becomes a portal through which readers watch the passage of elemental time as it eclipses human time. In a matter of days, the forces of shifting sands, sun, and wind erase any proof of violence against this group of Tigua people, even absorbing any cultural information beyond what are set up to become unpeopled ruins. Unlike Anzaldúa's "open wound" which grates and grates and can therefore never heal, this massacre is a wound that, in terms of physical evidence like blood or testimonies from survivors, is quickly healed and concealed by desert conditions, leaving too few traces of what was. The ruins become like scars with unknown stories, become spectral. Wylie asserts that spectral writing "is committed to bearing witness through a gaze at once direct, oblique, haunted and horror-stricken."[91] Here, despite the suggested lack of anyone to tell the story about this place and the atrocities carried out against the Tigua, the narrator is in fact telling this exact story. As Lee Clark Mitchell puts it: "the 'nothing' allegedly left behind [in the above passage] is belied

by the description itself, which etches its memento for later generations."⁹²
Such re-inscribing is common throughout the novel—in ghastly detail, "a catastrophic act of witness, embracing the real by tracing it in gore," returning readers to the past, but also returning the events of the past to the present.⁹³

Because the elemental desert can become a force of erasure, weathering things and making even recent pasts seem distant or even dead, there is a danger in discussing spectral deserts and Indigenous peoples, who are often misrepresented or dismissed through the "vanishing Indian" myth discussed in chapter 1, as specters of the past rather than contemporary communities with rich, diverse cultures and ancestral and contemporary relationships to the land. There is a harm perpetuated by the conflation of ghosts and the spectral, of Indigenous persons with the past, that I'd like to address. As Zapotec Indigenous scholar Lourdes Alberto writes, "nationalist pedagogies fossilize native and indigenous people within a previous temporality, a time before modernity. Within the linear telling of Western history, native peoples are celebrated as absent even though they exist very much in the present."⁹⁴ Wupatki National Monument, located in Northern Arizona, is a relevant example. The National Park Service's (NPS) landing page for Wupatki National Monument begins with a section called "Footprints of the Past," which states, "in the early 1100s during a time period of cooler temperatures and wetter seasons the ancestors of contemporary Pueblo communities created a bustling center of trade and culture."⁹⁵ The NPS uses the long history of Wupatki to serve as a relic, literal ruins of Indigenous people in the open desert that one can visit and walk around—but this place has a different story.

In 2014, several news articles were published about Stella Peshlakai Smith, who was then 89 years old, being the last Diné (Navajo) person to have a residence permit allowing her to live on her ancestral land. Legally, *The Washington Post* reported, Smith "has rights to live on the land because she was born there one month before the area was declared a national monument in 1924."⁹⁶ Confronted with her mortality, Smith's family fought for rights to remain on or return to Wupatki, which became "home to hundreds of Navajos whose ancestors returned to settle the area after a forced march [known as the Long Walk] to an eastern New Mexico internment camp" named Bosque Redondo, before Wupatki became a national monument.⁹⁷ Though she was living, most of the articles centered around Smith's death, after which "her family would have six months to vacate the property and an additional six months to collect any personal items that they have."[98] The news stories point out the cruel indifference, cloaked in legalities, of the NPS towards the family's deep-rooted relationship with the land, but they also feed into the "vanishing Indian" myth with headlines like "The last of the Navajos to live at Wupatki National Monument?" and "When 89-year-old Stella Peshlakai Smith dies, the Navajo presence at Wupatki National Monument will end forever." The stories and removal of Diné people from their land at Wupatki echoes past systemic violence and illustrates the current violence inherent in historicizing Indigenous groups, especially as many are presently seeking land return and restoration towards their communities' sovereign futures.

As spectral geographies, deserts provoke perceptual shifts about human and nonhuman temporalities—enable us to think *time through place*. They are polytemporal environments that expose the expansive scale of geologic time, erupt with elemental immediacy, and hold multicultural, multigenerational stories of human pasts, presents, and futures. These simultaneous temporalities produce a contrast to the notion of a timeless or empty desert land and contribute to the concept of desert abundance. The rest of this chapter is dedicated to revealing this abundance through an ecocritical lens, exploring how the language of fiction—through writing style, naming, and detailed world-building—provides opportunities to decenter the human experience and encourage us to (re)consider relationships with the many living and non-living things, including time, that create place.

Desert Abundance
Far from empty, the region commonly referred to as the Desert Southwest, and often in this chapter as the US-Mexico borderlands, has a profound fullness—an array of human cultures, histories, and spectralities, nonhuman forces and agencies, and possible futures—as vast as its landscapes. Desert abundance, against the void[99] (an understanding that has contributed to extractive, violent, colonial practices over the last five centuries), is an invitation to consider animals, plants, stones, stars, dust, elements, and forces—all that is nonhuman, all that is more-than-human—as integral agencies with which we are entangled, with which we are and have been in relationship. Desert distortion's processes of disorientation and reorientation, especially to

decenter the human, are vital processes for this kind of relationship-building, something Haraway refers to as "making kin."[100] This conscientious shift occurs over time, with deliberate practices that enable one to recognize the need for embodied and conceptual changes of perception with respect to places and our roles and responsibilities in them and to them. Desert distortion, a method of multiplicity, is one such practice, and radical animism and timefulness are a couple of others.

Through fiction, poetry, film, and visual art, this book is an intentional getting-to-know desert places. As you continue reading, I can only hope your understanding of deserts and their complexities deepens; if deserts are already familiar to you, I hope this work resonates and that you can bring your own experiences to it, and if they aren't, I hope they become less foreign. Familiarity requires time and begets fullness. Learning about or with something fosters familiarity, becoming a source of care, respect, and recognition of responsibilities to that something. Familiarization is crucial in the context of deserts because they are predominantly (re)presented as exotic lands comprised of rugged terrain and populated by strange but resilient creatures or as foreign environments that instill fear because of the people indigenous to them.

As Veronika Kratz explores, even the term "desertification," as used by the United Nations in the 1970s, was created to offer "a compelling story of environmental crisis that relies on a simplistic metaphor of desert advance wherein anti-desertification work seeks to halt encroaching desert sands."[101] Kratz argues that this framework "limits our ability to understand and respond to land degradation in arid regions by obscuring the colonial history of desertification and perpetuating a misunderstanding of deserts and drylands as bad or broken landscapes."[102] Essentially these tropes depend upon a certain terror of land-becoming-desert. These dominant narratives, framed and perpetuated by the language of settler-colonizers for centuries, continue to affect contemporary cultural imagination and current policy-making, which is why literature is so important. Through imagination and language, literature can cultivate an appreciation of desert abundance that a) challenges anthropocentric misrepresentations of deserts as barren backgrounds upon which action occurs and b) engages agential environments with which we are entangled. My readings of desert abundance in *Blood Meridian* are contributions to the conversation not just about the novel itself, but to how one encounters deserts in much of literature, art, and film.

CHAPTER 2

The use of language is key to revealing desert abundance in *Blood Meridian*, as the rest of this chapter will show. McCarthy's prose performs a literal fullness of desert places, filling pages with extensive sentences packed with detail, displaying vibrant environments of the terrestrial and celestial.[103] Referring to "vacillations" in McCarthy's writing that range from a tone of cold indifference to speculative wonder, Mitchell observes that *Blood Meridian*'s "shape-shifting instability of style disorients us, making our experience of the novel as unsettling as the kid's experience of the West itself."[104] Applying Mitchell's argument ecocritically, I argue that disorientation, instability, and unsettling are all conditions of desert distortion helpful for reflections and reorientations towards better relationships with deserts, in this case the palimpsestic (South)West.

Though the void may at first seem like the definitive depiction of desert environments in the novel, the text is also full of detailed descriptions of flora, fauna, elements, and forces, making the land familiar to readers over time, situating them in the milieu of desert abundance. Shaviro calls this writing style "an *erotics of landscape*, moving easily between the degree zero of 'desert absolute' and the specific articulations of water, mud, sand, sky, and mountains. It leaps from the concrete to the abstract and back again, often in the space of a single sentence."[105] Indeed, the narration's incessant movement shifts between curt, terse phrases about *the* desert—as "shoreless void" or "purgatorial waste"—and elaborate sentences about specific desert places loaded with bold imagery: "in a night so beclamored with the jackal-yapping of coyotes and the cries of owls the howl of that old dog wolf was the one sound they knew to issue from its right form, a solitary lobo, perhaps gray at the muzzle, hung like a marionette from the moon with his long mouth gibbering."[106] Desert world-building in *Blood Meridian* encourages readers to pay attention to the activities and details of nonhuman life and more-than-human things that thicken the places in the novel.

"Words are things,"[107] and names are words with which we world.[108] As discussed in the previous chapter, names carry historical, cultural, and personal significance—contain stories. The act of naming is an evocative practice, and, as Isabelle Stengers asserts, "is a serious, that is, a pragmatic business, when it means giving to what is named the power to induce thinking and feeling in a particular way."[109] Though the kid ironically remains nameless, *Blood Meridian*'s narrator saturates the rest of the novel with names, often paying specific attention to the nonhuman agencies of its desert places like towns, plants, animals, mountains, clouds, and even colors and sounds.[110] Naming becomes a way of knowing the land in this text, of scratching the surface of its abundance and representing its diverse actants. McCarthy's choice not to name is therefore equally important, becoming a way to mark not knowing. Captain White asks the kid, who has just been robbed, where the incident occurred; the kid responds, "They wasn't no name to it. It was just a wilderness."[111] Here the kid has no real relationship with the land on which he finds himself, so he generalizes it as a wilderness—a classic trope of desert landscapes, an abstraction of its harsh conditions and overwhelming vastness that feeds many classic "Wild West" aesthetics, from the twentieth-century films of John Ford and Sergio Leone to more contemporary representations in media like *Westworld* and *Mad Max: Fury Road*, and even the *Red Dead Redemption* game franchise. Non-naming in *Blood Meridian* is a deliberate evocation of the desert as space more than place, attributing it with awesome affective qualities but not acknowledging its diverse and heterogeneous agencies.

However, the novel engages desert-as-place more often than not, regularly including the activities of the sun, moon, and stars or filling the atmosphere with wind, rain, and snow. Readers encounter desert abundance through the power and procession of nonhuman presence. For example, the kid, making his way on foot through the snow high up on a desert mountain rim, must keep moving to save his toes from the elemental immediacy of frostbite, and, after a few days battling wind, hunger, and cold, he spots a fire in the distance, though "he could not judge how far it was."[112] Only upon his approach we learn:

> It was a lone tree burning on the desert. A heraldic tree that the passing storm had left afire. The solitary pilgrim . . . knelt in the hot sand and held his numbed hands out while all about in that circle attended companies of lesser auxiliaries routed forth into the inordinate day, small owls that crouched silently and stood from foot to foot and tarantulas and solpugas and vinegaroons and the vicious mygale spiders and beaded lizards with mouths black as a chowdog's, deadly to man, and the little desert basilisks that jet blood from their eyes and the small sandvipers like seemly gods. . . . A constellation of ignited

CHAPTER 2

eyes that edged the ring of light all bound in a precarious truce before this torch whose brightness had set back the stars in their sockets.[113]

Significantly, the fire in this passage was caused by a strike of lightning, an elemental force encountering the tree, and not human actors. This is a moment that acknowledges nonhuman assemblages and their possibilities. Further, the arc of this passage builds a dramatis personae of all who have gathered around the fire—beginning with a "lone tree" and ending with a "constellation of ignited eyes." In doing so, it populates this desert place with each new name and description of things celestial and terrestrial. The kid is welcome, but not necessary; his arrival has minimal impact on the ring of creatures who would still be there in its light and warmth, bearing witness, regardless of his attendance.

An iteration of this idea returns in fuller force in a later scene of what Shaviro describes as "material language," where the vastness of the desert environment levels all things with light, decentering the human through an "optical democracy":

> In the neuter austerity of that terrain all phenomena were bequeathed a strange equality and no one thing nor spider nor stone nor blade of grass could put forth claim to precedence. The very clarity of these articles belied their familiarity, for the eye predicates the whole on some feature or part and here was nothing more luminous than another and nothing more enshadowed and in the optical democracy of such landscapes all preference is made whimsical and a man and a rock become endowed with unguessed kinships.[114]

In this moment, where every thing is as impossibly yet equally lit as one another, an interconnectedness with desert abundance emerges through "unguessed kinships" that deanthropocentrize the desert. This concept is different from dehumanizing the desert, which many apocalyptic books and films depend on to create an antagonist out of the environment in a long-standing battle between nature and culture. Instead, deanthropocentrizing the desert provides opportunities to understand a fuller set of relationships, "a kind of perception before or beyond the human."[115] In his analysis of this passage, Shaviro writes, "the effect of the language is the same as the effect of the light. Minute details and impalpable qualities are registered with such precision that the prejudices of anthropocentric perceptions are disqualified. The eye no longer constitutes the axis of vision."[116] As I've established throughout this chapter, major perceptual shifts such as this are important for desert distortion, as they allow us to think through multiplicity and enable us to be better kin to our human and nonhuman relatives.

Decentering the human means understanding there are countless agential beings and forces that are always-already intra-/interacting with each other, and sometimes us. *Blood Meridian* welcomes an affirmation of the desert as a place where such interrelationships are not only important but abundant. Shaviro, still with respect to "optical democracy," continues, "this is not a perspective *upon* the world, and not a vision that *intends* its objects: but an immanent perspective that already *is* the world, and a primordial visibility, a luminescence, that is indifferent to our acts of vision because it is always passively at work in whatever objects we may or may not happen to look at."[117] Much like the revelation that the burning tree was going to be surrounded by lots of creatures no matter if the kid showed up or not, this reading pushes us to imagine how nonhuman and more-than-human assemblages function whether we witness it or not. This decentered perspective is a gift that both deep time and fiction give us, an imagining of abundant desert worlds before, beyond, and without us. For me, decentering is a speculative act that must imply a recentering—we can't take responsibility for climate change and social and environmental injustices if we keep humans homogenized and decentered. A return to human activity is quite literally vital to many human and nonhuman futures on this planet during the age of the Anthropocene. Through the process of decentering and recentering, of disorienting and reorienting, desert distortion examines the relationships of people from the land and people moving through the land, towards a thinking and working-with the land.

CHAPTER 3

ABOVE

DESERT AESTHETICS

Directed by Denis Villeneuve and released in 2015, *Sicario* stars Emily Blunt, Josh Brolin, and Benicio del Toro. The screenplay was the first written by an up-and-coming Taylor Sheridan, who went on to write for and direct films like *Wind River*, *Hell or High Water*, and has since risen to widespread fame as producer behind *Yellowstone*, *1883*, and *1923*. The director of photography is Roger Deakins, who is best known for his vision in Coen brothers classics like *The Big Lebowski*, *Fargo*, and *No Country for Old Men* and more recently *Blade Runner: 2049* and *1917*. Together, Sheridan's script and Deakins's cinematography complement Villeneuve's stylistic storytelling.

Blunt's character, FBI agent Kate Macer, is head of the Kidnapping Response Team in Phoenix, Arizona. Kate's dedication, and a recent raid in which her team finds dozens of dead bodies in the walls of a cartel house, catches the attention of Department of Defense contractor Matt Graver (Brolin). Matt invites Kate to join a special interagency task force, for which she must volunteer. Thus, Kate teams up with Matt and Alejandro (del Toro), a mostly silent character who is even more mysterious in motive than Matt. Their mission, as Kate understands it, is to quell cartel violence by taking down known bosses Manuel Diaz and Fausto Alarcón. What she doesn't know is that they will be traveling back and forth across the US-Mexico border to do so.

CHAPTER 3

The film, arguably without much dialogue between its three key protagonists, gives insight to their distinctive approaches to justice as they instigate the limits and liminality of the law. For Kate, this means doing things by the book; for Matt, it means by whatever means necessary; and for Alejandro, well, he's after those responsible for brutally murdering his wife and daughter. *Sicario* provides a contemporary dramatic depiction of tensions between US federal government agencies, state authorities, and Mexican drug cartels. It most successfully does this through its verticality, a mode of desert distortion explored throughout this chapter, which defamiliarizes desert places and interrogates hierarchical structures of law enforcement in the US-Mexico borderlands. Through stunning aerial shots that capitalize on surveillance technologies, e.g. infrared cameras, satellites, and drones, and nuanced stories about characters in differing positions of political power, *Sicario* deconstructs the empty desert of pop culture, which traditionally serves as a background, while reconstructing it as an agential environment conscripted to assist those who can operate from above it.

I'd gone to the theater to see *Sicario* knowing only that it was supposed to be an action film about narcotrafficking. I had expected an overdramatized or outdated portrayal, like those I've seen in countless classic Westerns or narco-dramas featuring an El Paso that I never recognize. While it does uphold the overdramatized single story of El Paso–Juárez as a violent hub of danger, I didn't expect its atmospheric intensities to evoke grief, distress, and even homesickness. This happened because I recognized the desertscapes of El Paso–Juárez and even Albuquerque (the story isn't set there, but many of the scenes were filmed in New Mexico). I could almost smell the creosote as I watched the monsoon clouds fill the screen with their promise of desert rain. I could feel the time of year. I was still living there when they started to put up the first iteration of the border fence under George Bush Jr.; I sped down Border Highway on my way to classes at UTEP; I visited Juárez with my grandma and had to wait the long time to get back across the bridge. Despite the dramatic license taken with the film's action, these visuals pulled me into memories of the cultural geography of my desert hometown.

And then there were moments where I didn't recognize it, moments of defamiliarization where I got to see it from an aerial perspective like never before. When Kate, Matt, and Alejandro take their first flight to El Paso, there is a shot of the mountains, noticeably green from recent rains, that starts

ABOVE

Figure 2: Still from *Sicario* from directly above the mountains. From this overhead perspective, the traditional Western aesthetic of horizon is challenged and an aesthetic of aeriality and the vertical is introduced. (Fair use.)

as a bird's-eye view before cutting to a directly overhead shot. We hover from a vantage point that accentuates the topography, staring down at the mountains from a *mezzo distance* that provides a perspective of the land as neither the hyperobjective desert[1] nor the intimate setting of individualized lived experiences. A slow, deliberate meditation on the terrain, this vertical viewpoint—not one that any character could have had from aboard the plane—is disorientating. Mountains, which wield their own vertical dominance over the ground, suddenly take up space on a different axis, their peaks pointed toward the viewer leaving us to discern their depths (see fig. 2). Viewing them this way, their lines and shadows create movement, pulling focus from any one center and showcasing the dynamism of desert environments. I had never seen the mountains like this before, and it moved me.

The film's aerial cinematography in scenes like this sets it apart from other post-Westerns[2] and challenges classic and neo-Western obsessions with open, horizontal space. On full display in any of the ten films John Ford directed and shot in Monument Valley, like *Stagecoach* (1939), or in the Andalusian stand-in for the American West Sergio Leone used for the Man with No Name Trilogy starring Clint Eastwood (1964–66), or even

CHAPTER 3

Figure 3: Still from *Sicario* showing a satellite image of the bottleneck of traffic into the US at the Bridge of the Americas. (Fair use.)

Figure 4: Still from *Sicario* showing an aerial view of the same bottleneck traffic contrasting with the task force's black SUVs headed into Mexico. (Fair use.)

Figure 5: Still from *Sicario*. An overhead view of a gridded neighborhood. (Fair use.)

Figure 6: Still from *Sicario* from an aerial perspective as the view shifts from suburban neighborhood to "undeveloped" desert land. (Fair use.)

CHAPTER 3

in the first season of the HBO series *Westworld* (2016), such stories provide a great sense of desert distance by way of horizon, especially through the plight of characters who must travel by foot, horse, wagon, train, or other vehicle across the land's expanses.

While Matt, Kate, and Alejandro do spend much of the film moving across the borderlands of the southwest, *Sicario* is far more interested in the vertical dimensions of its desert places, often framed by looking directly down upon them. Perspectival shifts, from horizontal to vertical and back again, are a technique of desert distortion the film uses to produce a new desert aesthetic, a way to build a dynamic relationship between the two axes, and therefore to create an experience of desert abundance, or the fullness of desert places, by way of dis-/reorientations that immerse viewers in a thick milieu of desert situatedness. The deserts in *Sicario* are not just open, "untouched," "empty" land—they are neighborhoods, cities, air force bases, borderlands. They shape and are shaped by their human and more-than-human inhabitants. They are storied.

Through the expert cinematography of Roger Deakins, the vertical vantages of the film allow us to experience its desert places in a variety of ways, and this is most often made possible by a position of privilege and detachment from the land that reveals the outsider perspective of federal agencies and their technologies used for aerial surveillance. For example, the interagency task force is equipped with satellites and helicopters that enable them to watch and move across the land and its people from above. After arriving in El Paso, Kate's first meeting with the rest of the team confirms that their immediate objective will take them into Juárez, Mexico—beyond their legal jurisdiction. Up at the front of the room, the man presenting this information uses a satellite image of the Bridge of the Americas/Puente internacional Cordova de las Américas that captures the aerial view of asymmetry of access at the US-Mexico border. Along with their intended route, it shows bumper to bumper traffic in an inverse bottleneck heading to the US, several lanes dispersing into a dozen on the right of the image, while the lanes on the left of the image, heading south into Mexico, require no such proliferation (see figs. 3 and 4).

The picture captures a two-dimensional moment of the region's multidimensional living reality; the binational El Paso–Juárez area is completely surrounded, for miles on every side, by the Chihuahuan Desert, creating

76

an interdependent economy and culture between the two major cities and their surrounding communities that connects through bridges like this one.[3] Crossing the border is an everyday activity; on foot and in vehicles, thousands of people cross for work, school, shopping, or visiting family and friends. But the satellite image used by the team fails to showcase this humanity, instead emphasizing how the government operates from a certain remove, a safe and tactical distance from the on-the-ground comings and goings of the place.

When the briefing is over and Kate decides, reluctantly, to proceed with their mission into Juárez, the film shifts gears and, instead of looking at a satellite image, we are above an El Paso neighborhood, seeing it from an overhead angle as a frame full of similar-looking houses bound by gridded streets soon pivots to include ever more "undeveloped" desert land. This establishing shot exposes the edges of suburban sprawl, where the structure of a built environment meets the natural environment, and eventually, slowly, the open desert takes over the screen (see figs. 5 and 6). The film's tone intensifies with the introduction of its signature sound, a low, grinding drone that is layered with the percussive rhythm of helicopter blades—a sonic complement to the area's abundant texture.[4]

The scene suddenly cuts to a landscape shot where the border fence forms a horizon across the screen, mountains in the distance behind and a Border Patrol vehicle in the foreground, to create a familiar representation of this desert place. Then it cuts to an aerial shot using the fence as the vertical axis, splitting the deserts of El Paso and Juárez evenly to the left and right of the frame—a unique way to view the border, as the only way to do so is from above. The aerial sequence continues to switch between perspectives of the border fence as horizontal and vertical, near and far, as if trying to find the best way to convey the fence's role in the vastness (see figs. 7–9).[5] Eventually the helicopters enter the frame over an oblique fence line, their tails straddling the border from above, a telling positionality that I explore through vertical hierarchies of power later in this chapter (see fig. 10). This scene encapsulates the sights and sounds of *Sicario*, the official invitation to its storied deserts.

Views from the ground interspersed with views from above—reorientations—continue in sequence as the team drives on El Paso's Border Highway, parallel to the border fence on their way to the bridge. The agents in Kate's vehicle gaze horizontally, through the latticed shadow of the fence at Juárez's

CHAPTER 3

Figure 7: Still from *Sicario*. A view with the border wall creating a horizontal axis. (Fair use.)

Figure 8: Still from *Sicario*. An aerial view with the road and border wall creating a vertical axis. (Fair use.)

ABOVE

Figure 9: Still from *Sicario*. An aerial view with the border wall creating a diagonal axis. (Fair use.)

Figure 10: Still from *Sicario*. A helicopter flies along the border fence above El Paso / Juárez. (Fair use.)

CHAPTER 3

colorful *colonias*[6] as one of the team members says, "There she is, the beast. Juárez."[7] The low grinding sound resounds. An aerial shot from the team's helicopter follows their five black SUVs as they pass somewhat frictionlessly into Mexico, while traffic heading into the US is just as congested as the satellite image from their briefing. Once in Mexico, the team is followed by several Policía Federal vehicles, and again the film alternates between synoptic and confined shots, conveying both horizontal and vertical perceptual experiences. From inside the vehicles, we see people playing wallball and hanging outside storefronts as the entourage propels through the streets, eventually driving by a bridge adorned with four naked, decapitated bodies.[8] This is the image Alejandro uses to welcome Kate to Juárez, and though it is a powerful depiction of a time when the city was plagued by such displays, it's not the most definitive visual of Juárez in this scene. After the team successfully acquires Manuel Diaz's brother, Guillermo, from a warehouse, they head back toward the bridge, and a few shots of Juárez from above display the city's incredible size. I argue that this vantage point, by way of a vertical mezzo distance that is further out than street level but close enough to omit the sky, defines Juárez more than the bodies hanging from the bridge because of its ability to increase awareness of the city's dense population, and therefore its multiplicity. The frame is full of houses, similar to the opening overhead shot of the gridded El Paso neighborhood on the northern side of the border. Homes and buildings of Juárez's 1.5 million people contour the land on which they are built, providing an opportunity for reflection about life in this desert city.

Sicario also experiments with both horizontal and vertical distances as a way to explore military presence as part of the desert atmosphere. Military use of the American West, and specifically its desert environments, has a long, convoluted, and problematic history that amplified during World War II. In his book *Dirty Wars: Landscape, Power, and Waste in Western American Literature* (2009), John Beck lists just some of these uses:

> The internment of people of Japanese origin in the West in the immediate aftermath of Pearl Harbor;[9] the location of America's atomic bomb project in Los Alamos, New Mexico; the progressive military withdrawal from public use of millions of acres of Western land; the hundreds of nuclear detonations at the Nevada Test Site

ABOVE

Figure 11: Still from *Sicario*. Kate Macer and Matt Graver have a heated conversation at the base after a shootout on the bridge. (Fair use.)

and elsewhere, and the subsequent poisoning by fallout of people and land; the plans for permanent storage of contaminated waste in the Western desert; the "war on drugs" and intensive policing of the international border with Mexico: all of these indicate some of the ways in which the West has been at war.[10]

Indeed, the militarization of the desert in *Sicario* is reflective of an active, contemporary pursuit to weaponize the border against certain bodies through the War on Drugs, surveilling it from above while demarcating the space from below. When the team returns from Juárez to the base in El Paso, Matt waits outside for Kate in the dirt parking lot, then asks her, "Got a little nutty, huh?" to which a vexed Kate says, "Nutty? Yeah, yeah, that was fucking illegal."[11] They're referring to the fact that, contrary to the ease with which they entered Mexico and despite the agents who were meant to wave them through, the team got stuck in traffic on the bridge returning to the US and shot several people wielding guns who were trying to get Guillermo back by force.

Unlike the shootout scene at the bridge, which was filmed through close-up and aerial shots, the argument at the base is filmed from a distant, steady angle along the horizontal axis, from which Kate and Matt become smaller parts of a larger composition. They are closely framed by chain-link fences topped with barbed wire, a black SUV on the left, the military base on the right, and Humvees and unmoving soldiers in the background. US Army and American flags audibly wave above them in the larger frame of monsoon wind and clouds, placing the audience within the desert situatedness of the base—not by viewing it from above, but from an adjacent afar (see fig. 11). Keeping a horizontal distance from Matt and Kate enables viewers to witness their discussion as if we're on the base with them; it's an invitation to feel surrounded by both the security of the base and its elemental desert location.

Military desert entanglements are a testament to the land's resilience and the effects of geopolitical ambition. The cinematography of *Sicario* uses vertical distances to examine the tensions between land and power, between human and nonhuman. As such, its aesthetics perform the hyphen between nature-culture. Toward the end of the film, the team successfully locates an underground tunnel used by the cartel. Their plan is to enter the tunnel, head toward the Mexican side of the border while creating a diversion so that Alejandro can make his way undetected into Mexico. They arrive in the area at dusk, decked out in protective gear and equipped with night vision goggles. On foot, they approach the tunnel's entrance as the last rays of light leave the sky, which is a stratified gradient from deep indigo to burnt orange. The distant mountains are a jagged black shadow overlaying the bottom third of the screen. As the team members navigate the uneven ground and walk away from the camera, their stark black silhouettes sink into and are absorbed by the horizon (see fig. 12).

Counter to the classic depictions of cowboys riding off into the sunset, the team are not moving horizontally in the vastness. Instead, they disappear into the desert underground, on a vertical axis. Even after the last helmet has descended beneath the frame, the shot lingers for a moment: a visual homage to the resilience of desert places, which, on a geologic timescale, swallow even the most violent of human endeavors in an instant.

Ultimately, *Sicario*'s vertical visuals have the ability to inform and influence how we understand the lived realities of desert places, and especially those along the US-Mexico border. Deakins's cinematography and Villeneuve's directorial vision incorporate different kinds of mediated viewing experiences through aerial and otherwise oblique angles using drone and satellite footage,

ABOVE

Figure 12: Still from *Sicario*. The silhouettes of the interagency task force walk toward the horizon to the underground tunnel at dusk. (Fair use.)

helicopters, and even infrared cameras to defamiliarize its environments. That is, such technologies can take the abundance of desert places I've been discussing throughout this book and transform it into spaces to be contained, monitored, and exploited with varying amounts of disregard for those who live there. What I appreciate about *Sicario* in this case is that, like with *Blood Meridian* discussed at length in chapter 2, there is evidence for both readings of deserts—as place and space, as void and multiplicity—which, like the horizontal to vertical oscillations, becomes a way for the texts themselves to perform desert abundance.

DESERT FROM ABOVE

Visually framing the US-Mexico borderlands from the interstices of entanglement, where its deserts can be navigated frictionlessly by those with the power and technology to do so, *Sicario* is a helpful text for perceiving the desert from above. The vertical aesthetics presented in the film mirror the hierarchy of power it engages. That is, access to a position higher up in the structure translates to having more power over people in desert places literally, through aerial surveillance and patrol, and through the privilege of being above the law. Further, *Sicario*'s vertical perspectives demonstrate this privilege by exposing the (ab)use of law and lawlessness in the US-Mexico borderlands, where that power historically has been assisted by the desert environment. As a result, desert conditions—especially distance and heat—can exacerbate the tension between law, power, and responsibility. The rest of this chapter investigates this vertical axis of power as represented in *Sicario* through various groups—federal agencies, cartels, police, and migrants—to expose the limits and liminalities of law enforcement.

Federal Agencies

Employed by US federal agencies, *Sicario*'s three key protagonists, Kate, Matt, and Alejandro, are all familiar with the Mexican cartel headed by Fausto Alarcón, whose cousin Manuel Diaz operates north of the border. Kate, recruited as liaison for the interagency task force led by Matt, is motivated to join them because she wants to find the people responsible for the dead bodies and explosion at the raid earlier that day. When she asks if this is the team's mission, Matt replies, "the men who are *really* responsible for today, yeah."[12] Kate is chosen for her "tactical experience" and a specialization "in responding to escalated cartel activity" and is briefly told that their next step is to retrieve Guillermo, Diaz's brother.[13] When Kate asks from where, Matt replies, with a dismissive hand-waving gesture and sideways glance at the other men, "the El Paso area."[14] Kate then inquires about the overall objective of the interagency task force; Matt responds, with another hand wave and a sort of smile, that their role is "to dramatically overreact."[15] Obviously, detailed information about what the task force is meant to be doing and why doesn't come readily to Kate, and the audience is mostly kept in the dark with her throughout the film, learning about her objectives as she does. Eventually we understand that this dynamic is intentional on Matt's part; someone like Kate has an approach to justice that abides by the law and would therefore prevent the team from carrying out their mission.

It isn't until they are on the flight to El Paso, a scene described at the start of this chapter, that Kate meets Alejandro, whose first words to her are "Have you been to Juárez before?"[16] A confused Kate asks Matt to confirm that they are going to El Paso. Matt, lying down in the back, feigns incoherence and pretends to be asleep. At this point Kate understands what Matt meant earlier when he said Guillermo was in "the El Paso *area*"—he was exploiting the proximity of the El Paso–Juárez border cities in order to tell the truth by omission. Thus begins Kate's crash course on how other federal agents abuse the limits of the law along the US-Mexico border in the name of justice. Loopholes, like calling Juárez "the El Paso area," set the stage for how the federal agencies who hired Matt and Alejandro intend to handle their transborder operations. They will be going into Mexico, beyond their legal jurisdiction. Significantly, this realization occurs to Kate as the team takes flight on the Department of Defense jet, literally ascending over the territory from Arizona to El Paso. It's then that we see the mountains from the vertical mezzo distance mentioned earlier. This cinematic detail emphasizes how power can be imposed from above. Through flight they occupy the aerial space as a way to navigate and control terrestrial desert places in a way that mirrors their status above the law.

Such an extrajudicial position enables the team to successfully employ a "state of exception" by declaring an emergency to stop Manuel Diaz and eventually Fausto Alarcón in Mexico by any means they deem necessary despite jurisdiction and otherwise legally binding conditions. Theorist Giorgio Agamben explains that "the state of exception is not a special kind of law (like the law of war); rather, insofar as it is a suspension of the juridical order itself, it defines law's threshold or limit concept."[17] In other words, the perceived threat to national security that cartel activity creates is enough to warrant the interagency task force who operate in a liminality of law(lessness).

For example, when Kate first gets a moment alone with Alejandro, she learns that he's not an American citizen and that he used to be a Mexican prosecutor. He tells her, "I go where I'm sent," which this time means from Cartagena, Colombia. More confused than ever, Kate frustratedly asks Matt if he or Alejandro are CIA, and as Matt tries to tell her that Alejandro's a "DoD adviser just like me," she knows better.[18] Matt once more employs truth-telling by omission and says, "Look, just pay attention to Alejandro, and if he says to do somethin' just do it."[19] Kate, trying to take a moral and legal stance, replies: "I'm not authorized to follow orders from Alejandro. Especially in Mexico."[20] Despite her initial protests and the lack of a transparent chain of command, Kate craves justice enough to go with them into Juárez, though she now better understands that Matt and Alejandro outrank her. Under the guise of national security, they head to Juárez. In the scene where they cross into Mexico, examined earlier in terms of horizontal and vertical angles of traffic on the bridge, their swift, uninterrupted entrance conveys their authority across the border, despite the fact that what they're doing there is otherwise illegal.

Throughout the film, the team, especially Matt and Alejandro, are almost always able to carry out their objectives without any major obstacles or setbacks. In fact, the only time they are forced to a halt is when they are coming back to the US and get stuck on the bridge. Despite positioning agents at the border who are ready to wave them through to the US, a car up ahead has broken down, and their plans to get back without incident are thwarted. They are temporarily leveled, unable to ascend. Surrounded by hundreds of others awaiting entry to the US, their presence creates serious tension and violence erupts. Several gunmen are shot and killed while trying to get Guillermo back, and Kate is forced to shoot someone to save herself—part of the reason for her angst with Matt once they're back at the base. The shootout on the bridge is the only time that Matt's task force is not comfortable in its role above the law. And even stuck on the ground, the team manages to retain its privilege as law enforcement, while the people they've just killed lie dead in the street with no answerability. The cartel members have become additional casualties lost in the norm of the area's narcoviolence. When a man over the radio says "This is gonna be on the front page of every newspaper in America," an agent in Kate's vehicle chuckles and replies, knowingly, "No it won't. They won't even make the papers in El Paso."[21] The already-violent environment operates here as a cloak for the illegal violence carried out by the team, a justification for the state of exception they are already exploiting.

At the post-shootout argument at the base, Matt feels secure defending what they did, even if it didn't go by the book. He informs Kate that she is there as a part of the team because her participation as an FBI agent gives them "the opportunity to shake the tree and create chaos."[22] The chaos, which they provoke but cannot control, is made possible by the current state of exception which is amplified by conditions of the desert environment. John Beck makes the argument that "the metaphorical construction of the desert, despite historical change, has remained largely consistent with the notions of vacancy and chaos, notions that enable the validation of particular cultural and political ideological positions."[23] Certainly, the desert environments of *Sicario* allow the team to shake the tree to suit their agenda with total authority from their position atop the hierarchy. Sometimes this is due to the remoteness of desert areas that they can exploit through their advanced technologies, as in the case of infiltrating the drug tunnel at night, and other times it's due to already-chaotic milieu, like their excursion into Juárez where they killed several men who are ultimately absorbed into the violent conditions of the desert city.

One way the team succeeds in shaking the tree is when they get the chance, in Matt's words, to "fuck with Manuel Diaz's wallet" by freezing his bank accounts.[24] To do this, they watch from a van in the bank parking lot as a woman makes a deposit into Diaz's account, arresting her immediately and learning that $9,000 is deposited into the account daily, for a current total of $17 million. Though Kate finally feels like they've conducted an operation legally that they can use to go after Diaz, Matt informs her that "it's a bogus bust"; their objective remains getting Diaz back to Mexico.[25] Once again, a frustrated Kate reminds Matt, "We have no jurisdiction in Mexico!" to which he simply holds his ground.[26] Kate takes the bank bust to her boss, hoping for some "semblance of procedure" to follow.[27] He responds, almost sympathetically:

> Kate, this isn't something that I dreamed up myself. I don't have the authority to hire advisors, or authorize joint agency missions, or fly agents from Air Force bases. Are you understanding me? These decisions are made far from here, by officials elected to office, not appointed to them. So, if your fear is operating out of bounds, I am telling you, you are not. The boundary's been moved.[28]

From his words, it becomes clear that the hierarchical structure of the federal government is built to keep those with the most power at the highest rungs. The people with the power to move the boundaries are able to make otherwise illegal decisions—like sending Matt and Alejandro into Mexico—while they remain at a comfortable distance from the daily activities and violence in the US-Mexico borderlands.

It's the people like Kate, hoping to carry out lawful justice, who find themselves further down in the food chain and therefore more at risk for personal and professional harm. After Alejandro completes his mission and kills Alarcón and his wife and kids in Mexico, he returns to convince Kate to sign documents that say everything was done by the book. He convinces her by holding a gun under her chin and suggesting he could make her death look like a suicide. This moment more than any other in the film reveals the lengths to which the federal government will go to protect itself, even from the individuals it employs and the policies it makes them swear to uphold. Federal agencies—including military branches—as well as groups like cartels and street gangs employ the practice of individual disposability in the name of serving the collective cause. The former group are supposedly bound by law, but *Sicario* shows that this means little when they can move the legal boundaries as they deem necessary.

Cartels

While federal agencies operate from above the law, cartels, by their very nature, are structured to operate outside of and against federal laws, evading their enforcement as often as possible. The more remote desert environments of the US-Mexico borderlands have historically served as places of business for mules and moguls alike, used for the same conditions of spacious land as government militarization efforts discussed earlier. As a creative representation of desert lawlessness—a central trope of the Wild West—*Sicario* produces many displays of dramatized violence based on the real border violences that took place in El Paso–Juárez at the start of the twenty-first century. In this way, the film reckons with the grave truth that drug cartels were able to cultivate immense amounts of unchecked power, rivaling federal authorities for a spot at the top of the hierarchy. Throughout this chapter I've suggested Kate Macer as a stand-in for the viewer because we often learn new information alongside her. Kate, as the film's moral compass, believes that finding and convicting known players like Manuel Diaz will quell cartel activity. Instead, just as she learns how extensive her federal employer's chain of command is, she also becomes better acquainted with the larger landscape of cartel activity and by the film's end realizes that the two groups aren't so different.

Part of this larger landscape includes the historical relationships between drug cartels and US federal agencies. This is explained in the film through the reference to Medellín, "the former narcoviolence hotspot supplanted by Ciudad Juárez in the 2000s" and international hub for illegal cocaine distribution from Colombia in the 1970s and '80s.[29] The first time Kate hears Alejandro referred to as Medellín, she is at the end of the underground tunnel into Mexico she wasn't supposed to be in. When she asks Matt what the name means, his response is as close to sincere as he ever gets: "Medellín refers to a time when one group controlled every aspect of the drug trade, providing a measure of order that we could control. And until somebody finds a way to convince 20 percent of the population to stop snorting and smoking that shit, order's the best we can hope for."[30] The bottom line for Matt Graver and his task force is that the Mexican cartels have become too heterogeneous to control. As long as this is the case, they pose a serious threat to the US government's position atop the hierarchy of power, changing the dynamics of international drug trade and the US War on Drugs. Matt's glorification of the Medellín Cartel in the face of newer, small-scale and less predictable cartel operations reveals the relationship federal agencies were accustomed to, when the cartel activity could be factored in as a controlled chaos.[31]

And though the film is driven by the need to shut down cartel activity, specifically the operations of the Sonora Cartel, *Sicario* provides only a few glimpses of cartel life, as we mostly experience the film through the federal team's point of view. In yet another similarity to federal agencies, the cartel structure has a vertical hierarchy that enables different distributions of labor, power, and safety/distance. Those who rank lower are the men being shot at on the bridge for trying to get Guillermo back—lying dead and unaccounted for by the US federal agents who killed them; they are the people whose bodies are hanging from the highway overpass, decapitated and presumed to be a part of the supposedly justifiable violence and even necroviolence incurred through inter-cartel activities.[32]

As that scene cuts back and forth between the dangling bodies and Kate's unsettled visage, a team member provides morbid commentary on the cartel powers that be: "It's brilliant what they do. When they mutilate a body like that, they make people think they must have been involved, they must have deserved such a death 'cause they did something."[33] While this may seem like insight into a cartel tactic, it's ironically no different from how the federal agencies treat people they deem expendable; the lower someone ranks, the more disposable they are, and—as we witnessed Kate held by Alejandro at gunpoint—with cartel or federal resources it isn't difficult to make people believe that they had it coming.

The only cartel members that *Sicario* spends any time with, apart from Silvio, a low-ranking member whose tragic plight as a corrupt cop is discussed in the next section, are the higher-ups Manuel Diaz and Fausto Alarcón, who are first presented as men who enjoy the fruits of their labors. When we meet Diaz, he is in his mansion answering the phone call about his frozen bank accounts as he watches his kids playing in the pool. This scene presents him as a successful businessman, a family man who lives well—not a man who kills for a living. And Alarcón, while demonized as a bogeyman for most of the film, is ironically the cartel member most fully represented as human even though he is only in one scene. When Alejandro finds him in Mexico, Alarcón is sitting enjoying dinner with his wife and two kids in his luxurious backyard. Alarcón calmly pleas with Alejandro about excusing the heinous murders of his wife and daughter, telling him matter-of-factly that their deaths weren't personal, just business. Like Diaz, he has no tattoos like the men brandishing guns on the bridge, and he has the look of a modern businessman. Both men, up until each is assassinated by Alejandro, clearly maintain their and their family's safety by keeping a literal and figurative distance from concentrations of violence in the border regions. They live in nice houses far away from cartel street activity further south from the border, and they operate from atop the extensive vertical hierarchy by which cartels are structured.

Police
State and local police have the unique position of being further down, towards the middle of the hierarchy, where they operate in ways that enable the liminalities of the law that benefit cartels and federal agencies. In other words, their given, though limited, authority places them within the political tensions of local, state, and international power structures where cartel and federal actions influence how they do (or don't do) their jobs. *Sicario*'s portrayal of cops on both sides of the border implies systemic corruption and abuse of the law.[34] During their mission in Juárez, one of the first things Alejandro tells Kate as they wait for their team to pick up Guillermo is to "keep an eye out for the State Police. They are not always the good guys."[35] This warning sets the tone for Kate and viewers to rethink relationships to state-sanctioned authorities and is reinforced when the team meets to discuss their objective in the drug tunnel. Matt tells everyone the cartels "use Mexican police for vehicle transport. If you see a uniform in the tunnel, consider him a bandit, too."[36] Two characters, Phoenix cop Ted (played by Jon Bernthal) and Sonora State police officer Silvio (Maximiliano Hernández),

exemplify the complexities of working for law enforcement and cartels who rule from the top.

The pressure applied to and performance demanded of police working for the cartel pushes officers to act outside the law. *Sicario* certainly provides its audience with the high-stakes situatedness of both Ted and Silvio, who have two very different stories, contributing nuance to conversations of police corruption. While off duty, Kate is picked up in a cowboy bar by Ted, who coincidentally happens to know her partner Reggie (Daniel Kaluuya). The pair drink and dance together before she takes him back to her place. As they get more intimate, Ted pulls his keys and a rubber bracelet out of his pocket and puts them on the table beside them. Kate spots the bracelet and realizes it is identical to the ones found wrapped around the cash deposits at the bank bust. As she connects the dots, Ted attempts to calm her down with an invitation to just talk about it. Instead, Kate tries to land a blow before grabbing her gun, and they get into a brutal physical fight, his hands squeezing her neck as he tells her, "This is you, you hear me? You did this."[37] Ted is clearly conflicted about how the situation has escalated, trying to shift blame while he continues to strangle Kate on the floor until Alejandro, just in time, appears with a gun pointed at the cop's head.

The next time we see Ted, he's in the back seat of a vehicle, his face swollen, bruised, and bloody. Matt is in the front asking questions, and Alejandro is outside the car, in charge of the beating. Matt asks, "How many other corrupt motherfuckers you workin' with on this side of the border?" and Ted confesses, "They came to me and they wanted details about our case, and yes, I did it, I gave it to them, but I never wanted anybody to get hurt. I woulda never gotten involved with them pieces of shit if I thought that there was any—."[38] His speech is interrupted by Alejandro violently grabbing his wounded head; they aren't falling for Ted's sob story. In fact, Matt asserts his power, reminding the corrupt cop that it's his decision whether Ted's daughter will get federal protection or not. Ted used his position to feed cartel intelligence and attempt to murder Kate, and even though he admits that the situation got away from him, he ultimately made a choice that puts his fate in the hands of the feds.

Like Ted, Silvio is conflicted. He also has a family, and it is clear from scenes interspersed throughout the film that he is just trying to get by. Whereas Ted gets one major appearance in the film, Silvio's arc is presented

CHAPTER 3

Figure 13: Still from *Sicario* where an overhead shot captures cartel members moving bricks of drugs into the trunk of Silvio's police car while he looks on. (Fair use.)

to us throughout *Sicario*, in almost sporadic vignettes of his home life. In the first of these, we see Silvio's son wake him up to eat breakfast and play soccer. It's obvious, from the way Silvio is pouring liquor into his morning coffee and the bucket of cigarette butts next to his bed, that he is going through tough times. But we don't know what this means until Matt Graver's team are in the tunnel and the scene cuts to an overhead shot showing bricks of drugs being moved into Silvio's trunk while he watches: he is working with the Sonora State Police *and* the cartel (see fig. 13). From Silvio's demeanor at home and during this transaction, it's safe to infer that this is not something he wants to be doing but has to do if he values his life and family. And unlike Ted—who gets caught and beat up, but will ultimately be partially protected by Matt for providing information—Silvio's illegal transgressions will cost him his life. His role as mule for the cartel eventually leads him to an even less fortunate role as guide for Alejandro, who kills him once Silvio's purpose is served.

An important difference between the two seems to be that Ted's decision to help the cartel was much more of a choice than Silvio's, which makes viewers empathize more with Silvio, especially as we watch his son wait for his father at the kitchen table or play soccer knowing he's dead. Portraying

Latinos as hardened criminals and gangsters has become the norm for films and shows about narcoviolence. People who live with it in their daily lives are represented with more humanity by *Sicario*'s characters Silvio, his son, and wife—even if they have very limited screentime. Actor Maximiliano Hernández, who plays Silvio, is proud that the character is able "to show the heart of the people who are caught up in this web, in this net, called the war on drugs . . . many of which have no choice."[39] Even with a uniform and an official car, Silvio is near the bottom of the hierarchy, which renders him disposable, an acceptable and inhibiting loss for the cartel and US federal agents.

Migrants
Predictably, migrants are grouped at the bottom of the vertical hierarchy explored by *Sicario*, as they are given the least amount of attention, yet there's evidence of how they are subjected to the authority of police, cartels, and federal agents as well as the harsh conditions of desert environments. Their main role in the film—serving as sources of valuable information about migrant trails in the Sonoran Desert—is introduced in one of its most harrowing scenes, where the imbalance of power is made abundantly clear. It's night, and Matt, Alejandro, Kate, and Reggie pull up to a border checkpoint where there are several police vehicles creating a blockade in the foreground and US Immigration and Customs Enforcement (ICE) buses creating one in the background. It's pitch black outside apart from the border checkpoint's yellow lights. As the team members exit the vehicle, a man greets them: "What's the deal, Matt? Why you holding up my transport?"[40] He's also upset that Matt has written him a huge check for Domino's, a bribe for interrupting the delivery of detainees that he's sure the auditors will catch.[41]

Matt tells the man it was Kate's call, using her position as an FBI agent to smooth things over despite her immediate correction. Then Matt and Alejandro head toward the buses while Kate and Reggie take a moment; Reggie asks about El Paso and without any further details Kate tells him, "We weren't in El Paso. We were in Mexico," and then walks past the police vehicles, slowing down as she takes in what she sees ahead.[42] Somber strings and vocals signal that we are about to witness something heavy with her as the camera follows behind Kate to reveal the situation. Before her, and us, are hundreds of migrants, literal huddled masses, all silently sitting on

CHAPTER 3

Figure 14: Still from *Sicario*. Kate Macer approaches the busloads of migrants that have been stopped for questioning. (Fair use.)

the floor underneath the lights, with armed Customs and Border Protection officers and plainclothes agents like Matt and Alejandro standing over them (see fig. 14). A sequence of shots, including a close-up horizontal pan, shows the migrants in their diversity—they are men and women, teenagers and elderly—and switches between Kate and the group to show her discomfort and their powerlessness at this moment. This part of the scene is filmed so that the camera angle looks down upon the migrants from Kate's level and up to Kate's level from their seated position, visually reinforcing the hierarchy.

During this scene we learn that Alejandro and Matt are interested in the migrants who were picked up around Nogales because they might be able to tell them things about the land, specifically the location of a drug-running tunnel, that they wouldn't otherwise know how to find. In other words, they are using migrant experiences as a source for reliable information, a position that contradicts the initial portrayal of the migrants as silent and powerless. Echoing the complexity of Silvio's situation as a police officer in Sonora, *Sicario* here posits a brief but more complex understanding of migrant experience, shining a light on how the US federal agencies, specifically Border Patrol and ICE, treat these people—rounding them up and deporting them by the busload as "illegal aliens"—and putting that perspective into conversation with their human stories, ones that often include risking their lives to get away from oppressive conditions in their home countries.

ABOVE

Once Alejandro has spoken to some of the migrants to figure out what they might know, the team lets all the others go back to their buses. The next day, the chosen few end up discussing different border crossing routes with Alejandro as Matt looks on confidently. Congregated in a desert motel, the migrants, all men, are evidently unaware of the purpose their knowledge is serving, as one can discern by the cries of "No!" when Alejandro points to a location on the map and announces, "this is our spot."[43] Unsure why Alejandro wants to go where it is most dangerous, one of the men tries to warn:

> This is drug land. The only people who cross there are mules and *pollos*. It keeps Border Patrol away. Never cross where there are tunnels.
> (Alejandro): You know this area?
> (Migrant): For years it was the best place to cross. Here you can walk easily to Highway 86. There is water and shade.[44]

Alejandro, knowing they are getting helpful information, asks the man to mark the tunnel for them. He tells Alejandro that "they hide the entrance behind an old car" and then spots it on the satellite image.[45] In this scene, beyond assisting the team to carry out their mission, the man is sharing from a collective migrant history, revealing the land's storied deserts, detailing how the place on the map has served migrant crossings in the past and how this has changed recently. The place that used to be the easiest to cross had a highway, water, and shade—all vital factors for success in the harsh desert environments of Southern Arizona—but is now incredibly dangerous as the man confirms what Matt and Alejandro already know: drug cartel activity and narcoviolence have pushed migrants into the even more hazardous peripheries of the Sonoran Desert.

The motel scene is the last we see and hear of migrants in the film, but it's enough for us to learn that they've adapted their knowledge and thus their on-the-ground navigation of the desert terrain based on threats from both federal agencies and cartels. In the next chapter, I further analyze how migrants' horizontal journeys through the Sonoran Desert are at odds with the vertical, imposing authority of Border Patrol in Luis Alberto Urrea's *The Devil's Highway*. In both texts migrants face fatal consequences if they can't navigate land successfully, which is a tactic designed by groups higher up on the hierarchy. The dangers posed by cartel presence would be deterrent enough, but Prevention Through Deterrence (PTD), a US governmental "strategy that since the 1990s has deliberately funneled people into the desert," creates even more difficult conditions for migrants to contend with as they head north.[46] Cultural anthropologist Jason De León argues that "nature has been conscripted by the Border Patrol to act as an enforcer while simultaneously providing this federal agency with plausible deniability regarding blame for any victims the desert may claim."[47] In other words, Border Patrol have found a way to use the desert as an ally to weaken or kill migrants in the most extreme desert conditions, often alleviating themselves from any culpability.

Consequently, distance from migrant deaths in desert places has become increasingly common, while paradoxically it was proximity to the US-Mexico border that set PTD into motion. In 1993, Silvestre Reyes, former Chief Patrol Agent of the El Paso Sector, had the idea to line the border with roughly 400 agents for twenty miles, in essence forcing migration from the urban areas of El Paso–Juárez into further, more remote areas of the Chihuahuan Desert. This effort was called Operation Blockade and later renamed Operation Hold the Line, and lasted two weeks, causing a stir just as the Clinton administration was getting ready to sign the North American Free Trade Agreement (NAFTA) with Canada and Mexico. Out of apparent concern to quell the controversy at the border, then Attorney General Janet Reno called Chief Reyes to try and get him to end the operation on account of "political consequences, international ramifications."[48]

It was during this conversation that Reyes asked Reno to observe it for herself. He told her: "Come and visit El Paso . . . because you are making these statements, with all due respect, without knowing the difference that it's made in El Paso."[49] And so, after a day of meeting with El Paso locals and hearing what they had to say about the new strategy, Reno went back to Reyes impressed and determined to have him discuss his efforts with President Clinton. Reyes didn't yet know how the operation would, as De León puts it, "evolve into a large-scale policy that would strategically use the natural environment and subsequently become the foundation for border security in a post–9/11 world."[50] Being present in the El Paso area not only changed Reno's mind—it ultimately led to Operation Gatekeeper in San Diego and Operation Safeguard in Arizona.

ABOVE

Former Commissioner of the Immigration and Naturalization Service (INS) Doris Meissner was at the forefront of these new plans for patrolling the border. In a 2018 *Radiolab* podcast mini-series called "The Border Trilogy," Meissner explains, "the thinking was that it [the desert] would be a natural geographic ally that would take care of the rest."[51] In the interview she admits that government measures to force migrants into remote areas of the desert did not completely deter people from trying to cross the border into the United States. And though today she feels "deeply ambivalent" about the thousands of deaths caused as a consequence of Prevention Through Deterrence, her position of power atop the political hierarchy demonstrates the comfort and privilege of her distance from the realities migrants had to face.[52]

Taking up Agamben's idea of the state of exception, understood as "the process whereby sovereign authorities declare emergencies in order to suspend the legal protections afforded to individuals while simultaneously unleashing the power of the state upon them," De León grounds the concept in the geography of the US-Mexico borderlands, replacing the word "state" with "space":

> The US-Mexico border has long existed as an unspoken space of exception where human and constitutional rights are suspended [by the State] in the name of security. Border crosser deaths are justified by a person's lack of citizenship (i.e., exceptional status), his or her commission of a civil offense, and the hypocritical desire to protect the United States from the very people we rely on to pick our strawberries, pluck our chickens, and valet-park our cars. Lacking rights and protections when they illegally cross into sovereign territory, undocumented people are killable in the eyes of the state.[53]

For De León, it is accurate to understand the area of the borderlands as a *space of exception*. In this space, as in too many others, citizenship outweighs humanity, and claims of threats to national security override human rights. Though *Sicario* is ultimately a dramatic film informed by narcoviolence and is certainly not a documentary, the film fuels an expressive engagement with what the space of exception of the US-Mexico borderlands feels like for those in charge of enforcing it from above.

CHAPTER 3

FROM THE TOP

Discussing *Sicario* as a whole and why working on the film appealed to him so much, actor Maximiliano Hernández emphasizes, "It's brutal, it's unflinching. . . . It's to make you feel uncomfortable and say look, look how horrible this was—you know, or how horrible this is. And that's what provokes thought."[54] And I agree that it is incredibly uncomfortable. It's uncomfortable to watch a mysterious hitman like Alejandro torture or hunt down one person while somewhat arbitrarily saving another. It's uncomfortable to see that the FBI is overpowered by officials far from the violence affecting the US-Mexico border. It's uncomfortable to see someone like Kate Macer, vigilant as she is about doing things by the book, participate in less-than-legal operations of an interagency task force.

Importantly, the majority of the film's characters are people with some form of legal authority doing things that are illegal, disrupting comfortable alignments of morality with legality. In addition to revealing the (ab)use of the law by federal agencies, the film shows the rival scope and power that the cartels have. Rather than follow bosses Manuel Diaz or the elusive Fausto Alarcón through their day-to-day operations, we learn their capacity through information about daily bank deposits, corrupt cops, and the house filled with dead bodies during the raid. The film is dedicated to telling an important story: the narcoviolence that took place along the US-Mexico border, especially from 2007 to 2012, proved the law has limits it is willing to transgress and enabled a politics of threat that has endangered migrants in the space of exception through strategies like Prevention Through Deterrence.

Ultimately, the vertical hierarchy of power, examined here through groups ranked from "top" to "bottom" as represented in the film, aligns with the vertical perspectives produced through *Sicario*'s striking cinematography. Through disorientating bird's-eye shots which view the landscape from directly overhead, panning aerial shots which make the atmosphere palpable, and the use of infrared and night vision mediated lenses, *Sicario* creates a vertical desert aesthetic that defamiliarizes the traditional, horizontal cinematic deserts in order to present them anew as both place and space. That is, the film's affinity with filming from above provokes an engagement with spatial treatments of desert places that can only be accessed through a place of privilege. This approach allows audiences distinctive ways to view and therefore deconstruct the deserts of pop culture as backdrops while reconstructing them as agential environments that demonstrate desert abundance. Whether they are urban or rural or north or south of the border, *Sicario*'s vertical storytelling establishes desert environments as full of people and things, geopolitical, biopolitical, and human-nonhuman entanglements, and contributes a more comprehensive, multidimensional representation of deserts as places of multiplicity and possibility—and thus as storied deserts legible through the tactics of desert distortion.

CHAPTER 4

AGAINST

The aim of distortion writ large is to engage, reveal, and produce ways of appreciating the value of life and death on this planet. It is especially interested in working toward better futures in the face of anthropogenic climate changes and intensifying biopolitical conflicts. To that end, desert distortion is a technique to favor and foster complex understandings of desert places—as storied and abundant—through embodied and conceptual perspectival shifts achieved by the ongoing processes of (dis/re)orientation, (de)familiarization, and (de/re)centering. So far, I've established how borders are a generative case study for this technique, as each of the previous chapters wrestles with the US-Mexico border to some extent—whether as a settler invention imposed upon peoples *from* the land, as a postwar demarcation of territory created *through* legislature over time, or as a space of exception which those in power exploit as a "zone of lawlessness" from their position *above* the law. Keeping notions of horizontality in mind, this chapter engages the Border and its proliferation of borders, investigating their systemic violence *against* bodies that in turn must work *against* borders for survival. Specifically, my analysis focuses on Luis Alberto Urrea's *The Devil's Highway: A True Story* (2004) and Alicia Gaspar de Alba's *Desert Blood: The Juárez Murders* (2005), both useful works for examining how the changing socioeconomic and political

CHAPTER 4

climates of the 1990s affected and still affect people in and migrating to the US-Mexico borderlands today.

The turn of the twenty-first century preserved a geopolitical climate teeming with ways to dissolve and reconstruct the US-Mexico border in ways that those with the most power saw fit. In 1993 Mexico, Canada, and the United States signed the North American Free Trade Agreement (NAFTA), essentially leveling trade barriers between the three countries. Taking effect in 1994, the agreement paved the way for large-scale industrialization and exploitation for corporate profit along the US-Mexico border, especially through the use of maquiladoras, factory plants and warehouses where workers assemble and produce goods to be exported. In short: NAFTA influenced factories in the US to close down and enabled maquiladoras in Mexico to open up. The new "American-owned transnational factories" in Mexico depended upon cheap, exploitative labor, and their workforce was overwhelmingly made up of women.[1] Maquiladora working conditions are notoriously arduous—in addition to long hours and meager pay, employees are often subjected to poor ventilation, restricted bathroom access, exposure to toxic chemicals, and high risk of injury. In analyzing the language of NAFTA, critical legal theorist Elvia R. Arriola argues that its policies privilege "more rights for the investor than for the worker or migrant laborer," an issue that became increasingly apparent throughout the 1990s and into the current century.[2] As more women moved to Ciudad Juárez seeking opportunities to make a living and provide for their families, an increasing amount of violence towards women in the area, including assault, rape, and murder, surged.

Coinciding with the implementation of NAFTA and an increased amount of violence against women, who were disappearing at unprecedented rates, another set of events was drawing national attention towards the US-Mexico border. In 1993, the US Border Patrol in El Paso launched Operation Hold the Line, a two-week show of force that fended off illegal border crossings from Ciudad Juárez and surrounding areas into El Paso "in an effort to bring a level of control to the border" that the region had never seen before.[3] As discussed in chapter 3, though it was initially a threat to NAFTA, Operation Hold the Line was so effective that it fed directly into the launch of San Diego's Operation Gatekeeper in 1994, a "massive undertaking, involving the construction of walls and fences along parts of the border that were easier to cross and dramatically increasing the Border Patrol's personnel and the technology it uses for border surveillance."⁴ Both operations were effective at decreasing apprehensions in their respective major cities, though "apprehensions overall continued to rise as the flow of undocumented immigrants shifted from El Paso and San Diego, where Border Patrol strength had been increased, to other sectors on the Southwest border less well manned."⁵

In response, the Tucson sector in Arizona launched Operation Safeguard in 1995 and the McAllen sector in Texas launched Operation Rio Grande in 1997. Each of these subsequent operations implemented measures from prior ones, "including the installation of landing mat fence and stadium style lighting . . . night vision scopes, additional sensors" and allocating funds to more personnel, purchasing helicopters, and new cameras.⁶ Such strategies in the name of national security, like Prevention Through Deterrence (PTD), the Secure Fence Act of 2006, and the border wall itself, are the lasting legacies of these operations that have forced an uncountable number of migrants to their deaths as a result of using alternative, more remote routes.

Published only a year apart, Urrea's *The Devil's Highway* and Gaspar de Alba's *Desert Blood* depict two very different experiences of desert entanglements, though both concern living and dying in the US-Mexico borderlands. Additionally, both authors grew up in border towns—Urrea was born in Tijuana before moving to San Diego at three years old, and Gaspar de Alba was born and raised in El Paso. As such, they contribute complementary perspectives that give insight into ways of thinking about multiple, emergent borders in addition to a singular, fixed, and official, capital "B," Border. Where *The Devil's Highway* explores the rugged terrain of the Sonoran Desert in Arizona that gives the book its name, *Desert Blood* exposes discrepancies between urban and suburban settings in the Chihuahuan Desert in El Paso–Juárez; *The Devil's Highway* is an account of twenty-six men traversing fatal desert conditions, while *Desert Blood* focuses on missing and murdered women in Ciudad Juárez; the desert environment in *The Devil's Highway* has a hand in taking lives, while the desert of *Desert Blood* participates to a greater degree in obscuring deaths. This chapter emphasizes how each text informs the ways that borders are used against certain bodies and how certain bodies in turn work against borders.

A reminder here that national borders are invented. Invented but not imaginary—a descriptor which takes away from the many lives lost as a real consequence of their enforcement—and as such they foster the creation of complex border regions, which "is neither country," in the words of Victor Ortíz, but "a sociopolitical landscape of dramatic historic and economic dynamics defined by a pervasive dislocation, which is experienced very differently by the individuals and institutions involved."[7] To demonstrate this disparity, in the previous chapter, I showed how vertical *distance*, whether aerial or organizational, enables people with power to pull strings—in *Sicario* the US-Mexico border becomes just one such string. This chapter argues that *The Devil's Highway* and *Desert Blood* conversely contain elements of *nearness* through a mode of horizontality engaging on-the-ground, moment-to-moment activity, which does not afford such privileges. Historian Julian Lim posits that "we need not accept the state-centric premise that borders are fixed, constant, or unproblematic. . . . The region straddling the US-Mexico international line has thus always remained both borderlands *and* bordered lands, providing thoroughfares for certain kinds of crossings while shutting out others."[8] Framed through desert distortion, what follows is an exploration of the various borders presented in *The Devil's Highway* and *Desert Blood* through an analysis of horizontal, immanent engagement with desert places and an examination of how those borders interact with and against human bodies, and vice versa.

BORDERS IN *THE DEVIL'S HIGHWAY*

> They trotted along the road, Mendez in the lead, the other two gangsters taking up the rear. Nobody told the walkers anything. They thought they were going to jump a big fence and hide in trees as helicopters bore down. But they ran in sand, slipping and struggling, and they dropped into a dry wash and up the three-foot bank on the north side, and they stepped over a dropped and rusted barbed wire fence.
> "Los estados unidos, muchachos."
> "That's it? That's the border? This is North America? It don't look like much!"
> —Luis Alberto Urrea, *The Devil's Highway*, 103

Author Luis Alberto Urrea explains the contemporary magnetism of the north for Latin American people as something akin to the draw of the

West that birthed Manifest Destiny in the nineteenth century and informed Frederick Jackson Turner's Frontier Thesis in his 1893 essay "The Significance of the Frontier in American History." Urrea, who was born in Tijuana, Mexico, and moved to the US as a toddler, succinctly boils the mythos of a few hundred years down to just a few sentences:

> In North America, the myth tends west: the cowboys, the Indians, the frontier, the wild lands, the bears and wolves and gold mines and vast ranches were in the west. But in Mexico, a country narrow at bottom and wide at the top, **the myth ran north**. The Mayas pushed north, and the Aztecs pushed north once they'd formed an empire. Later, the Spaniards pushed north. The wide open spaces lay northward. The cowboys and Indians, the great Pancho Villa outlaws, the frontier, lay north, not west. That's why norteño people are the cowboys of Mexico—not westerners. The Spanish word for "border" is, after all, frontera. The frontier.[9]

For many, this directional shift, *south→north* instead of *east→west*, may be a new way to engage thinking about the US-Mexico Border, an example of desert distortion, or a disorientation that creates an opportunity for reorientation, as readers reimagine it less as a fixed line and more as a porous beacon of myth and promise through which, instead of looking down into (or sometimes onto) Mexico, they are invited to look "up there, above," from Mexico. When one applies the characteristics of the western frontier to the US-Mexico Border—with a capital "B" to signify the official international Border separating Southern Arizona and Northern Mexico since the Gadsden Purchase was finalized in 1854—in such an act of desert distortion, things immediately become less settled. Then, the Border begets borders.

This section highlights key examples of such borders, material and immaterial, in *The Devil's Highway*. For the Wellton 26,[10] the stakes of crossing the Border pale in comparison to the many other borders, material and immaterial, the men find themselves up against during their arduous navigation to the north. In fact, they are noticeably underwhelmed by the physical presence of the Border, the obstacle they'd always envisioned so much grander in their imaginations: "*That's it? That's the border? This is North America? It don't look like much!*"[11] Like the men of the Wellton 26, readers may be under the

CHAPTER 4

impression that most or even all illegal border crossings are accompanied by immediate action from Border Patrol or soldiers of so-called vigilante justice. However, the construction of a border wall stretching from California to the southernmost tip of Texas that has become a familiar contemporary component of the US-Mexico borderlands ecology was not yet erected, and so this just wasn't the case for the group in 2001 when they were making their journey. Following his description of a warning sign once placed in Sasabe, Sonora, by the Mexican government, Urrea proffers, "There is no real border here, just a tattered barbed wire fence, a dusty plain, and some rattling bushes."[12] In these examples, the Border itself does not physically perform in a way that matches the felt and far-reaching consequences of its very existence. Instead, the Border, as transcendent, monolithic bio/necropolitical entity, produces a multiplicity of borders, which in turn become active forces that impact certain bodies more than others. Thus, those affected in the desert environments of the borderlands must find ways to work against borders while confined to modes of horizontality at the low end of the hierarchical structures of power.

Based on his extensive research, including interviews with survivors and Border Patrol agents, Urrea's *The Devil's Highway* is a work of creative nonfiction recounting the Wellton 26's journey in 2001. The group, whom the author describes as "walkers" in order to reinforce their mode of horizontal navigation through the land, begins their trek south of the US-Mexico border and makes its way north into Arizona along a stretch of the Sonoran Desert known as the Devil's Highway, or *El Camino del Diablo*.[13] Most of the men die or go missing during the journey, woefully guided by a man called Mendez for whom the task was too great. Urrea's compelling writing style weaves the stories of the Wellton 26 so that in reading it we bear witness to the brutalities they face as they come up against a number of emergent borders, physical and psychological. As a result, Urrea often adjusts the book's focus to discuss the border-at-hand, resituating readers again and again to address the immanent conditions that threaten the group's survival, detailing their on-the-ground struggles through the immense desert region.

In a mode of perpetual horizontality, migrants walking on foot must constantly contend with physical, or material, borders, whether they are constructed by human design or are the natural geographic features and elemental conditions of a desert environment. In the first case, Urrea describes

Border Patrol agents known as "signcutters," who are trained to track walkers using key strategies like setting up "drags" and reading things like displaced pebbles and walker footprints as signs. Essentially, drags are the agents' way of wiping the slate of desert floor clean, like a Zen garden for catching walkers. Urrea describes the process:

> Drags are created by bundles of five car tires attached to a frame, looking somewhat like the Olympic rings. Every few days, a truck chains a drag to its back end and drives the roads, ironing the sand into a smooth surface. The drags tend to cut east/west. Since the illegals head north, they are forced, sooner or later, to cross a drag. The Devil's Highway itself is the Mother of All Drags.[14]

Drags are borders just as likely to bear consequences for walkers as their stepping across the US-Mexico border itself. Creating a smooth space along the roads forces walkers to inscribe upon it, taking advantage of the fact that the migrants are earthbound by horizontal movement. Drags also expose the ranking order in the vertical hierarchy discussed in the previous chapter—even though both agents and walkers leave distinct traces upon the land, only the agents may do so with authority. Agents set up the conditions by which the land becomes legible to them as it remains illegible to most migrants. Legibility, as discussed in chapter 1, is a key concept of storied deserts; the abundance, possibility, and multiplicity of desert places emerge and are revealed through sustained entanglement with the land. This means, in addition to their ability to "read the land like a text" and "search the manuscript of the ground for irregularities in its narration," signcutters contribute their own narratives to the desert places they patrol.[15]

The signcutters aren't the only group who read the land and its manifold material borders like a text, skills crucial in a place where every moment spent away from water or shelter, exposed to the elements, matters. *Guías* (guides), too, must know how to read the land. Also known as *polleros*, they are responsible for leading groups of walkers, or their *pollos*, from Mexico to safety in the US. Some guías are more successful than others. Though Mendez, the guía for the Wellton 26, had successfully taken groups north before, his usual route was through Southern California, a much different text to read than the Sonoran Desert in Arizona. Just a week before he set out with the Wellton 26, Mendez had successfully led a group through the Devil's Highway, his newly assigned territory, though they ended up getting busted. During the second, failed, and fatal group attempt documented in *The Devil's Highway*, navigation by unfamiliar landmarks coupled with inhospitable desert conditions explain why the group suffered as long as they did. According to Urrea, the group "didn't know that Mendez was in uncharted territory. He probably knew it, but seemed to think he could work out the puzzle of the landscape."[16] Mendez was never going to figure out the puzzle of the landscape because he didn't have the experience of walking through the land that would have made it familiar and therefore legible to him the same way it is for trained agents and other more experienced guías.

Eventually, Mendez leads the group up into the Growler Mountains, which quickly become the most immediate and prominent material border between the walkers and their success, which here means survival. Signcutters were able to determine that due to his left leg having "just a little less thrust than his right," the guía had veered and misled the group.[17] Not only was Mendez ignorant of the desert place he was trying to lead them through, he was also unaware of the way his own body interacted with the terrain. The guía, unable to attune to the land or his body, "always cut to the left."[18] According to Urrea:

> [Mendez] was clearly aware that Ajo and salvation lay over the unforgiving mountains to his right. He repeatedly tried to climb over the Growlers, dragging the crew up until they foundered, and then fell back, to hit the burning grit and bake as they rested. Then another slog north until a mild-looking slope presented itself, and they tried again, only to be foiled by the heat and the deceptive nature of these desert mountains. Just when they thought they were topping the summit, a higher ridge or peak appeared.[19]

With their increasingly weakened condition—exhausted, dehydrated, and unable to escape the all-pervasive heat—the men are guided more and more by the physical features of the land than by their guía Mendez. Drained of energy and morale, Urrea describes how "they followed the land, now tired enough to only want to flow downhill."[20] The nature of their journey, walking on foot, emphasizes the harshness of horizontality which mandates that geographical borders must be encountered head on in the elemental desert. No matter how high up in the Growlers they find themselves, the men remain unable to ascend its peaks or transcend its borders to get to safety.

Despite the incredible distance the Wellton 26 must walk, desert expanse becomes claustrophobic through its immediate and unrelenting oppression of their human movement. With regard to Mendez, Urrea describes that "the arroyos and gullies dulled his mind. It was all walls. There was no break."[21] No break, and in the vast expanse of desert country, Urrea conjures walls, borders. Without the physical ability to withstand its extreme conditions, the walkers and their guía are boxed in by the rocks, the sand, the heat, and even the light, which work against their bodies and fill the vastness.

As an example of desert distortion, *The Devil's Highway* defamiliarizes the horizontality of desert vastness, exploring it as a heterogenous place instead of a homogenous, or open, space. The idea of deserts as stifling runs contrary to the established aesthetics of the rocky landscapes of the American Southwest that have long served the national imagination as unwavering symbols of open roads and total freedom. Evidence of this aesthetic can be found in travel writing, visual art, car commercials, and films alike, as all have long capitalized on the horizontal openness of the region's desert places, turning isolation into liberation. Migrant experiences refute the common equation of openness and freedom, revealing the important interrelationship of privilege and place—the American Southwest is a place of freedom for whom?

From their battle against the physical borders of the Growler Mountains, filled with harsh desert conditions like extreme heat and vastness, emerge psychological borders between expectations and reality. Most of the Wellton 26 were from tropical Veracruz and had never even seen a desert before—a common situation as walkers often use guías because of their own lack of experience with the terrain.[22] With no reference points from which to understand what walking through the Sonoran Desert would entail, the chasm between their imagined journey and their lived experience grew as the group walked on. Further, Mendez's expectations clearly underestimated the stakes, as he led the group "into a blank map with landmarks etched in transient memory, known by obtuse Coyote descriptions," that are only helpful if one is truly familiar with its desert environment, not operating from a distance.[23] Urrea points out how painstakingly near to salvation the group was: "he was only about five miles off."[24] Despite being lost, Mendez repeatedly and

CHAPTER 4

inaccurately assures the group that there were only a few more steps, days, or deserts before they reached their desired destination: "'It's just a few more miles,' Mendez told them, but they already understood that he was wrong."[25] The scale of distance demanded by place in this instance is difficult to process. He does not know this specific land well enough, and the border between what he thinks will be the journey versus what the journey actually entails tragically proves to be fatal for fourteen men in the group.

Even information that the men know well enough becomes subject to change due to an onset of immaterial borders between clear thinking, remembering, and forgetting. These borders surface with disorientation from heat, dehydration, and exhaustion and endure with the survivors well after they are rescued. This announces itself in the survivors' stories as

> their accounts of the following days fade into a strange twilight of pain. Names are forgotten. Locations are nebulous, at best, since none of them, not even the Coyotes, even knew where they were. Nameless mountains loomed over them, nameless stars burned mutely overhead, nameless demons gibbered from the nameless canyons.[26]

Repetition of the word "nameless" suggests an enduring psychological barrier that inhibits their ability to orient themselves in space and time. In chapter 2, I discuss namelessness as a tactic in *Blood Meridian* that marks the act of not knowing intimate information about a place, person, or event. Namelessness in *The Devil's Highway* serves this purpose too, as most if not all of the men, including Mendez, were not familiar with the areas they were traveling through. Additionally, I argue that this namelessness helps emphasize the psychological impacts of experiencing extreme desert conditions even after the fact; the survivors are unable to remember any specific names or locations, yet the affective intensities of their experience remain accessible.

It's clear from Urrea's work that the walkers spend much of their journey in the liminal space between life and death, the ultimate mortal border that threatens them at every step of their journey: "You are now at the borderline, standing before the abyss. One more step, and you cannot return. Another border crossing."[27] Ultimately it is this border that makes migrants who are struggling hope for La Migra to find them, no matter the legal consequences;

whatever penal reprimand is in order, it is worth living for. Urrea writes that walkers "often gave themselves up when they realized the western desert had gotten the better of them."[28] And this is by design. Jason De León writes extensively about the Border Patrol's implementation of Prevention Through Deterrence (PTD), "an infrastructural funnel along the US-Mexico border that intentionally directs people toward the desert."[29] As De León points out, the Border Patrol have increasingly used desert places as "a tool of boundary enforcement *and* a strategic slayer of border crossers . . . violence has been outsourced to mountains, extreme temperatures, and thousands of square miles of uninhabited terrain."[30] This is the larger context that the Wellton 26 find themselves within, the one that enforces the Border against migrants through a proliferation of physical and psychological borders that their bodies must work against to survive, borders that have cost thousands of migrants their lives.

BORDERS IN *DESERT BLOOD*

Published in 2005, *Desert Blood* is a work of fiction informed by the staggering rise of violence against women that plagued the El Paso–Juárez area in the 1990s. The book follows the journey of protagonist Ivon Villa, a professor of Women's Studies, as she returns to her hometown of El Paso with hopes to adopt a child.[31] When readers first meet Ivon, she is on a plane from Los Angeles learning about the *feminicidios*, the ongoing crisis of murdered and missing women, from an issue of *Ms.* magazine. As she descends into the milieu of the border town in the book's opening pages, her verticality and distance are exchanged for horizontality and nearness. With this transition to horizontal storytelling—an act of desert distortion—Ivon and readers are set up to encounter the immediate dangers of gendered violence[32] being carried out against women along the Border, on the ground. Sometimes this is in the specific context of unethical working conditions of maquiladoras, which I discuss later in this chapter and include monitoring menstruation, requiring workers to take pregnancy tests, and firing pregnant employees. Other times, like when Ivon's teenage sister Irene is kidnapped, Gaspar de Alba is addressing the broader threat to women in the area as targets of sexual violence. *Desert Blood*, like *The Devil's Highway*, contains proliferations of material and immaterial borders that emerge from the enforcement of the Border itself. As a continued demonstration of the multiplicity and possibility of desert places—storied deserts—my analysis of Gaspar de Alba's novel here provides examples of geographical and legal borders that the women in the novel must, not always successfully, work against.

In the borderlands, the geographical is always-already geopolitical. At the end of the twentieth century, women from across Latin America were coming to Juárez to work at the maquiladoras and provide for their families. Terribly low wages have meant that the workers often live in colonias, unincorporated sections of a town or city with few to no amenities like electricity and running water. The distance between these "poorly served shantytowns that sprang up in the desert and hills southwest of Juárez" and the factories created a border that women had to go up against daily despite dangerous and sometimes deadly conditions.[33] Maquiladora workers often travel in the dark hours of morning or night, walking through stretches of desert between colonia and maquila, in order to ride company buses to and from work.

When Ivon and her cousin Ximena go to Juárez to pick up Cecilia after her shift, they are unable to find her. Cecilia is a pregnant maquila worker who has agreed to let Ivon adopt her baby. Ivon suggests paying Cecilia a house visit to check on her, but Ximena rejects the idea immediately: "she lives in a colonia way out in Puerto Anapra. Wild horses couldn't drag me there at night, ésa. No roads, no electricity. Just a black hole of danger, especially for women."[34] The pair are not willing to brave the border between the maquiladora and the colonia, the same border that other women who work at the factories have no choice but to cross. The same border that deprives women of their safety based on time of day or night and their distance from anyone who would be able to hear or see them in trouble, let alone help.

In addition to oppressive working conditions in the maquilas and a lack of basic amenities in the colonias, desert places connecting work and home become increasingly threatening, especially to women traveling alone and on foot—horizontally. In the 1990s, the Chihuahuan Desert had seemingly become a burial ground for hundreds of women, many of whom, just like their killers, were never found or identified. In *Desert Blood*, readers learn about *rastreos*, or searches for bodies, through Father Francis and his nonprofit Contra el Silencio.[35] Joined by volunteers primarily comprised of family and friends of the missing and murdered women, Father Francis leads groups through the desert areas around Juárez, which in turn become difficult geographical borders to cross. Unlike Mendez in *The Devil's Highway*, the priest in *Desert Blood* is an effective guide because he has spent so much time walking through the land that he can discern the different terrains of places like Lomas de Poleo.

When interviewed for a local television show called *Mujeres Sin Fronteras*, Father Francis breaks down the land into three categories: "the sandy terrain," "rock and limestone," and "scrub brush and thorn bushes."[36] Each entails characteristics, like extreme heat and light or even scorpions, that warrant one's attention to the elemental immediacy of desert place. Of the third terrain, which is the most difficult to navigate, Father Francis warns that "the whole panorama can change in a matter of minutes, so it's easy to get lost."[37] The desert landscape itself thus constructs borders preventing groups like Contra el Silencio from successful searches—in this case through disorientation as much as heat or distance. Further, because the groups must travel by foot it is easier to lose their bearings, so they are instructed to look to the nearby peak of Mount Cristo Rey, which has a forty-foot statue of Christ on the cross as a vertical marker for reorientation.[38]

Through the lens of desert distortion—which requires processes of (re/dis)orientations in order to understand the complexities and possibilities of desert places—I suggest that as readers and characters alike navigate the events, entanglements, and disorientations of the text, Gaspar de Alba repeatedly relies on prominent landmarks of the El Paso–Juárez area as ways to reorient. The landmarks include the aforementioned Mount Cristo Rey and Franklin Mountains as well as built structures like the ASARCO smelting stacks and El Paso's Border Highway. Of course, the most significant is the Rio Grande, the so-called "natural border" that lends its shape to the Border itself as seen on maps depicting the region since the 1850s.

Gaspar de Alba uses the river's liquid qualities to mirror both the flow and tension of identity and culture between El Paso and Juárez. For example, Ivon's sixteen-year-old sister, Irene, goes missing after attending a party in a Juárez colonia, but not before she swims back and forth across the Rio Grande: "She breast-stroked and back-stroked back and forth across the river, daring the Border Patrol vans cruising the black bridge to take her in so she could laugh at them and tell them she was an American citizen."[39] Irene both embodies and literally swims in the tension between the US and Mexico. She becomes the hyphen in Mexican-American, much as the river is the hyphen connecting El Paso–Juárez. She infiltrates the Border. When

CHAPTER 4

Ivon finds out Irene is missing, she visits her ex-lover Raquel and learns that she was the reason Irene was at a colonia in the first place. Raquel recounts that Irene was "playing wetback . . . no *mojado* would be swimming like that, back and forth, like it was a swimming pool."[40] The fluid border of the Rio Grande that Irene takes pleasure being enveloped in speaks to the liquidity of identity that comes with being from a place so liminal as a border town. Internally, Irene struggles at the party because she isn't Mexican enough to be accepted, but externally she looks Mexican enough to fit the physical and racial profile of many of the women who have gone missing in the area: "Teenagers with dark skin and dark hair, slim and short."[41] During the rastreo, this thought hits Ivon as she looks at what is left of a body. She thinks about the people who took Irene, and how they might not know that Irene had never worked at a maquila; "all they saw was another thin, dark-skinned, dark-haired young Mexican woman, and didn't realize she was a Mexican with the privilege of US citizenship."[42] Irene, like many Chicanx people of the area, is not culturally either/or; she is both/and—a complex reality that national borders by design cannot accept, but one that desert distortion is helpful for thinking-with.

Viewed from a legal perspective, the Border signifies a limit, a jurisdiction, to the application of the law and commitment to justice for all. Sometimes, as in my analysis of *Sicario* in the previous chapter, this limit is transcended by governmental powers atop the hierarchy. Other times, as in *Desert Blood*, local officials on either side use jurisdiction as a way to cease or plead ignorance about investigations that may be connected to cartel violence and especially the feminicidios. This legal approach works against the otherwise integrated cultures of El Paso and Juárez, two cities isolated together in the northern Chihuahuan Desert that are economically, socially interdependent. With regard to her missing sister, Ivon mentions several times that "the authorities on both sides are washing their hands of this situation" and "acting like it's not their jurisdiction," referring to regulations that disable them from continuing the investigations.[43] She begins keeping notes about her sister's case and readers learn that neither the El Paso nor Juárez police are officially committed to taking the case on. In a section titled "facts," Ivon writes that the most the El Paso police can do is "call her a 'Missing Person,' and since it happened across the border, they have no jurisdiction over there," and the authorities in Mexico argue that "because Irene was last seen sitting on the

El Paso riverbank, this is a probably a case for the American authorities, not the Juárez police."[44] It becomes obvious that the law is not going to cross the Border to save Irene, but that it has itself *become* a border, an obstacle to finding the young girl and countless others.

Gaspar de Alba also explores the abuse of legal authority through the novel's villain, known as El Guero or Lone Ranger until it is discovered that he is really a Border Patrol agent and Chief Detention Enforcement Officer Captain J. W. Wilcox. Hiding in plain sight as someone who wields the power of letting people cross the border into the US and authorized to cross back and forth as he sees fit, Wilcox, readers learn, runs a snuff business in which kidnapped women, often maquila workers, are tortured, raped, and killed for online entertainment. It's Wilcox's crew who have taken Irene into captivity. The way the character exploits his position both protects and enables him to continue his operations without scrutiny. Even after his death, Wilcox is honored with a twenty-one gun salute while Ivon's testimony against him is questioned.[45] Whether it's the local police force throwing their hands up in the name of jurisdiction or Wilcox's hiding in plain sight, nearness to the Border becomes an excuse for eschewing legal responsibilities at the cost of countless lives.

BODIES IN *THE DEVIL'S HIGHWAY*

> Their arms were too heavy to lift. They couldn't get their watches up to their eyes. The heat was heavy. The sunlight weighed a thousand pounds. Their mouths were as dry as the soles of their feet: their tongues were hard and dense and did not want to bend. They sucked and sucked at the insides of their mouths, but they couldn't raise any spit.
> —Luis Alberto Urrea, *The Devil's Highway*, 159–60

The Wellton 26's journey, navigated on foot, horizontally, through the rough, hot, and dry terrain of southwestern Arizona, tests the limits of the human body against intense nonhuman forces like heat and light. Urrea provides staggering and detailed descriptions of the strain and change that the men's bodies undergo as they remain in near constant movement, entrenched in a battle with an alien environment that offers no reprieve. The Devil's Highway reminds them of its

CHAPTER 4

inhospitality with each step: "The sand was deep enough that they slid back a half step for every step they climbed and it didn't take long for their thighs to start burning."[46] Working twice as hard, the men lose stamina twice as fast in order to move forward at all. Further, they spend the majority of their journey on the high ground of the Growlers, initially intent on "baffling the Migra's drag system" before becoming completely lost and disoriented.[47]

Heading for higher ground had previously worked for their guía Mendez, though that was on a different journey through the Quitobaquito Hills, where evading the Border Patrol was easier because the "ground was so rough and crooked that all you had to do was squat under a paloverde or a mesquite, or hug a creosote. Mexican skin, from the air, is hard to tell apart from the ground."[48] In that situation the walkers were able to use their horizontal mode of movement as an advantage over agents who searched for them from a vertical vantage point. However, the trek through the more extreme terrain of the Growler Mountains in the middle of May makes hugging creosote seem almost wholesome and suggests that the Border Patrol aren't the only authorities operating against walkers in the area. As discussed at length in chapter 2, desert elemental conditions have the power to produce literal, embodied senses of distortion—especially changes in perception—that push bodies towards their phenomenological limits, which this section explores through the walkers' experiences in *The Devil's Highway*.

Heat is as inescapable in the text as it was for the men of the Wellton 26. Numerous references, including different ways that walkers try to fend it off, litter the pages. The book rightfully holds a great reverence for how heat affects and interacts with the human body and dedicates ample attention to its very real elemental agency, but it's Urrea's explanation of the six stages of heat death, or hyperthermia, that I'd like to focus on here. In it, he breaks down the agonizing process and conveys the range of effects that bodies face. With the first stage, heat stress, Urrea writes, "the heat becomes personal," while the next stage, heat fatigue, brings with it the flesh of the world as it tears at one's flesh: "the air comes to your lips and pulls water from you. Every breath dries out your nose, your sinuses, your mouth, your throat" and, through some sort of heat-crazed body scan, the awareness of one's own embodiment becomes overwhelming, jarring.[49]

During the third stage, heat syncope, fever makes one cold and turns skin pale while Desolation—Urrea's own word for and personification of "the desert"—"has begun to edit you. Erase you."⁵⁰ Heat cramps are next, a crucial stage because "eighty percent of lost walkers can still be saved if the Migra spots them."⁵¹ During the fifth stage of heat exhaustion, one's brain may attempt to shut the body down to "try and tend to damage control," but eventually they'll experience "tunnel vision . . . second degree burns from lying too long on the ground" and "your memories are conflated with your dreams."⁵² Urrea notes that this is when people first understand they need to drink their own urine. During the last few stages, one begins to experience intense hallucinations, which demonstrate a limited physiological and psychological capacity for coping with extreme heat. The final stage of hyperthermia is heat stroke, when blood vessels burst and body temperature soars. The author reveals that walkers will sometimes strip nude at this point:

> Once they're naked, they're surely hallucinating. They dig burrows in the soil, apparently thinking they'll escape the sun. Once underground, of course, they bake like a pig at a luau. Some dive into sand, thinking it's water, and they swim in it until they pass out. They choke to death, their throats filled with rocks and dirt. Cutters can only assume they think they're drinking water.⁵³

These and other descriptions in *The Devil's Highway* are equally baffling and horrifying. What must it be like to mistake sand for water during the last throes of one's life? Ultimately, heat death can be understood as a great leveler for understanding human finitude in the face of elemental immediacy—the six stages "are the same for everyone. It doesn't matter what language you speak, or what color your skin."⁵⁴

In a desert place like the Growler Mountains, light joins heat, intra-acting with rocks, plants, animals, and humans with intensity—"instant and profound."⁵⁵ The longer a human body is exposed to sunlight, especially without access to water or sufficient shelter, the more of a threat it becomes. In fact, Urrea calls hyperthermia "death by sunlight," acknowledging the light as an adversary against walkers due to its reflectivity in the mountains and its partnership with heat which provides no respite.⁵⁶ The author contends that Mendez had made three major mistakes since the outset of the group's journey: "First, he'd gotten started too early, and they'd been precooked by extra hours in the sun. Then he'd taken the wrong turn at Bluebird. And now,

CHAPTER 4

he started walking in the light."⁵⁷ Notably, two of the three mistakes involve underestimating the agential force of light; paying attention and working with the light as much as possible could have given the Wellton 26 a better chance at survival.

Though exposure to sunlight is ultimately fatal for some of the men, Urrea paints a more complex picture of light's role in desert abundance that understands its necessity and impact beyond the human:

> It opened certain blossoms and closed others. The desert was full of color, though they couldn't see it from the valley where they awoke. . . . The last bats sipped their last saguaro nectar. The first hummingbirds swarmed up from Mexico and took their place. . . . Rattlesnakes eased from dens and unfurled in the light, soaking up the day's warmth. Tarantulas backed timidly into their burrows. Scorpions wedged themselves in dark crevices.⁵⁸

In this description readers witness the fullness of a desert place, a transition between its nocturnal and diurnal rhythms as its ecosystem is guided by the dawn's light. Tragically the walkers were led by someone who "decided to break with the pattern," resulting in a physical struggle where light and heat perform against their bodies and become life-threatening.⁵⁹ However, these observations are a testament to light's significance as it conducts the flora and fauna of desert places, all of whom have adapted with it, through extreme temperatures and aridity.

To contend with intense elemental desert conditions, guías have developed techniques to keep migrants going as long as possible. When bodies inevitably start to give out, one of the methods used to make walkers dependable again is to give them drugs and fat-burners, which creates a false sense of strength, energy, and capability. Sometimes cocaine is used "to make them walk faster and longer. Of course, cocaine helps their hearts explode, too."⁶⁰ Other times, Urrea writes, "low-rent Coyotes were using a new chemical prod to speed up their walkers. It turns out that ephedra-based diet pills are cheaper, effective, and easily available. The apparent Coyote favorites are over-the-counter 'fat burners.'"⁶¹ These are obviously dangerous approaches, as they bestow already taxed bodies with even more physiological duress. In truth, the possibility of dying due to drug usage becomes yet another force working against walkers, though it is evidently worth the risk for guías.

Even without drugs, when heat and light encounter human bodies through elemental immediacy, they create disorienting experiences of distance and time. As the body tries to fight against increasing fatigue and delirium, perceptual shifts destabilize and defamiliarize one's sense of spatiotemporality; with prolonged exposure to the elemental forces of desert environments, miscalculating one's location or the amount of ground left to cover can lead to misjudged uses of resources like water and energy, and are essentially fatal. For instance, Urrea writes, "Ten trees a quarter mile apart can look like a cool grove from a distance. In the western desert, twenty miles looks like ten. And ten miles can kill."[62]

In a situation like the Wellton 26's, where every step is a struggle and no one is familiar with the terrain, desert vastness can make the land threateningly illegible. It is this illegibility that lends itself to representations of *the* Desert that this book works hard to think against. Even so, for anyone contending with unfamiliar spaces of desert environments by way of walking, a purely horizontal perception of distance and time can become dangerously abstract—a disparity between human and nonhuman scales that renders the former inadequate. Urrea describes the passing of time in experiential terms as the walkers begin another torturous day and wait in the heat for Mendez to return: "Six o'clock in the morning took ten hours to become seven o'clock. A week later, it was eight o'clock."[63] And while this description nearly reads like nonsense, it conveys an alternative sense of temporality based on felt intensity as opposed to accurately accounting for standardized units of measuring time. In a disorienting relationship with the land and its elemental forces, the body undergoes changes that are difficult for the mind to comprehend. There is not always a reorientation, which of course decreases one's chance of survival.

And what of the people who fail to find respite? The reality is grim. Animals and environmental conditions of desert places like aridity and heat work against their bodies even postmortem. In a matter of days, bodies can be transformed beyond recognition. Urrea reveals, "the nature of desert death is such that forensic evidence is quickly obliterated. The body mummifies. In one of the million ironies of the desert, those who die of thirst become waterproof. Their fingers turn to stiff leather, and the prints are unreadable."[64]

CHAPTER 4

In De León's *Land of Open Graves*, he argues "the postmortem events that affect the bodies of migrants in the desert are a form of necroviolence largely outsourced to nature and the environment but intimately ties to Prevention Through Deterrence, territorial sovereignty, and the exceptional (i.e., killable and disposable) status the US government ascribes to undocumented border crossers."[65] Referring to experiments using dead pigs as proxies for human bodies, De León writes about the various ways that the bodies were eaten, skeletonized, and torn apart by coyotes, domestic dogs, and especially by turkey vultures.[66] After detailing timelines, usually days to weeks, that the bodies endured necroviolence due to animals, he concludes: "constant physical movement and destruction of body parts and personal effects suggests that with enough time, a person left to rot on the ground can disappear completely."[67] An inability to identify bodies is perhaps one of the most disturbing consequences of desert death. It keeps Border Patrol agents from having to think of bodies as people with names and families and friends and dreams and dignity. It obscures the stories that they carry, is an erasure.

As evidence that identification of the bodies is of political and economic importance, Urrea reports that an unidentifiable body found in Arizona is billed to the state's taxpayers, while an identifiable body is paid for by the Mexican government, taking what is often its first plane ride back to Mexico.[68] The act of racializing migrant bodies postmortem is equally intriguing—the fourteen dead bodies of the Wellton 26 were identified as white, a privilege they would never have been afforded legally or otherwise while alive. Urrea mentions this as a "final surprise" and he writes that "file after file says the same thing . . . all of them have been listed in death as WHITE MALE."[69] This recounts the notion of racial passing in death discussed in chapter 2, where *Blood Meridian*'s villains, the judge and John Glanton, contemplate whether or not a man's head they've just severed could pass for that of Gomez. When the judge responds "no" because the dead man is *sangre puro*, this demonstrates how the scrutiny that Indigenous, Mexican, Latinx bodies undergo while alive is often just as present when they're dead.[70] These examples show that violence against racialized and gendered bodies doesn't end with a person's life, but can persist after death.

The Devil's Highway is an interesting look at the adult male migrant experience in southwestern Arizona facing and creating borders as they engage with the roughest parts of the Sonoran Desert. Urrea also attests to the trials that women migrants and their children have to face in the desert, albeit briefly. In fact, according to his research with the Border Patrol, "all the agents seem to agree that the worst deaths were women and the children."[71] Toward the book's end, after imparting that no one will ever know if Mendez meant to mislead his group—desert them in the desert—or whether it was just plain stupidity, the author reminds the reader of the many ongoing and unsolved murders of women around Juárez, "still being slaughtered and abandoned in desert lots, rotting and mummifying where their rapists and torturers dropped them."[72] He does this, without holding back in his morbid descriptions, to illustrate the disparities of gendered violence.

BODIES IN *DESERT BLOOD*

> Were these crimes happening to men, were men being kidnapped, raped, mutilated, and dismembered, no matter what their class, we would already know the answers to the question of "Who is killing the women of Juárez?"
> —Alicia Gaspar de Alba, *Desert Blood*, 323

Before an exponential escalation of cartel violence made Juárez one of the most dangerous cities in the world at the beginning of the twenty-first century, hundreds of women in the 1990s became the victims of feminicidios that plagued the area. These acts of brutal, gendered violence took the form of kidnapping, rape, murder, and mutilation either before or after death. Further, desert vastness and elemental forces allowed many, whether killer or victim, to remain unidentified; bodies were disposed of and left to decay in unfrequented parts of the Chihuahuan Desert, and the limits of law to track down and prosecute those responsible were tested and exploited. The increase in feminicidios was aided by oppressive conditions of poverty and political strife in Mexico and Latin America that drove people from their homelands in search of refuge and opportunities for work.[73]

NAFTA's implementation took advantage of these dire circumstances for migrants, many of whom were not local to the US-Mexico borderlands, and by 1999 there were over 300 maquilas in Juárez. It's hardly coincidence, then, that the murdered and missing women in the area were often maquiladora workers, a workforce that until the turn of the century was primarily made up of women, who fit the "gendered tropes of global capitalism" which view the ideal worker as "cheap, docile, dextrous, and female."[74] According to Melissa Wright, in 2001 there were "thirty-one hundred maquiladora facilities in Mexico, with a total employment of more than one million workers. Almost one-fourth of these workers are employed in maquiladoras located in Ciudad Juárez, and approximately 60 percent of these employees are women."[75] Perceived by businesses as the ideal demographic for the hard labor, "the economic, political and gendered forms of violence faced by maquila workers represent the ways in which working class women from the global South have been constructed as docile and cheap, therefore, producing a narrative that justifies and perpetuates the continued devaluation and exploitation of their bodies and their labour."[76] As an embodiment of their rank in the hierarchy of power, women are kept in a mode of horizontality working on the factory floor of the maquilas while their male supervisors often watch them from above. While I am not proposing to define maquila workers solely through the lens of victimization nor condemn the city of Juárez only as a place to be feared, my work in this chapter demonstrates that the area was a violent and devastating place for women and especially maquila workers at the end of the twentieth century, especially because of its location in the Chihuahuan Desert.[77] This is just as important a part of the storied deserts in the US-Mexico borderlands as any other, as histories influence futures.

Throughout *Desert Blood*, Gaspar de Alba provides examples of how gendered violence specifically targets women's bodies and especially as a condition of working for the maquiladoras in Juárez. Literary scholar Tereza Jiroutová Kynčlová, analyzing the characters of Cecilia, who is forced to hide her pregnancy and give up her child in order to keep her job, and Elsa, who is artificially inseminated by a doctor at the maquila who tests out an experimental contraceptive,[78] explains that they both "engender the systematic and systemic exploitation practices that capitalism and androcentrism apply to women's productive and reproductive bodies."[79] At one point in the novel, Ivon and fictional television host Rubí Reyna discuss women's reproductive capabilities as their only form of power to work against the system that's working against their bodies. Rubí tells Ivon, "most of these young women are migrants . . . they're the easiest workers to exploit. They don't unionize, they don't complain, they'll accept whatever wage they get," to which Ivon suggests that the fact "they can *get* pregnant" is "the threat they pose when they come this close to the border."[80] Ivon is correct here: because of the proximity to the US and the ability to bear children, women's menstrual cycles and the possibility of pregnancy became a biopolitical concern for maquiladoras in the borderlands. Even though the practice "violates Mexican law and has been hard fought by local and international labor organizations," many maquilas in Mexico have continued to impose regular pregnancy testing and even monitor menstruation cycles.[81] There is no ethical justification for subjecting workers' bodies to these procedures; it is all so that the companies can optimize productivity as they continue to take advantage of young and abled women for maximum profit.

In addition to exploitation of women as workers, the objectification and sexualization of women's bodies contributed to a significant disregard of the increasing number of feminicidios. This issue presents itself in *Desert Blood* during Rubí Reyna's show, *Mujeres Sin Fronteras*, when her guest Paula del Rio, "founder of an organization that advocated for the protection of women against sex crimes and domestic abuse in Juárez," adamantly explains "were these crimes happening to men, were men being kidnapped, raped, mutilated, and dismembered, no matter what their class, we would already know the answers to the question of 'Who is killing the women of Juárez?'"[82] To del Rio's point, attitudes of indifference with regard to violence against women's bodies are often rooted in a patriarchal system that keeps women at the lowest end of the hierarchical power structure and a deep suspicion of their sexual prowess: "Circulating through the media and by word of mouth—as onlookers try to determine if the murder victims were prostitutes, dutiful daughters, dedicated mothers, women leading 'double lives,' or responsible workers—is the question: 'Was she a good girl?' The question points to the matter of her value as we wonder if she is really worthy of our concern."[83] In the plight to locate her sister, Ivon becomes increasingly frustrated because everyone thinks the former ran away for a boyfriend or because she was asking for it. Even one of the pictures of Irene she wants to use for her missing persons flyer is judged inappropriate by Father Francis because her red lipstick, which looks black in print, "Sends the wrong message."[84] When Ivon challenges this assertion, saying the photo is helpful because it shows what Irene was wearing the night she was kidnapped, he sticks to his point by first informing her that often the killers change the women's clothes and second that if people "see a picture of someone that to them looks like a prostitute,

CHAPTER 4

they won't have any sympathy for her."[85] Ivon has no choice but to concede, and the flyers are made with Irene's graduation picture on them instead.

The Devil's Highway establishes that "bodies" is a word used by the Border Patrol to mean living migrants that have crossed the border. In *Desert Blood*, the word most often refers to women who have been ruthlessly killed, and they are hardly even called that because of their incomplete and fragmented state. Most of the victims, if they are found, must be identified by their remains, which takes months and requires sending the remains to Chihuahua City, which many families can't afford.[86] Ximena describes the findings of her first rastreo:

> They weren't even bodies, just bones and clothing scattered across a radius of like 300 yards. . . . Someone in the group found a plastic Mervyn's bag that had a trachea and a bra inside it. Someone else spotted a spinal column in some weeds. . . . We found a pelvis, another skull . . . and a black tennis shoe that still had part of a foot inside it.[87]

Ximena's harrowing list of body parts that the group found scattered across the desert environment clearly establishes the extent of the violence committed against women. Describing what she finds in pieces symbolically abolishes any hope of the person being whole again. Unfortunately, their decomposition is often aided by desert conditions. Elemental desert forces like heat and wind can further fragment these bodies, or what is left of them, and desert vastness creates the necessity for rastreos, which can only cover a certain amount of space at a time, further obscuring the bodies and their chances of being found.

The feminicidios are a devastating testament to how women, especially migrant, working-class women, are valued precisely for their supposed lack of value; they are deemed to be of little worth and endlessly expendable. These are characteristics that Gaspar de Alba uses to link the women's bodies and pennies in *Desert Blood*. In lieu of a preface, the novel includes a disclaimer in which the author explains that as an invented detail, the role played by pennies adds "a metaphorical dimension to the story."[88] Physically, the pennies are repeatedly found to be a cause of severe sickness or death to the targeted women. Some of them are fed pennies, causing zinc poisoning, but there are also instances where the pennies are placed postmortem in the mouth, throat, vagina, or rectum as a symbol of their worth and an implication of the maquilas.[89] Figuratively, the men who kidnap Irene refer to maquila workers as pennies and to Irene and another American as a nickel, transforming different women into currency.[90]

Eventually, Ivon pieces together that the novel's villain Captain J. Wilcox, or El Guero, is involved in running a website called Exxxtremely Lucky that specializes in live streaming the murders of kidnapped women and girls, extending the penny metaphor.[91] In Gaspar de Alba's own words, pennies "signify the value of the victims in the corporate machine; the poor brown women who are the main target of these murders, are, in other words, as expendable as pennies in the border economy."[92] Indeed, equating pennies and maquila workers conveys their perceived low worth. Thus the author illustrates how countless women can be and are made into currency of the most insignificant value, reinforcing their status at the lowest point of the structural hierarchy of power.

The author's use of pennies incorporates another connection to the ways copper was used against bodies in the El Paso–Juárez area: ASARCO, or the American Smelting and Refining Company. The history of the El Paso ASARCO site goes back as far as the 1880s, but it wasn't until 1910 that the company began smelting copper. For many generations of people living in the area, the dual chimney stacks, measuring 612 and 828 feet tall, stood simultaneously as "towering symbol[s] to some of economic power and jobs, and to others, including some former ASARCO workers, of pollution, environmental degradation, and illness."[93] Located between Border Highway, the University of Texas at El Paso, Mount Cristo Rey, and the historical neighborhood called Smelter Town or "La Calavera" (The Skull), the plant was notorious for "contaminating central El Paso with dangerous metals, and for secretly and illegally burning hazardous waste."[94] Juárez, too, was heavily affected, as the air pollution and chemical contamination produced by the company was not subjected to border enforcement.[95] Readers of *Desert Blood* are informed about the toxicity of the soil surrounding the smelter facilities and maquiladoras when Father Francis prepares his group for the rastreo and warns them not to touch anything in Lomas de Poleo with their hands because there is likely to be radioactive waste left over from local industry.[96] According to Public Health scholar Marianne Sullivan, "Over its operating

CHAPTER 4

lifetime, El Paso produced copper, lead, cadmium, zinc, and antimony," until it was suspended in 1999 due to environmental concerns.[97] *Desert Blood*'s events take place a year before and include ASARCO often to reference how the company's actions have committed violence against local residents on both sides of the border. To accentuate the refinery as a place of harm, Gaspar de Alba makes it the headquarters for Captain Wilcox's kidnapping and snuff film operations. Thus, environmental injustices compound with the feminicidios and the impacts of NAFTA that brought thousands of people to the El Paso–Juárez area.

DESERT HAUNTOLOGY

> *My heavy metal album.*
>
> *I like it that the gorgeous cover looks like a Pink Floyd record.*
>
> *Almost won the Pulitzer.*
>
> *It weighs heavy on my heart.*
>
> *Almost impossible to discuss it anymore.*
>
> *The ghosts of the forgotten enter the room sometimes.*
>
> *The book has made me many friends—some enemies.*
>
> *Border Patrol agents sometimes give me gifts.*
>
> *We all want a fair shake.*
>
> *We all need a witness.*
>
> *WWJD: Who Would Jesus Deport?*
> —Luis Alberto Urrea, about *The Devil's Highway*

The storied deserts of these texts show the horizontal, immanent engagements with the land as bodies act against borders and borders act against bodies. In addition to the migrant experience, Urrea addresses the surveillance and militarization of the so-called Desert Southwest, especially near the area of the Devil's Highway, and Gaspar de Alba emphasizes the role of maquiladoras and ASARCO in creating the conditions of exploitation and pollution, adversely affecting communities on both sides of the border. These situations place readers amidst the milieu of the necropolitics of the region and are part of the diversity of desert abundance.

To this end, this chapter has argued that *The Devil's Highway* and *Desert Blood* both present the US-Mexico borderlands as a place heavily impacted by violence unfortunately aided by the conditions of its vast, arid landscapes. *The Devil's Highway* showcases the battle between migrant men and the toughest of terrains of the Sonoran Desert, whereas *Desert Blood* more subtly implicates the Chihuahuan Desert environment as a sort of siren call for the rape, torture, and murder of hundreds of women. Both representations contribute to a fuller understanding of what I term a desert hauntology, where the spectral presence of human and nonhuman violence and its victims saturates the land.[98] This includes what Jason De León calls necroviolence, which, as addressed in chapter 2, is "specifically about corporeal mistreatment and its capacity for violence."[99] And though the desert places in these texts are spectral, teeming with death, there is often an inability to mourn the dead because there are so many bodies that cannot be found or identified, so many questions that will go unanswered and therefore fail to provide closure and assist grief.[100] De León uses clinical psychologist Pauline Boss's term "ambiguous loss" to describe this inability.[101] A desert hauntology acknowledges the centuries of racialized, gendered, and colonial violences and their lasting influences through trauma and place. It is a phrase meant to speak to the ways one encounters the spectral in connections with land, individual and collective memories, and embodied experiences.

To illustrate how desert hauntology manifests through embodied experiences, I turn to *The Devil's Highway* and *Desert Blood* for their descriptions of the thick, pervasive, unmistakable smell of death. Urrea describes the scent in a scene with the women working for the consulate who keep the files of the Yuma 14/Wellton 26. As one takes out a file, "The stench sneaks from the baggie. The women tell you that they go home with the smell on

CHAPTER 4

their skin, in their hair and clothing. Sometimes, when several packets have arrived in their office, they can't wash it off, even hours later. A year after death, files still reek faintly of spoiled flesh."[102] The thickness of the smell lingers. It illustrates a lasting entanglement with the environment and the people who have perished.

A similar encounter takes place in *Desert Blood*, when Ivon is in the shower trying to wash off the smell of Cecilia's dead body she encountered earlier during the autopsy. Trying to recover and cope with the abrupt and intense deaths of Cecilia and her unborn baby, Ivon "needed to scrub the scent of death off her skin but could not remove the image of Cecilia's body from her mind, a permanent stain on her memory."[103] When Ximena asks her if the shower helped her feel better, Ivon replies, "Cleaner, anyway. I couldn't get that smell out."[104] In both texts, death's smell attaches itself to the skin and holds on for much longer than the consulate women or Ivon are comfortable with. Smell requires proximity. One must have been near enough to death for the scent of it to stick. Further, it remains psychologically imprinted with memories of being close to death or a dead body.

On an environmental scale, smell serves as an indicator of what comprises the atmosphere of a place. In *The Devil's Highway*, smells help to tell the walkers they are farther north in Sonoita, meaning they are getting closer to the Border.[105] In an anecdote about one of the survivors who suffered severe nerve damage, Urrea states that the man was working one day, "cooking, and he put his hand on the griddle. He didn't notice it frying until everybody smelled the stink."[106] Smell provides modes of interacting with the environment that other senses cannot. It fills in gaps of a story about a place. Far from the enchanting aesthetic of the Old West's big blue skies and vast horizons, the environment in *Desert Blood* is fraught with odors imposed upon El Paso–Juárez by governments and corporations like the maquiladoras and ASARCO. Her borderland setting includes "night air . . . laced with diesel fumes . . . from the Phillips *maquila*" and a Rio Grande that "stunk of sewer."[107] In fact, ASARCO's lasting powers remain through its exuding exhaust: "even though ASARCO had shut down operations in January [1998], the air still smelled of refinery soot and chemical fumes."[108] The author's attentiveness to the olfactory assures that readers acknowledge the insidiousness and impact of a lingering toxicity that people of the region, no matter on which side of the border, cannot escape.

Gaspar de Alba describes the twin stacks of ASARCO as "sentinels of death."[109] Indeed, structurally they lend themselves to this metaphor, signifying many fatal injustices over the course of the twentieth century. Once towering over El Paso and Juárez, the stacks haunted the region, dwarfing those who dwelt near to them and representing the plant's detrimental health effects on the local populace over many generations. These vertical beacons of "progress" stuck out, stark, amidst the horizontal sprawl of symbiosis. When *Desert Blood* was published in 2005, ASARCO had already been shut down for six years. ASARCO's use of toxic chemicals and hazardous waste has a lasting impact on the area to this day. To illustrate its enduring presence, Gaspar de Alba includes stories of Ivon's grandparents, who were forced to live in the impoverished community known as Smelter Town, where they subsequently fell ill and died from cancer and tuberculosis.[110]

As explored earlier, these fictions mirror difficult truths about the area. According to NPR's John Burnett, "a landmark study by the Centers for Disease Control in the early 1970s found that more than half of the children living within a mile of the smelter had levels of lead in their blood four times today's acceptable limit. The lead study was so influential that it contributed to the EPA's decision in 1973 to phase lead components out of gasoline."[111] Production was suspended in 1999 and in 2013, the chimney stacks were demolished, leveled to the ground.[112] Even with the chimneys gone, for many they remain erect in memory, and their pollution still haunts surrounding residents, unsure if their tumors or their children's reduced motor skills are due to the plant or not.[113]

Whether it's the pervasive smell of death, ongoing chemical contamination and pollution, or a government-sanctioned commandeering of areas of land with few inhabitants, out of the Desert Southwest emerges a desert hauntology. It beckons us to pay attention; yet, much like any hyperobject, it eludes our capability to grasp it entirely. The desert hauntology proposed here also includes the US-Mexico border as witness and actant against migrant bodies. It both causes and marks generations of trauma inflicted upon people who've found themselves entangled with it. My analysis of *The Devil's Highway* and *Desert Blood* applies desert distortion as a way to view the various acts of violence committed through borders and against bodies confined to horizontal modes of literal and sociopolitical navigation. Through their stories of place and people living and dying in the Sonoran and Chihuahuan

CHAPTER 4

Deserts, both books rely on conveying the horizontal experience of desert places as a way of understanding them more fully and creating a more comprehensive picture of violence across the borderlands at the end of the twentieth century and into the twenty-first.

CHAPTER 5

WITH(OUT)

"Every attunement is a tuning up to something, a labor that arrives already weighted with what it's living through. The intimacy with a world is every bit about that world's imperative; its atmospheres are always already abuzz with something pressing."

—Kathleen Stewart, "Atmospheric Attunements," 448

Desert distortion, as explored throughout this book, is a technique for knowing arid lands and their communities differently, that is, more intimately. It is especially interested in the relationships between multiplicity, possibility, stories, and place, thus exposing desert abundance materially and ideologically, and decentering outdated approaches concerned with lack. To this end, both distortion and abundance emphasize *being-with*, while traditional Western takes on desert spaces, landscapes, or "the Desert" writ large have for centuries focused on being without. With these tensions in mind, this chapter puts two artists in conversation with one another in order to think with their work as it concerns desert placemaking. As James Turrell and rafa esparza have radically disparate approaches, juxtaposing them here provides an opportunity to address and even reify the desert aesthetics of the past century that are rooted in the legacies of settler colonialism and investigate how those are perpetuated or pushed back against. Turrell's pieces are often designed with an emphasis on the individual's perceptions of light and space, and his work is so affective precisely because of its minimalist meticulousness; esparza's work, on the other hand, is fundamentally centered around culture and community with a vested interest in identity, belonging, and larger discourses about race, gender, and sexuality. Though both have a variety of works to examine, in the analysis that follows, I discuss those that seem most relevant to the project of desert distortion in how they invite the elemental as a collaborator: Turrell's Roden Crater Project and esparza's work with adobe bricks and panels.

JAMES TURRELL AND ATMOSPHERE

Since the 1960s, artist James Turrell has been working with how light, space, and human perception relate with and constitute one another. Turrell began with projections using electric light in the darkened room of his California apartment to create striking optical illusions of light and shadow. Before long, he felt that "closing off the studio from outside light . . . resulted in the needed darkness but also a certain stuffiness" and decided to begin working *with* natural light instead of fighting against it.[1] Though some of his works, most notably Ganzfelds and Perceptual Cells, have continued to use electric light exclusively in order to disorient the viewer's depth perceptions and generally disrupt the mechanics of seeing, Turrell also began creating structures called Skyspaces, which are "specifically proportioned . . . with an aperture in the ceiling open to the sky . . . [and] can be autonomous structures or integrated into existing architecture," so as to invite the celestial to the viewer's perception.[2] There are currently over eighty Skyspaces installed all over the world (in at least nineteen countries), and, while they demand a collaboration with air, sky, light, and perceiver, Turrell's magnum opus is the Roden Crater Project, which works with these same elements, only on a larger scale.[3] The crater is deeply situated in the so-called Desert Southwest, just an hour's drive northeast of Flagstaff, Arizona, and adjacent to the Painted Desert, where the artist has been working on it for more than fifty years since he spotted it from above: one man's ever-expansive experiment with desert placemaking.

In 1974, James Turrell used the money from a Guggenheim Fellowship to buy "gasoline for his airplane in order to look for what amounted to a huge alternative outdoor space—a location in the desert of the western United States where he could take his art directly into nature."[4] Turrell recalls the journey that took him seven months of systematically flying around the American West: "Each of the places I saw from the air generated thoughts for pieces. It was a process that could have gone on forever.... It was also an important time because I was moving out into territory where I didn't feel too comfortable. In the desert, the work gets lost; it just disappears."[5] The artist eventually caught sight of Roden Crater, a cinder cone volcano that drew him in. Michael Govan speaks of Turrell's fascination with the harsh terrain as a "desert obsession," one which Turrell has been able to indulge in from above as on land for the last few decades.[6]

Turrell's Roden Crater, in all of its site specificity, evokes attunement to the nonhuman desert atmosphere. The project is designed around intensifying daily celestial events like sunrise and sunset, the position of the North Star, and the weather. Additionally, it is designed to have a person attune to less frequent events like equinoxes and eclipses. In all, the massive undertaking is predicated on a very particular set of values as well as conditions with which one can better understand the phenomenological position of being human in a more-than-human desert world. As discussed in chapter 2, deserts are places readily associated with changes in perception, embodied senses of distortion, because they so often produce extremes of heat, cold, light, and distance. The sensual embodiment of distortion thus lends itself to a more affective understanding of desert distortion as a broader concept, giving rise to desert aesthetics which often attempt to link the two.

Two life experiences influenced Turrell's work early on: aviation and studying phenomenology. Both require sustained attention to (dis/re)orientation, attunement/detunement, (de/re)centering—skills and processes that are crucial underpinnings of desert distortion. Turrell the pilot, influenced by his father's life as an aviator, began flying small planes at the age of 18. Aviation is crucial to his arts practice, and he has often said that his airplane "has served as his studio."[7] Flying also exposed Turrell to dramatic shifts in visual perspective required to fly, and especially the phenomenon of sky myopia, where the eyes are unable to focus because there is nothing for them to focus on, and celestial vaulting, where the sky seems to close in around one as opposed to expanding ever outward (see fig. 15). In his own words, Turrell has stated that flying has "changed [his] perspective and sense of territory" and "afforded [him] different vantages.... But with this vantage came responsibility."[8]

CHAPTER 5

Figure 15: Celestial vaulting at the top of the eye of Roden Crater. (Photo credit: Celina Osuna.)

Due to his range of perceptual experiences and encounters, Turrell has honed an incredible ability to translate his own familiarization with the initially unfamiliar. Though the results of replicating these phenomena are precisely what make his work so intoxicating, I can't help but think about the alignment between verticality and authority as discussed in chapter 3. Just as in *Sicario* where the officials are the ones who operate from above and get to call the shots, Turrell spotted this place and decided he would like to own it—and succeeded. Turrell's discussion of "territory" actually imbues his outlook as one from a position of power and with privilege that is important to keep in mind.

As a student at Pomona College in the 1960s, Turrell was fascinated by the work of Maurice Merleau-Ponty, whose pivotal text *Phenomenology of Perception* (1945) defines phenomenology as "a study of the *advent* of being to consciousness, instead of presuming the possibility as given in advance."[9] Merleau-Ponty's emphasis on the individual's felt embodied experience becomes paramount for Turrell, who is a master of creating a set of conditions by which each experience of a work is highly singular. With a Turrell space, the viewer is confronted with their individual embodied process of visual perception that ultimately defamiliarizes seeing. Turrell's interest in Merleau-Ponty's phenomenology stemmed from "concern with the act of perception more than the crafted object" and combines "artistic practice and scientific experiment to create a transformative experience by turning vision back on itself in order to see seeing."[10] When studying James Turrell, "to see seeing" becomes the ultimate refrain by which all of his work is measured, precisely because the atmosphere of his works emphasizes perception itself, its process rather than a specific art object. Through a desert phenomenology, one understands the power of atmosphere. In her work on atmospheric attunements, Kathleen Stewart writes: "It is not an effect of other forces but a lived affect—a capacity to affect and to be affected that pushes a present into a composition, an expressivity, the sense of potentiality and event."[11] For Turrell, the sense of potentiality and event just happens to be attuned to celestial events like sun and moon cycles. His concerns seem largely about the continuation of such cycles beyond human temporality, and yet he's dedicated most of his life to trying to construct ways through which humans can see and feel such things for themselves.

Further, Turrell uses light and space as materials to intensify what German contemporary philosopher Gernot Böhme has called a "phenomenology of light."[12] For Böhme, who is largely concerned with aesthetics, atmosphere, and architecture, a phenomenology of light means "studying those selfsame laws of nature relative to the sense of the eye. In which case, you soon discover that you cannot stop at colors. You have to take all the phenomena of light into account—the glow, the brilliance, the flickering, shadow, and lots of other things besides."[13] Turrell's ganzfelds, as designed interiors that use only electric lighting to immerse viewers entirely, depend heavily upon his precise programming of such phenomena. The phenomenology of light is thus taking place between his programming and the perceiver. On a much grander scale, however, Roden Crater has various components that consist of interior and exterior spaces situated in a particular place, inviting the "lots of other things besides" that emerge from its design to incorporate and accentuate celestial and atmospheric elements of light, land, and shadow.

It is all these other things that contribute to the atmosphere in which one finds the work. And part of what makes them so intriguing is that their atmosphere is incredibly intense and therefore demanding of one's attention. Even when not visiting a large crater that's been excavated and manicured to create exceptional visual and auditory experiences, atmosphere is influential in a Turrell space. What sets a place like Roden Crater apart is the way it allows and encourages one to attend to atmospheric attunements, what Stewart states is an act of "chronicling how incommensurate elements hang together in a scene that bodies labor to be in or to get through."[14] The names of the chambers which often include cardinal directions, the apertures which are built to include natural light and phenomena, and even the various materials like limestone, basalt, marble, and volcanic cinder rocks or ash, are all curated to heighten one's attention to atmosphere.

DESERT PHENOMENOLOGY AND RODEN CRATER

Using Böhme's phenomenology of light and Stewart's atmospheric attunements as two helpful nodes for thinking-with the more-than-human world, I suggest Roden Crater is a venture of desert phenomenology, an embodied experience of desert distortion that explores and reveals the relationships between humans and the more-than-human desert elements, constituting its own conditions of time, space, atmosphere, and agency. In other words, the project is at once concerned with the spatial and temporal nears and fars of desert place, its elemental immediacy or intimacy and its immensity. Though Roden Crater is still a work in progress, the massive project has spaces designed to let the sunlight, moonlight, and starlight in, and it has spaces meant to wrap you deep in the subterranean reverberations of the earth, as some of the spaces will even have underwater elements.

As a key aspect of his phenomenology of light, Böhme asserts "the space that light creates is the space of distances, extent, remoteness from me," and the crater as situated in a rural part of the high desert of Arizona amplifies a sense of great distance and remoteness.[15] Yet Turrell is equally interested in proximity as another type of distance, as he "encourages viewers to see in ways that are haptic, as if they could feel light with their eyes, like pressure on the skin of visual perception."[16] Importantly, "much of what he is trying to do at the crater involves pulling the visual qualities of the sky down to the surface," a collapse of distance that renders the celestial nearly tangible.[17] For instance, looking up through the eye of the crater as the first stars begin to appear in the sky almost makes one feel like the aperture exposing the night sky is a circular piece of fabric pinned to the middle of the ceiling punctured by tiny dots of flickering lights. Bringing down the celestial to the haptic grasp of the human eye is central to Turrell's design.

Roden Crater is multiscalar, simultaneously immense and immediate: sitting in the Crater's Eye or walking around the Crater Bowl, one feels at the center of this magnificent desert spectacle while also feeling impossibly far from the center of the solar system, galaxy, or universe. The open desert atmosphere transforms distance and time so that a desert phenomenology means being at once centered and decentered in the vastness. Stewart posits that "what affects us—the sentience of a situation—is also a dwelling, a worlding born from an atmospheric attunement"; one becomes aware of human bodily limits and of the various other bodily limits of light, rock, plant, and animal; one attunes or even detunes, orienting and then perhaps disorienting and reorienting.[18] In his own words, the artist says:

> I feel I'm taking in this space in the Painted Desert, where you see exposed geology—a stage set of geologic time. And in that stage set of geologic time I then want to make spaces that engage celestial events in light.... These pieces are performed by the rotation of the earth and the motion of planets so that they will keep themselves performing long after I'm gone.[19]

Writing about the project in 2013, astronomer and director of the Griffith Observatory in Los Angeles Ed Krupp describes a few of the spaces in detail that speak to Roden Crater's very specific sense of place:

> The tunnels, chambers, and apertures Turrell has designed there are intended to sample moments from the sky that will open the mind's eye through optical revelation. In fact, the axis of the roughly elliptical mountain runs intercardinally, from the northeast to the southwest, and accommodates the summer-solstice sunrise, on which Turrell intends to orient the not-yet-built East Space. Each year, in June, when the sun rises out of the Painted Desert, it will shine through nearly nine hundred feet of what is now unexcavated volcano to the Sun and Moon Space, which has been built. There, it will illuminate a massive wedge of black marble, fifteen and a half feet high and thirteen feet wide, in the center of the circular room.[20]

Here Krupp carefully conveys the various ways that the celestial, terrestrial, and atmospheric are invited to convene at Roden Crater. What might also come across is the vast spatiotemporal scale at which this work is operating.

CHAPTER 5

In early 2019, Turrell announced what *The Wall Street Journal* called "a new master plan" for Roden Crater as the artist partnered with Arizona State University (ASU) to see the project to its completion.[21] The article is a testament to the work that Turrell has completed since Krupp was writing about the crater and lists updated and highly specific plans for the crater spaces:

> One 8-foot-deep pool will reflect every sunrise. In a light-spa complex, bathers will dive under a barrier, emerging outdoors looking out across the horizon. In the fumarole, the volcano's secondary vent, Turrell imagines a brass bath where transducers hooked to a radio telescope will broadcast the sounds of passing planets and the Milky Way underwater. In another space a visitor will sometimes be able to see his or her shadow with the light of Venus. An amphitheater is on the drawing boards too, as well as a wine cellar.[22]

Sights and sounds of the celestial abound. Air, earth, water, and light—the elemental—as conveyed above are amplified by the structural settings and conditions of this desert place. Over the course of time, Turrell's objectives have become so much more than to see seeing and have proceeded full throttle towards atmospheric attunements with the more-than-human. The twenty-first century has transformed the naked-eye observatory into an enormous apparatus to *feel feeling*. The goals are ambitious and in their consideration of the more-than-human have in turn perhaps become demanding of a more-than-human timeline for construction. As part of the first major phase, according to the project's website at the time of writing this book in 2024, "six spaces were completed, including two of the most difficult, the shaping of the Crater Bowl and the Alpha (East) Tunnel. The Sun & Moon Chamber, East Portal, and the Crater's Eye, are joined by the Alpha (East) Tunnel and a connecting tunnel to the Crater Bowl . . . when complete, the project will contain 24 viewing spaces and six tunnels."[23]

As another part of the Roden Crater Project's expansive nature, while the optics of light and space are still a large focus, all kinds of felt intensities are produced from engaging with water as well as air, which carry sound and light at different frequencies. Such felt intensities constitute a haecceity, or thisness, of a desert phenomenology. In *A Thousand Plateaus* (1980), Gilles Deleuze and Félix Guattari discuss the idea of haecceity in terms of individuation:

A degree of heat is a perfectly individuated warmth distinct from the substance or the subject that receives it. A degree of heat can enter into composition with a degree of whiteness, or with another degree of heat, to form a third unique individuality distinct from that of the subject. What is the individuality of a day, a season, an event? A shorter day and a longer day are not, strictly speaking, extensions but degrees proper to extension, just as there are degrees proper to heat, color, etc. . . . A degree, an intensity, is an individual, a Haecceity that enters into composition with other degrees, other intensities, to form another individual.[24]

The haecceities individuated in a Turrell work are demonstrated vividly here. When one is standing beneath an aperture at Roden Crater or in a Skyspace, one is also experiencing a being-with the amount of daylight, heat, and wind (in short, climate and atmosphere) of that given moment. Turrell has created a built environment, some conditions with certain criteria—things like aperture size, structure shape, and LED colors and color changes—that are meant to entangle with the natural environment's elements and forces. This world can be noisy, rainy, sunny, cold, and the world might even produce ruptures—new individuations—like a plane flying above and leaving a trail within the aperture's view. However, attuning to the dissipating trail overhead, just like to the clouds that come and go in desert skies, shows how haecceities are constantly changing, individuating and re-individuating. One evening leaving the "Air Apparent" Skyspace on campus I encountered a fox, which had seemingly taken refuge in the cinder and sheltering plants that surround the structure. Some evenings I was the only person there; other evenings groups of friends or colleagues would wander in. Rarely, but sometimes, it rained. Desert phenomenology reveals desert abundance, reveals how the land is storied.

One of the most challenging aspects of writing about Turrell's work is that it produces a phenomenological self-awareness that I carry with me long after I've left the space that I can't seem to convey or arrest in words. Richard Andrews describes it well: "walking across the crater and around the rim, one feels the paradox that underlies this work, that human perception conditions our understanding of the universe and allows us to see ourselves as simultaneously dwarfed by the immensity of our surroundings and made vast by our ability to use the crater as an immense oculus."²⁵ What Andrews calls the paradox of the work I understand as the multiple modes of being-with desert place that are at the heart of this book. As established throughout this project, desert distortion is an act of de-/refamiliarization, de/re/centering, dis/reorienting, a way of knowing and feeling differently. It is a technique that reveals desert abundance, multiplicity and possibility. It allows humans to engage with the various human, nonhuman, and more-than-human assemblages of which we are a part.

Throughout each chapter, I've argued against thinking about the Desert Southwest as barren, and I avoid using words like "remote" because that is the kind of thinking that has led to hundreds of years of enslavement, physical and cultural violence, and environmental injustices towards communities who call desert places home, especially Indigenous peoples. The consequences of the empty desert mentality explored throughout this book—a process which Voyles terms wastelanding—are still acutely felt in communities near mining sites, sites for dumping hazardous waste, and of course along the US-Mexico border:

> Wastelanding reifies—it makes real, material, lived—what might otherwise be only discursive. Like race, which is a social construction made material by the embodied consequences of racism (threats and acts of violence, foreshortened life expectancy, incarceration, under and uncompensated labor, inequalities in wealth accruement, and so on), ideas about the value of environments are manifested by the material consequences of environmental destruction (or, in the inverse, by environmental protection).²⁶

In much Western scholarship and pop culture depictions, the desert horizon, where its mountain ranges greet its big skies, has an aesthetical grandeur that tends to eclipse or mystify the stories, values, and futures of Indigenous peoples who come from the land. Attuning to this, detuning from the myth of the open, uninhabited American West or of the "vanishing Indian," makes it clear that inequity and violence based on ethnicity, race, gender, and nationality continue throughout the so-called Southwest today.

As previously mentioned, Turrell used Guggenheim money to literally fuel his search for the perfect place to take his art out into the desert landscape. In 1974 he flew for seven months across the West, from the Rocky Mountains

WITH(OUT)

to the Pacific Ocean and from Canada to Mexico. His desired site required "a crater or a butte that rose from a surrounding plain to a height of between 600 and 1000 feet" because he was eager to "engage artistically" the phenomena of "celestial vaulting and its counterpart in the concave earth illusion—visual impressions that are especially evident from the air."[27] He acquired Roden Crater in 1977, three years after seeing it for the first time. The story at once amazes and troubles me. It's reminiscent of the government's choice to test nuclear bombs in the deserts of New Mexico and Nevada due to the right conditions, one of which was of course "underpopulation." Roden Crater was chosen from above by the artist for its relative remoteness to any major cities and its specific geological attributes. Yet at the foot of the volcano are remains of a Hopi settlement, and more than 100 square miles of land Turrell owns is adjacent to the Navajo Nation, which encircles the Hopi Reservation in northeastern Arizona.

For all of its attention to the events of earth and sky, it is at the time of writing this still unclear to the public what role Roden Crater or its creator has planned for its surrounding residents, human or nonhuman. In addition to specifics about the crater spaces, Jay Cheshes writes about how Turrell has continuously acquired land surrounding the crater, which is mostly made up of ranchland, "buying plots 10 to 40 acres at a time, amassing a buffer against development, snapping up fallow tracts from investors who were duped in a big land fraud in the 1950s" and successfully keeping the skies out there dark.[28] Cheshes discusses Turrell's plans to release a fragrance and even dishware in the near future.[29] Presumably these endeavors help the artist to raise funding to fuel construction at the crater. And that is all aside from completing other large projects around the world such as "Ta Khut Skyspace" in José Ignacio, Uruguay (2021), "Skyspace Espíritu de Luz" in Monterrey, Mexico (2022), "Night Raiment 2024" in Basel, and "Skyspace" for the newly built Children's Hospital in Zurich, Switzerland (2024). According to the project's website, "Fundraising is underway to complete the construction and open Roden Crater to the public," but there is no mention of a potential date and no information about how increased tourism might impact the area.[30] Turrell's partnership with ASU and the Skystone Foundation seems to be the only major collaboration with local communities on the crater, which for decades has been attracting people to see it even without ever officially opening to the public.

CHAPTER 5

I have found three significant mentions of Hopi people being involved in the project as of 1992. The first was in Richard Andrews's essay of that same year, when he states, "Hopi stonemasons will build some of the structures that contain the viewing spaces, reinforcing connections to the history of the place."[31] The second is in an issue of Pitzer College's student newspaper, *The Other Side*, also from the same year, in which author Chris Michno discusses the two-week trip that thirteen students took from California to Flagstaff "in order to meet with Turrell, his mentors, associates, and others who could offer information relevant to the Roden Crater Project or to the regional history."[32] In his piece, Michno declares:

> the Hopi have offered their support of Turrell. A result of that interaction will be a Hopi Kiva space in Roden Crater designed with the help of the Hopi. Another aspect of that relationship, from which we benefited, was the participation of a Hopi elder in our project. Gene Sekaquaptewa spent a great deal of time with our group explaining Hopi religious and moral philosophy.[33]

The third mention also involves Gene Sekaquaptewa, who was a Hopi Chief of the Eagles Clan briefly captured on film for Carine Asscher's *Passageways*, released in 1995. Sekaquaptewa doesn't speak, only chants at the beginning and end of the film, but Turrell does attribute the North Space "which is pretty much Gene's design" to the elder before explaining that the Eastern space "has the physical connection to the Hopi Shrine that Gene goes to and is so important to him because the furthest north sunrise physically connects to that on its alignment."[34] Of course, that was twenty-five years ago, and a lot can change in that time. None of the press pieces released in 2019 mention Turrell's current relationship with the Hopi people or any of his neighbors up near Flagstaff, and there is no such info on the website.

One of the five field labs that went up to visit Roden Crater as part of the collaboration with ASU was taught by Wanda Dalla Costa, an architect and member of the Saddle Lake First Nation in Alberta, Canada. Dalla Costa's lab, "Indigenous Stories and Sky Science," included a four-day trip with visits to "Navajo Technical University, Chaco Canyon, Wupatki National Monument, Sunset Crater and [students] got a full-day experience of the Hopi reservation."[35] The field lab I participated in also visited Wupatki

WITH(OUT)

National Monument and Sunset Crater Volcano National Monument, though we did not get to speak to any Indigenous experts or community groups while in the area, and I can't help but feel that we missed the context that Dalla Costa's lab benefitted from including. To celebrate the work of the field labs, ASU held a Roden Crater Student Showcase complete with exhibitions by students inspired by thinking through Turrell's magnum opus and our respective courses. The artist joined us on campus, spoke with Ed Krupp about his love of light and his practice, shook hands, talked, and took pictures with students as we all tried to process just exactly what was happening around us.

I keep coming back to Dalla Costa's questions about voice and community: "We'll ask ourselves, 'Whose story is this, and how do we make it have value for the community?'"[36] Undoubtedly the embodied experience of being at Roden Crater was transformative and profound. I've spent years reading about the crater in books and online, and I check its social media accounts for the day they announce its official opening to the public—but being there, walking the tunnel up from the Sun | Moon Space towards the circular aperture and watching it turn slightly more elliptical with every step forward, whispering words of awe to a classmate as we both tried to take it in, there is no way to feel that except to feel it. Our group included then ASU Director of Student Engagement Megan Workmon, who drove our SUV and sang opera as dusk turned to night inside the Crater's Eye. Her grand voice's "Ave Maria" joined the already thick desert atmosphere as we were encouraged to walk around the space and notice the changes in acoustics and watch the stars appear above. Certainly this is haecceity, an encounter of desert phenomenology. It attuned us to each other, to the black volcanic cinder arranged in a perfect circle at our feet, and to the arrival of a breezy February evening chill in the high desert. There is value in this for an individual interested in perception and relationships of the human and more-than-human.

As both a shared group experience and a highly individualized experience, our visit to Roden Crater has changed my understanding of light, space, and time; in many ways its yet-to-be spaces still confound me because I'm limited in my ability to visualize them or understand how they will work. And then there are the parts of me that cannot quell the bubbling echoes of Dalla Costa's question: "Whose story is this, and how do we make it have value for the community?" Eventually, I form my own: Do the celestial and terrestrial scales at which Roden Crater operates decentralize the human too far? As someone interested in decentralizing the human in order to better understand the more-than-human world of beings, environment, and phenomena, an affirmative answer is contrary to my usual provocations. But not to instigate the community component of Roden Crater, its local situatedness, is an incomplete understanding of its significance to desert cultures, stories, and futures, and would perpetuate the erasure enabled through centuries of bias in favor of written outsider histories of that land as opposed to valuing Indigenous lifeways, including oral and tribal traditions.

One of Edward Abbey's most famous passages from *Desert Solitaire* is a striking description of his longing to merge with the desert environment. In it he asserts his presence thusly:

> I am here not only to evade for a while the clamor and filth and confusion of the cultural apparatus but also to confront, immediately and directly if it's possible, the bare bones of existence, the elemental and fundamental, the bedrock which sustains us. I want to be able to look at and into a juniper tree, a piece of quartz, a vulture, a spider, and see it as it is in itself, devoid of all humanly ascribed qualities, anti-Kantian, even the categories of scientific description. To meet God or Medusa face to face, even if it means risking everything human in myself. I dream of a hard and brutal mysticism in which the naked self merges with a non-human world and yet somehow survives still intact, individual, separate. Paradox and bedrock.[37]

Though his words are carefully chosen and his tone is convincing, to renounce the cultural apparatus in favor of the natural one in this way is to assume that the natural is devoid of its own cultures and that the category of human is somehow separate from what is natural. Both assumptions are of course false. Further and more importantly, to merge in the way Abbey craves—paradoxically maintaining an individuated self and becoming-other—is to lose one's humanity entirely, which actually does nothing for understanding the important interrelationships of human and nonhuman agents and intensities. And all of this is to say nothing of Abbey's racist and problematic views on who should be allowed to live where; the author was outspoken in his views about race, especially when it came to Indigenous peoples of the desert places he so often claimed ownership of.[38]

WITH(OUT)

Raj Patel, writing in 2013, suggests that "we're surrounded by catastrophic narratives of almost every political persuasion, tales that allow us to sit and wait while humanity's End Times work themselves out. The Anthropocene can very easily become the Misanthropocene."[39] This is the trap that Abbey's polemic falls into, and no doubt the reason why so many of the near-future apocalypse tales like *Mad Max*, *Dune*, *Parable of the Sower*, and *The Water Knife* seem to fit within the desert landscape as wasteland. Though at present it is unclear how Turrell's masterpiece enfolds or engages its human residents, Roden Crater strangely and beautifully confronts its visitors with the possibilities and limits of human perception and experience in ways that are more in line with Haraway's Cthulucene, which "entangles myriad temporalities and spatialities and myriad intra-active entities-in-assemblages—including the more-than-human, other-than-human, inhuman, and human as humus" than with the Misanthropocene described above.[40] It is neither a setting of desert apocalypse nor a desert utopia, but an instrument for desert phenomenology and attunement that reveals relationships between humans writ large and the more-than-human landscape that constitutes its own atmospheric conditions, even as it currently lacks the infrastructure to strengthen human kinship with one another.

RAFA ESPARZA AND "BROWN MATTER"

At a time in his life when he was seeking guidance, Los Angeles artist rafa esparza asked his father to show him how to make adobe bricks. esparza learned from his mother that his dad, Ramón Esparza, was once an adobe brickmaker in his home state of Durango, Mexico. It was there that he built his first house with the material. Working with his father, who initially struggled with his rafa's queer identity, was, according to him, "very peaceful. . . . I think of it as a first step in mending our relationship"; it was a time in which the pair underwent a "very rich bonding experience in laboring with the land."[41] Since then, Ramón has been involved in many of his son's projects that use adobe as an essential, elemental material.[42] In 2014 the father-and-son team taught other family members how to work with the adobe, and after a few months they had 1,500 bricks ready for the piece. *Building: A Simulacrum of Power* was commissioned by Clockshop, a nonprofit organization working with California State Parks to turn Bowtie, a former railyard and postindustrial space, into an urban park. It was the first time that esparza incorporated the adobe-making process as part of his arts practice. Six years later, Ramón led rafa's first large-scale adobe-making project, and throughout the last decade rafa has traveled to many different communities to make adobe bricks and build relationships. For the artist, teaching others to make the bricks is "maybe the most queerest aspect of this work because it's been that way of holding a space with someone without having verbal communication, but building a bond with [them], has been something that I've been actively replicating with groups of intentionally like queer artists of color."[43]

Where James Turrell mostly left museum spaces because creating giant apertures in the ceilings became less and less practical, esparza initially left gallery spaces out of frustration for who their audiences were, and weren't. Instead, he started doing site-specific performances, like *Building*, linked to lived experiences of a place, drawing "the art public's gaze to the site *from* the site."[44] Born and raised in Los Angeles, esparza is deeply invested in his community, its histories, and futures there. The land and understanding one's relationship to it is central to his practice, whether performance or visual art. Eventually he returned to gallery spaces, but with the intention of transforming them into spaces that reflect him and other Brown, queer artists.

The recipe changes with the ecology, but, as a combination of earth and water, adobe has been used as a building material around the world for thousands of years. In the Desert Southwest, adobe-style homes (also known as Pueblo Revival) are prevalent, though many of them are now constructed out of materials like stucco, stone, and wood in order to achieve the look of adobe on the outside without its internal mutable properties. Because they are cured by baking under the sun and not fired in a kiln, "adobes are known to contract and expand depending on their surrounding climate and humidity, thus retaining their organic character even when formed into a building."[45] esparza's adobe bricks are made by mixing clay-rich soil, horse dung, hay, and water (which in the earlier works was sourced from the Los Angeles River); they are made of earth, of place, and as such are understood to have their own agency. The artist says that a large factor in bringing adobe into his art practice is because it is "material that's alive, this material that has the potential to kind of like self-implode . . . it's never really stable."[46] This description speaks to desert distortion as a method of encountering the more-than-human with which emergent, productive relationships are made possible.

Though not all of his performances, paintings, or installations involve adobe, this chapter focuses exclusively on key earlier works that do. Brief engagements with *Figure / Ground: Beyond the White Field* (2017), *Tierra. Sangre. Oro.* (2018), and *Staring at the Sun* (2019) demonstrate esparza's ability to work with the agential material in co-creating a desert atmosphere. Here the classification of desert refers less to a specific biome—Los Angeles is technically a Mediterranean climate—and more to a shared history, sense of identity, and aesthetic across the US-Mexico borderlands, where Brownness is ever present and to be celebrated. In his own words, his "interest in browning the white cube—by building with adobe bricks, making brown bodies present, and collaborating—is a response to entering traditional art spaces and not seeing myself reflected.'"[47] The whiteness of institutional spaces is found in both the physical galleries, which often have bright white walls, and in the colonial histories of whiteness that such places uphold.

The adobe material and esparza's constructions thus defamiliarize art museum experiences by filling the blank white gallery spaces with the textures, the abundance, of desert atmosphere, which includes cultural components as much as it does materiality of desert place. The adobe bricks and structures, most often made in collaborative sessions with family and friends, also "reflect the durable, functional form prevalent across Mexico and its former lands in the Southwest. . . . [M]aking the bricks alludes to their community's history."[48] The bricks "combine blue-collar drudgery and artistic 'practice' with a sense of *tierra*, a word with poetic reflections of soil, earth, land, and dirt."[49] No matter where he is installing the adobe pieces, the process of brickmaking with community is a special, intentional part of his practice—for esparza "this is, I feel like, where the work is happening, is when we're making the bricks."[50]

Figure / Ground: Beyond the White Field (2017)

In 2017, esparza and sixty-two other artists showed their work for the Whitney Biennial in New York City. *Figure / Ground: Beyond the White Field* turned the John Eckel Foundation Gallery into an adobe rotunda featuring five other artists invited by esparza: Beatriz Cortez, Joe Jiménez, Dorian Ulises López Macías, Eamon Ore-Giron, and Gala Porras-Kim.

CHAPTER 5

Writer and curator Alicia Inez Guzmán describes walking into the space and immediately smelling the adobe earth before noticing how the rotunda "created its own microclimate."⁵¹ In a longer essay about the installation, Guzmán writes, "uneven adobes cover all the walls, making curved lines from hard angles . . . an undulating surface that deviated from the linearity of the walls that lay beneath."⁵² The fixed nature of gallery walls is contrasted by the adobe's vulnerability. Sturdy enough to stay in the form of bricks yet not completely collapse underfoot, the material is still subject to change, to contract, to expand, to crumble, in its elemental, storied way. It does produce an earthy scent, it will leave traces of dust on your shoes, and it completely changes the atmosphere of a museum space.

Guzmán describes how esparza's installation was "respite after walking the streets of Chelsea to arrive at the Whitney's new location in the Meatpacking district. . . . Esparza's adobe offered the brown and the gritty, dirt remade into building blocks. Walking into *Figure / Ground* is walking into a room where one is immersed in the earth, without being underground."⁵³ Like Turrell's, esparza's work is in many ways about creating a set of conditions that evoke a certain awareness and being-with place. Unlike with Turrell's work, this embodied experience is highly sociopolitical, bringing comfort to someone like Guzmán who is visiting New York City from her home in New Mexico and making a place for those who, like the artist, very rarely see themselves and their cultures represented in institutional spaces.

The very fact that esparza used the opportunity of showing his work at the world-renowned exhibition at the Whitney to create a platform of inclusion for artists from his community is a testament to his community values as an artist. In his own words, "the white cube was transformed into a brown, round space that held everyone's works inside it," and, as a result, the gallery space becomes decolonized, defamiliarizing before he refamiliarizes what such a space should and could look like, and presenting an inclusive platform for their futures.⁵⁴ But it's not just esparza and his invited artists/collaborators that travel all the way to the East Coast for the exhibit; the adobe bricks and panels it uses have traveled across the US, too. This idea amused esparza, who enjoyed the ability to "take a piece of L.A." with him to New York, especially because he "can't think of any other time when they're really surrounded by that much earth."⁵⁵ *Figure / Ground* demonstrates the power of adobe to create desert atmosphere—desert placemaking that values an intimate connection with earth, land, and soil in a way that can become easy to ignore when one lives in a densely populated, urban setting that depends upon disconnection from the natural as part of its assumed progress. Having worked with adobe for over ten years as a part of his arts practice, esparza has been "emphasizing or focused on the generative abilities of soil and how it sustains all life on this planet."[56] The rotunda is a reminder that storied matter intra-acts, can create deep connections, with the earth.

Tierra. Sangre. Oro. (2017–18)

The bricks from *Figure/Ground* were sent to yet another "foreign" destination for a group exhibition in Marfa, Texas, titled *Tierra. Sangre. Oro. (Earth. Blood. Gold.)*. *Tierra* featured works by Carmen Argote, Nao Bustamante, Beatriz Cortez, Timo Fahler, Eamon Ore-Giron, Star Montana, Sandro Cánovas, María García, and Ruben Rodriguez. Each artist's work, whether directly or indirectly, is in conversation with adobe as storied, "brown matter."[57] Cánovas, García, and Rodriguez, for example, spent two months with esparza "mixing adobe and molding bricks, to produce tons of building material that he used to create a rich ground for his peers and Ballroom's visitors."[58] Fahler and esparza worked with adobe and cinder block molds, "colliding those two dissimilar building modes. The resulting stacks and structures become bodily proxies, occupied by found objects, cacti, and colorful appendages."[59] Montana's four portraits of female-identifying people of color are held up by "four hulking adobe structures … named in honor of Aztec deity Coatlicue, the mother of the gods, the sun, the moon and the stars."[60] In all, *Tierra* consisted of some 2,000 adobe bricks that served as flooring and foundation for many of the pieces.

In addition to the sections of floor covered with bricks and the above collaborations, esparza worked with Beatriz Cortez to build an archway out of adobe, inspired by Mayan architecture. It was constructed last, but became the entrance through which visitors had to enter the space:

> visitors are invited to pass through an entry point of the artists' own creation, and to move through the galleries from north to south, towards the border and Mexico. Most of the bricks for this monumental structure were made by Don Manuel Rodriguez, an expert adobero living in Ojinaga, Mexico, and were brought over the border particularly for this sculpture.[61]

The artists had "used it to reorient the way visitors enter the white-turned-brown cube."⁶² Reorientation, a key tenet of desert distortion, means here that people entering the space presumably had some expectations and presuppositions that the artists wanted to both challenge and make them aware of. By focusing on how to reorient someone's movement and perception, a borderlands ecology emerges that encourages visitors to engage with the work's Brown aesthetics.

The adobe bricks of *Tierra* fit well within the desert aesthetic of West Texas, as opposed to in a museum in New York where they obviously seem to be from somewhere else, yet the packed earth holds intrigue for visitors to Marfa in much the same way—by pulling focus to the irregular shapes of the earthy material and the environment they create. Marfa has only recently become a place where the "white international art world" convenes.⁶³ Noting the disparity between who the place attracts and how impoverished the county is, esparza sought to create a literal foundation—he covered parts of the floor with the adobe bricks—"as a vehicle for having conversations and for inviting other brown artists and artisans to work with [him] and with each other to consider land and how to create within each other's spaces. There is a performativity to this way of working; it informed what we made."⁶⁴

As with *Figure/Ground*, esparza's opportunity to exhibit his work became one for his community at Ballroom Marfa. These choices make clear esparza's desire to uphold the importance of being with and engaging community. His choices contrast conventional desert aesthetics, for example those that prop up a lone, solitary, male figure like "the man with no name." Instead, his work speaks more closely to a value system that centers community and its connection to place, one much more aligned to actual desert lifeways and that can be considered as a foundational practice of many Indigenous peoples from the region who formed their epistemologies and cosmologies in relationship with the land, as relative. In thinking about both approaches, part of the work I hope this book does is highlighting this value system through concepts like storied deserts, desert abundance, and close readings of texts from and about the US-Mexico borderlands.

Staring at the Sun (2019)
esparza began his career drawing and painting, but he switched abruptly to performance art when he stopped feeling that the canvas could express his

frustration with treatment of Brown and queer people in his community. In his own words, "I turned to performance after I came out. It created a rupture, and it impacted every aspect of who I am."[65] After a while, he began to "experiment with adobe as a surface . . . brown matter, brown material," and the adobe is now a sort of a hallmark for rafa's experimentations.[66] Using the brown, lively adobe as a canvas, as opposed to a traditional stretched white material, got him excited about painting again. The use of adobe as a canvas means that the skin color of any portrait subjects or base color for any landscapes would be brown by default, a drastic and powerful conceptual and perspectival shift from the carte blanche that is the white canvas—an act of desert distortion. In 2019, his exhibition *Staring at the Sun* opened at MASS MoCA in North Adams, Massachusetts. According to the museum's official site, the exhibit allowed him "to design a brown space and to simultaneously engage, create images, and build narratives intrinsic to his use of land—brown matter—as context, surface, and content."[67] Unlike *Tierra. Sangre. Oro.* and *Figure / Ground*, this exhibition contained only esparza's works. It was, however, still storied, still peopled, as many of the panels depicted portraits of his close family and friends.

When my friend and I arrived at its double doors, we first saw an adobe panel hanging on the wall straight ahead, with a well-known image on it of Mexican laborers being sprayed with DDT at the Hidalgo Processing Center in Texas during the mid-1950s (see fig. 16). The painting is based on a piece of documentary film by photographer Leonard Nadel:[68]

> It is 1956. A queue of Mexican immigrants stands at a processing station in Texas, about to be admitted to the United States as part of the bracero guest worker program. They are naked, clothes in hand, waiting for a masked attendant to douse them with DDT, an insecticide whose use would be banned in the US just sixteen years later.[69]

This is the image that greets me as I walk into the gallery space lined with adobe, which otherwise had felt inviting, like the sense of respite that Guzmán refers to, as we stepped into the museum from the cold and snow outside. The rendition of the bracero workers being fumigated with toxic pesticide makes very clear that trauma and violence is part of Latinx experiences in the US, especially along the border. It is a reminder

CHAPTER 5

Figure 16: *Border Wash—after Leonard Nadel,* 1956 (2019). Adobe panel and portrait of bracero workers being sprayed with DDT at the Hidalgo Processing Center in Texas during the 1950s. Part of rafa esparza's exhibition *Staring at the Sun* at MASS MoCA. (Photo credit: Celina Osuna.)

of the way that communities of color, especially in the so-called Desert Southwest, have been systematically subjected to violence for centuries, and still are. This, too, is part of a borderlands ecology, the tendrils of which have only multiplied and intensified with the arrival of the twenty-first century. It is powerful to witness this iteration of the story so far from the Sonoran Desert (where I was living at the time), or the Chihuahuan Desert (where I'm from), during a frigid December day in the Northeast: an encounter with a piece of my heritage, in material and image, hanging on the wall of a giant museum.

My friend and I turned to walk further into the space and saw several more adobe panels hanging on the wall. The floor was tiled with adobe, too, and I reveled in the fact that I could see how the bricks closest to the walls retained their separation from one another while the ones in the middle of the space had been compacted, blending together now through the gradual

Figure 17: *Tierra Rara Sancha: No soy de aquí ni de aya*, 2018. Acrylic on adobe panel with portrait of San Cha. Part of rafa esparza's exhibition *Staring at the Sun* at MASS MoCA. (Photo credit: Celina Osuna.)

process of visitors walking on them. It felt like the earth because it was the earth. Some of the mounted slabs of adobe had portraits on them and some didn't. Two of them I recognized as artists San Cha and Sebastián Hernández, esparza's friends from Los Angeles (see figs. 17 and 18). Another two were portraits of his family members. The colors, bright red for San Cha's dress

CHAPTER 5

Figure 18: *Sebastian as Chalchiuhtlicue*, 2019. Acrylic on adobe panel with portrait of Sebastián Hernández. Part of rafa esparza's exhibition *Staring at the Sun* at MASS MoCA. (Photo credit: Celina Osuna.)

and brilliant blue for Hernández's blouse, pop against the brown material, emphasizing it. Up ahead, four large adobe panels are placed side by side, cut irregularly at the top to make up the canvas for a piece titled . . . *we are the mountain*. On it, a figure in green is reaching toward the top of the brick while, grabbing a piece of chain-link fence, looking at the viewer (see fig.

Figure 19: . . . *we are the mountain*, 2019. Acrylic on adobe panels with portrait of someone grabbing a chain-link fence. Part of rafa esparza's exhibition *Staring at the Sun* at MASS MoCA. (Photo credit: Celina Osuna.)

19). One can assume the person is climbing over the fence, but they might also be destroying it. This is the sort of ambiguity that esparza's works perform doubly through the materials he uses.

The curator for the exhibition, Marco Antonio Flores, told the *LA Times*, "The interesting thing is that for [esparza] to create portraits out of material that breaks and cracks, you think, what does that tell us about portraiture?"[70] Tending to his practice means tending to his community, to land, to the earth, and understanding that fixity can sometimes mean what you allow to persist and can more importantly provide an illusion of permanence in the face of finitude. What does it mean to paint a portrait of a loved one on a surface that will likely crumble and fade? What does it mean to embrace and work with dust and dirt? Gwyneth Shanks observes, "Dust and dirt also connote a more broadly defined set of assumptions about poverty, disease, deprivation, lowliness, and mortality. Meanwhile, its absence connotes not only cleanliness but also morality."[71] Certainly, esparza is challenging these connotations. For him, working with dust and dirt is an embodied practice that brings bodies, particularly Brown and queer bodies, together in a rewarding labor with land and each other. Perhaps this is another point where likening esparza's adobe works to Turrell's massive excavation of Roden Crater troubles me. Even when esparza is presenting solo work he is seeking to make his communities more visible. He made the adobe bricks with family and friends long before the blocks ever arrived in a museum space; the making is just as important as the final exhibition product.

Having branched well beyond Los Angeles, esparza continues to create work for exhibitions beyond those discussed here, maintaining a connection to the element of earth and the history of the broader region of the US-Mexico borderlands by working with adobe and using it in spaces and in ways that visitors may not have ever encountered it before. He has also begun writing a book about his adobe works, which at the time of this book's publication is still in progress. esparza's taking hundreds or thousands of adobe bricks to build installations like those I've examined is desert placemaking. And encountering adobe in this way, in such contexts, is encountering a large history of Brown people in the Desert Southwest. Travis Diehl astutely asserts, "Such is Esparza's knack for incorporating violent colonial histories into work that gathers, rather than destroys."[72] It is using art as a chance to gather and confront the past while thinking and performing possible futures.

Here I'd like to return to the discussion at the outset of this book, which turns to Indigenous communities who have built and sustained intimate relationships with desert land and place. esparza's practices often align with and embrace how "Indigenous logic moves between relationships, revisiting, moving to where it is necessary to learn or to bring understandings together. Eventually this process, a synthesis, leads to a higher reflective level of thinking."[73] As Gwyneth Shanks hopes, along with myself and many others, esparza's work produces

> ... a new ground from which to imagine a museum predicated upon alternative aesthetic practices, cultural histories, and models of acquisition and display. Such a future might honor art of the global south, minoritarian artists and museumgoers, and challenge museums' practice of claiming ownership over objects, artists, and art movements through conventional acquisition and archival procedures. Esparza's adobe pavers frame a materialized desire for a future

WITH(OUT)

Figure 20: Adobe bricks beneath your feet. Taken at rafa esparza's exhibition *Staring at the Sun* at MASS MoCA. (Photo credit: Celina Osuna.)

different from the now, marking a mode of transformation in which that future is made actual, if only for the duration of a performance.[74]

And indeed, on a near-freezing winter afternoon in Massachusetts, it was in his constructed adobe space where I was so warm. I studied, felt, and smelled the adobe bricks, scattered around the space, hanging on the wall, wearing away below my boots—comforting me.

DESERT ABUNDANCE

Putting Turrell in conversation with esparza is a provocation to examine art and desert placemaking as approached from two very different positionalities, but with some overlapping intentions of working with the more-than-human. Both artists have interests in collaborating with the earth and its material conditions, yet Turrell's Roden Crater seems to favor the individual's convenings with light, sky and ground in situ while esparza's adobe creations invite communal efforts both inside and beyond a designated, institutionalized art space. Desert aesthetics are created and engaged by each of the works examined in this chapter—some of which play into the land's great distance, exploring its textured and vibrant atmospheres, and some that seek to reflect and reclaim connections to place disrupted by colonization, the establishment of borders, and the extractive efforts of institutions. Yet even with the differences between Turrell and esparza, their desert aesthetics—desert phenomenology and brown matter alike—are achieved, or at least revealed, through the lens of desert distortion, which illuminates borderlands ecologies and desert abundance and pushes back, in a serious way, against outdated desert aesthetics of emptiness and wasteland that perpetuate real harm against desert people and places to this day. In a discourse historically dominated by deserts as places, or really spaces, of lack, ones defined by being-without, it is my sincerest hope that the art considered here, alongside the other texts examined throughout this book and the methodology of desert distortion, offers wide-ranging opportunities to reflect and explore the values of being-with, of desert abundance.

BEYOND

Nearly ten years have passed since I began the work that has become *Desert Distortion*, and I'm writing this conclusion from my office desk, which happens to be in the same building where I took my undergraduate English literature courses nearly twenty years ago. I walk the same halls, drive most of the same streets to get here, and, even a few years since moving back, find myself constantly assessing what has changed and what has stayed the same in this storied desert. It's been a privilege to teach students here, to speak with them about their own connections and disconnections to this desert borderland region. Every course, no matter the main topic, is an opportunity to empower them and remind myself that if we don't take it upon ourselves to tell stories about where we live, and where we come from, others will continue to do so in ways that are harmful at worst and inaccurate at best.

The borderlands ecology in which I presently find myself informs my thinking and being as I reflect on my relationships to this place. The border fence, which didn't exist when I was growing up, has become a giant metal wall adorned with concertina wire looped in so many layers that it makes it difficult to imagine a time, past or future, without it. The city stretches so far to the east now that I may as well be from another part of the country because I have no reference points to make it legible to me yet. The bridges for crossing to and from Juárez have long lines of vehicles going both ways, a change from days when the lines to get into Mexico were slight. The freight train clunks along the tracks and the sound of its horn pierces through the city's quiet atmosphere at night. My grandmother's house is still as much of a time capsule as ever; the battered lattice and sun-bleached exterior betray the fact that it's still got an interior full of original curtains and matching wallpaper, with furniture and a functioning fridge that's older than I am. I'm still getting used to seeing the words "El Paso Strong" everywhere—painted on business buildings and neighborhood walls, displayed as decals on vehicle windows, and even welcoming visitors at the airport. This slogan became the city's refrain in 2019 in the wake of a racialized mass shooting that killed twenty-three people, injured twenty-two more, and demonstrated that the dangers of xenophobia and anti-immigrant rhetoric are very real. The incident profoundly disrupted the community, and yet people found new ways to connect and create that have shown our strengths in the face of adversity.

When I began this research, I didn't know that I'd end up back here; I only knew I wanted to write the book I wish had existed to guide me. I wanted to write about desert places in a way that appreciates their stories, celebrates their complexity, and recognizes their abundance. Ultimately this became the work of desert distortion—to analyze texts and explore possibility, abundance, and futurity through the embodied complexities of living, dying, and dreaming in deserts imposed upon by colonial practices like erasure, extraction of natural resources, exploitation of labor, and erection of geopolitical borders. This is a project concerned with both desert aesthetics and their lived realities, with an aim to understand how these interrelate and even shape one another. Engagement with desert distortion decenters traditionally dominant tropes primarily concerned with violence and wasteland and realizes that those are just two of many facets that constitute the borderlands ecologies of the so-called Desert Southwest. Throughout this book, distortion is a concept of play, experimentation, perspective, and difference; at its broadest level, it is a technique employed to embrace the multitudes of experiences and interpretations of desert texts and desert places so that we can become better kin to the land and one another.

There are a few practical aims that *Desert Distortion* offers to help readers make the perspectival shift from lack to abundance. As addressed in the introduction, the first suggestion is the linguistic move to expel or at least marginalize the use of "the desert" when referencing a specific desert place. "The desert" as such is a term that presupposes inferior conditions of arid places (such as low population density or a perceived lack of usefulness) and conjures tropes of wasteland, emptiness, and void. Instead, I encourage readers to reserve "the desert" for reference to the lineage and aesthetics of those very tropes that have produced myths about and perpetuated harm against human and more-than-human desert communities the world over. Some alternatives include using the name of the specific desert place, pluralize to "deserts" when applicable, or even add a word so that the phrase becomes something like "desert places." These approaches not only combat the monolithic image of a vast and empty desert space, they are also much more aligned with the understanding that the earth's deserts are diverse and unique places distinct from one another even as they share some qualities that categorically group them together.

Another practical application of desert distortion emerges from the book's structure, which uses prepositions as chapter titles to guide the textual analysis therein and to illuminate a diversity of desert positionalities. Historically, it is an attention to verbs that excites critical theorists, due to their ability to conjure action and perform with language. By emphasizing prepositions, I hope to draw attention to (un)situatedness, or how things connect, disconnect, reconnect, with actions, how they become (re-/dis)entangled. Prepositions help determine what's at stake because they are essentially words for relationality. Maybe your breakfast is *on* the table, but it is also *in* the kitchen and *from* a grocery store. Which prepositional phrase one uses doesn't negate the existence or truth of all others, but it does highlight and prioritize one relationality above others even if only temporarily. With so many prepositions to choose from, I have accepted that selecting some means leaving others to be explored. The ones I have chosen—from, through, above, against, with(out), and beyond—assist with situating my arguments and demonstrating how desert distortion operates. They resonate most with my current approach to the borderlands ecologies of the US-Mexico border, realizing desert distortion as a generative mode of revealing desert agency and abundance in order to unsettle stale portrayals and produce ways of knowing deserts differently, dynamically. Changing analytical perspectives from chapter to chapter requires reorienting and sometimes disorienting shifts in thought, and reaffirms the complexities inherent in this book and the literature, people, and places it concerns.

Alongside the mode of analysis driven by prepositions, major concepts emerge in each chapter that build the book's lexicon and construct a constellation of desert distortion's theory and praxis. It is my hope that these concepts—storied deserts, elemental immediacy, desert aesthetics of verticality, desert hauntology, and desert phenomenology—provide readers with fruitful, applicable ways to think with and realize the multiplicity and possibility, or abundance, of desert places. For example, while storied deserts was initially written as a key idea of this manuscript, which has a regional focus, it became incredibly useful at a more global scale while working with my colleague Aidan Tynan on an edited volume interested in interdisciplinary scholarship about the world's deserts. We even decided to name the collection *Storied Deserts: Reimagining Global Arid Lands*, and that book absolutely puts the concept to work through its range of content and attention to specific, localized histories of desert narratives in literature, film, and politics. If this or any of the other key concepts listed above resonate with scholars, activists, or artists in ways that help transform individual or collective perceptions towards better desert futures, I would consider that a resounding success. This is the most I could wish for.

Inevitably, and despite my best efforts, there will be gaps in this text just by the very nature of having to choose which primary and secondary sources to focus on at the expense of others. Some of this book's limits include insufficient discussions of the histories of, for example: the 15,000–20,000 Chinese and Chinese American migrant workers who in the nineteenth century were exploited for labor as they helped build the Transcontinental Railroad across the Sierra Nevada and the 5,000–6,000 who worked on portions of the Southern Pacific Railroad in Arizona; the Buffalo Soldiers who were stationed at Fort Huachuca in Arizona at the end of the nineteenth century and into the twentieth, and who had to contend with racism from within the US Army even as they waged battles on its behalf with Indigenous groups in the area like the Lipan, Mescalero, and Warm Springs Apache, as well as the Comanche and Kiowa[1]; the establishment of internment camps for Japanese and Japanese American people during World War II as part of Executive Order 9066 issued by Franklin D. Roosevelt; and downwinder communities across the intermountain west, especially Diné (Navajo) people, who since the mid-1900s were and still are affected by cancers and other diseases resulting from radiation exposure to nuclear bomb testing and the extraction and waste of radioactive materials like uranium. This very brief list is just a glimpse at the desert abundance present in the American Southwest, as each of the groups mentioned have contributed to an ever-expanding borderlands ecology of the region. Undoubtedly, as my research on deserts has evolved, I have concretely learned that there are impossibly many cultures and histories to become intimately familiar with—though it excites me greatly with respect to what future desert-based projects are possible.

And it's on this thought that I'd like to conclude by turning to the current and developing discourse of Desert Humanities/Desert Studies. Though the argument behind much scholarship in these fields is still often predicated upon pushing against narratives of emptiness and erasure, the research I find most exciting and inspiring is invested in establishing conversations around the complexity and value of desert placemaking. With regard to the deserts of the American West, books published in the last decade—Gary Nabhan's edited collection *The Nature of Desert Nature* (2020), Jada Ach's *Sand, Water, Salt: Managing the Elements in Literature of the American West, 1880–1925* (2021), Gary Reger's *Wild, Weird, West: Essays on Arid America* (2024), Kyle Paoletta's *American Oasis* (2025), and *The Invention of the American Desert* (2021) edited by Lyle Massey and James Nisbet—have truly begun to foreground desert agency and drawn attention to how deserts, real and imagined, have been encountered, experienced, and expressed over time.

I've already mentioned *Storied Deserts*, but that volume, as well as texts like Diana K. Davis's *The Arid Lands: History, Power, Knowledge* (2016), Natalie Koch's *Arid Empire: The Entangled Fates of Arizona and Arabia* (2023), and *Deserts Are Not Empty* edited by Samia Henni (2022) signal aims for more critical consideration of the world's deserts and their communities, drawing attention to local engagements which then foster comparative analyses at a global scale. At the time of writing this conclusion, projects like Brahim El Guabli's book *Desert Imaginations: A History of Saharanism and Its Radical Consequences* and Brittany Meché's book *Desert Black: Arid Lands and Imperial Democracy in the Transatlantic World* are already on my "to read" list, even though at least one of them is still forthcoming.

I am grateful that, from the time I started piecing together this manuscript until the time I submitted the final draft to the press, much of this scholarship has surfaced for me to be in conversation with. I am also very appreciative of conversations in classrooms, at conferences, and in everyday life where people—strangers, colleagues, friends, family—have shared their outlooks on desert places with me. Sometimes they share about their first time experiencing a desert place; other times they might share about living in one. Sometimes they share joy from seeing their home place represented; other times they ask me about my home place. Sometimes they have questions I can answer, and more often they have questions that spark my curiosity. All of these discussions have helped to shape this book and to encourage its completion. Desert distortion is a methodology predicated on perception and possibility, offered throughout as a way for thinking critically and carefully about arid environments and their human and more-than-human communities. Its applications go well beyond this book, which I hope will carry the power to make legible how local intimacies are required for just environmental futures, especially in arid places—revealing desert abundance.

NOTES

ABOUT

1. Aidan Tynan, *The Desert in Modern Literature and Philosophy: Wasteland Aesthetics*, Crosscurrents (Edinburgh University Press, 2020), https://doi.org/10.1515/9781474443371.
2. Traci Brynne Voyles, *Wastelanding: Legacies of Uranium Mining in Navajo Country*, 1st ed. (University of Minnesota Press, 2015), 15.
3. See Celina Osuna, "Color, Place, and Memory in Silko's Gardens in the Dunes," in *Reading Aridity in Western American Literature*, ed. Jada Ach and Gary Reger (Lexington Books, 2020), 223–42; Doreen Massey, *For Space* (SAGE, 2005), 141.
4. Timothy Morton, *Being Ecological* (The MIT Press, 2018), 10.
5. Thinking here of Edward Casey's extensive works on phenomenology of place. See Edward S. Casey, *Getting Back into Place: Toward a Renewed Understanding of the Place-World* (Indiana University Press, 1993); Edward Casey, *The Fate of Place: A Philosophical History* (University of California Press, 1996).
6. Anna Lowenhaupt Tsing, *The Mushroom at the End of the World: On the Possibility of Life in Capitalist Ruins*, Edition Unstated (Princeton University Press, 2015); Jeffrey Jerome Cohen, *Stone: An Ecology of the Inhuman* (University of Minnesota Press, 2015).
7. Tsing, *The Mushroom at the End of the World*, xviii.
8. Celina Osuna and Aidan Tynan, eds., *Storied Deserts*, 1st ed. (Routledge, 2024).
9. Osuna and Tynan, *Storied Deserts*, 1.

NOTES

10. "Green," in *Keywords for Environmental Studies*, ed. Joni Adamson, William A. Gleason, and David N. Pellow (New York University Press, 2016), 128–29.
11. Szerena Szabo and Jane Webster, "Perceived Greenwashing: The Effects of Green Marketing on Environmental and Product Perceptions," *Journal of Business Ethics* 171, no. 4 (2021): 719–39, https://doi.org/10.1007/s10551-020-04461-0.
12. Szabo and Webster, "Perceived Greenwashing," 720.
13. Steve Mentz, "Brown," in *Prismatic Ecology: Ecotheory Beyond Green*, ed. Jeffrey Jerome Cohen (University of Minnesota Press, 2013), 193, https://doi.org/10.5749/j.ctt5hjk31.3.
14. Scott Slovic, *Getting Over the Color Green: Contemporary Environmental Literature of the Southwest* (University of Arizona Press, 2001), xvii.
15. Slovic, *Getting Over the Color Green*, xvii.
16. Sarah D. Wald, et al., *Latinx Environmentalisms: Place, Justice, and the Decolonial* (Temple University Press, 2019), 3, 1.
17. Steve Mentz, *Ocean* (Bloomsbury Publishing, 2020), xviii.
18. Lawrence Buell, "Foreword," in *Prismatic Ecology: Ecotheory Beyond Green*, ed. Jeffrey Jerome Cohen (University of Minnesota Press, 2013), x, https://doi.org/10.5749/j.ctt5hjk31.3.
19. Mentz, "Brown," 193.
20. Mentz, "Brown," 193.
21. Mentz, "Brown," 194.
22. J. T. Roane and Justin Hosbey, "Mapping Black Ecologies," *Current Research in Digital History* 2 (2019), https://doi.org/10.31835/crdh.2019.05.
23. Sara Ivry, "Historian J. T. Roane Explores Black Ecologies," *JSTOR Daily*, February 14, 2024, https://daily.jstor.org/historian-j-t-roane-explores-black-ecologies/.
24. Jada Ach and Gary Reger, eds., *Reading Aridity in Western American Literature* (Lexington Books, 2020), 2.
25. Tynan, *The Desert in Modern Literature and Philosophy*, 2.

CHAPTER 1

1. Gregory Cajete, *Native Science: Natural Laws of Interdependence*, 1st ed. (Clear Light Publishers, 2000), 211.
2. There are countless examples of settlers and governments utilizing the

NOTES

deserts of the American Southwest as spaces for environmentally destructive practices. Perhaps most notable are militarization and the testing of nuclear bombs in the twentieth century including dropping the first atomic bomb at the Trinity Site in New Mexico; the mining of uranium, copper, coal, silver, and lead throughout the region which has caused contamination and radiation exposure to surrounding communities; and crude oil and natural gas extraction which create unsafe amounts of air and terrestrial pollution.

3. Senate of California, "Journals of the Legislature of the State of California at Its Second Session: Held at the City of San Jose," 1851, 15.

4. As examples, James J. Rawls writes that Shasta County "in 1855 offered five dollars for every Indian head presented at city headquarters. Subsequently, one resident reported that he saw men bringing to town several mules laden with eight to twelve Indian heads. A community near Marysville in 1859 paid bounties that were collected by public subscription" (James J. Rawls, *Indians of California: The Changing Image*, 1st ed. (University of Oklahoma Press, 1984), 185).

5. Rawls, *Indians of California*, 171.

6. For an in-depth analysis of the "noble savage" concept, see anthropologist Ter Ellingson's *The Myth of the Noble Savage* (University of California Press, 2001) in which the author explores "the fundamental myth is that there are, or ever were, any actual peoples who were 'savage,' either in the term's original sense of 'wild' or in its later connotation of an almost subhuman level of fierceness and cruelty . . ." and how "the myth itself deceives us by claiming to critique and offer an exposé of another 'myth,' the existence of Savages who were really noble" (xiii). For discussions about the term's problematic perpetuity, see Frances Peters-Little, "'Nobles and Savages' on the Television," *Aboriginal History* 27 (2003): 16–38; M. J. Rowland, "Return of the 'Noble Savage': Misrepresenting the Past, Present and Future," *Australian Aboriginal Studies* (Canberra), no. 2 (January 1, 2004): 2–14, https://doi.org/10.3316/ielapa.449221711277109. In her chapter, "Civilization Is Poison to the Indian: Missionization, Authenticity, and the Myth of the Vanishing Indian," in *Coming Full Circle* (University of Nebraska Press, 2013), 71–99, Suzanne Crawford O'Brien writes, "as late nineteenth-century authors described the demise of Native populations, dwelling painstakingly upon the gruesome details, dissecting both flesh

and experience, their printed observations acted as proof of the dominant cultural myth: *the Indians were vanishing*" (98).

7. Gail Guthrie Valaskakis, *Indian Country: Essays on Contemporary Native Culture*, Indigenous Studies (Wilfrid Laurier University Press, 2005), 76. Here Valaskakis is quoting from Margaret Atwood's 1972 text *Survival: A Thematic Guide to Canadian Literature* (105).

8. Philosopher Gilles Deleuze offers the concept of multiplicity against the dialectic of the one and the many, asserting that multiplicity "must not designate a combination of the many and the one, but rather an organisation belonging to the many as such, which has no need whatsoever of unity in order to form a system" (182). For them, doing away with the opposition of the many and the one makes it possible to account for variety and difference of multiplicity: "everything is a multiplicity in so far as it incarnates an Idea. Even the many is a multiplicity; even the one is a multiplicity. That the one is *a* multiplicity (as Bergson and Husserl showed) is enough to reject back-to-back adjectival propositions of the one-many and many-one type. Everywhere the differences between multiplicities and the differences within multiplicities replace schematic and crude oppositions. Instead of the enormous opposition between the one and the many, there is only the variety of multiplicity—in other words, difference" (182).

9. Defined by Rob Nixon as "a violence that occurs gradually and out of sight, a violence of delayed destruction that is dispersed across time and space, an attritional violence that is typically not viewed as violence at all . . . a violence that is neither spectacular nor instantaneous, but rather incremental and accretive, its calamitous repercussions playing out across a range of temporal scales" (*Slow Violence and the Environmentalism of the Poor* (Harvard University Press, 2011). 2).

10. Valaskakis, *Indian Country*, 217.

11. Writer and literary critic Gerald Vizenor (Minnesota Chippewa, White Earth Reservation) defines "Native survivance [as] an active sense of presence over absence, deracination, and oblivion; survivance is the continuance of stories, not a mere reaction, however pertinent. Survivance is greater than the right of a survivable name. Survivance stories are renunciations of dominance, detractions, obtrusions, the unbearable sentiments of tragedy, and the legacy of victimry." "Aesthetics of Survivance:

Literary Theory and Practice," in *Survivance: Narratives of Native Presence* (University of Nebraska Press, 2008), 1, http://ebookcentral.proquest.com/lib/asulib-ebooks/detail.action?docID=452198.
12. Tynan, *The Desert in Modern Literature and Philosophy*, 17.
13. Tynan, *The Desert in Modern Literature and Philosophy*, 17.
14. Tynan, *The Desert in Modern Literature and Philosophy*, 8.
15. Tynan, *The Desert in Modern Literature and Philosophy*, 8.
16. Tynan, *The Desert in Modern Literature and Philosophy*, 42.
17. Sometimes the vocabulary is overwhelming; currently the wealth of terms to categorize agential life and nonlife beyond humans includes but is not limited to nonhuman, posthuman, more-than-human, other than human, and inhuman, each producing their own specific discourses.
18. Serenella Iovino and Serpil Oppermann, "Material Ecocriticism: Materiality, Agency, and Models of Narrativity," *Ecozon@* 3, no. 1 (2012): 83, https://doi.org/10.37536/ECOZONA.2012.3.1.452.
19. There are multitudinous critical theory texts directing their attention to other than human agencies and their importance and entanglements with anthropogenic forces that were published at the start of the twenty-first century. These include: Jane Bennett, *Vibrant Matter: A Political Ecology of Things* (Duke University Press, 2010), https://doi.org/10.1515/9780822391623; Serenella Iovino and Serpil Oppermann *Material Ecocriticism* (Indiana University Press, 2014);Robin Wall Kimmerer, *The Serviceberry: Abundance and Reciprocity in the Natural World* (Scribner, 2024); Eduardo Kohn, *How Forests Think: Toward an Anthropology Beyond the Human* (University of California Press, 2013); Isabelle Stengers, *Cosmopolitics*, Posthumanities 9 (University of Minnesota Press, 2010); Kari Weil, *Thinking Animals: Why Animal Studies Now?* (Columbia University Press, 2012), https://doi.org/10.7312/weil14808. All published in 2015, Anna Tsing's *Mushroom at the End of the World*, Jeffrey Cohen's *Stone: An Ecology of the Inhuman*, and Richard Grusin's *The Nonhuman Turn* (University of Minnesota Press) solidified a certain and crucial shift towards understanding more-than-human, nonhuman, inhuman, and posthuman worlds.
20. As an additional example of the value of inseparability of stories, education, and lived experiences from Indigenous perspectives, Oscar Kawagley, a Yup'ik (also written as Yupiaq) anthropologist and teacher, writes that

traditional Indigenous educational "processes were carefully constructed around mythology, history, the observation of natural processes and animals' and plants' styles of survival and obtaining food, and use of natural materials to make their tools and implements, all of which was made understandable through thoughtful stories and illustrative examples" (*A Yupiaq Worldview: A Pathway To Ecology and Spirit*, 2nd ed. (Waveland Press, 2006), 2).

21. Valaskakis, *Indian Country*, 76.
22. Robin Kimmerer, *Braiding Sweetgrass: Indigenous Wisdom, Scientific Knowledge and the Teachings of Plants* (Milkweed Editions, 2013), 179.
23. Cajete, *Native Science*, 182.
24. Iovino and Oppermann, *Material Ecocriticism*, 2014, 2.
25. Josh Jones, "Hear the Only Instrumental Ever Banned from the Radio: Link Wray's Seductive, Raunchy Song, 'Rumble' (1958) | Open Culture," April 18, 2017, https://www.openculture.com/2017/04/the-only-instrumental-every-banned-from-the-radio-link-wrays-rumble-1958.html.
26. Jones, "Hear the Only Instrumental Ever Banned from the Radio."
27. Valaskakis, *Indian Country*, 73. Here Valaskakis is quoting Richard Hill's "One Part Per Million: White Appropriation and Native Voices" (1992, 21).
28. I'd also like to acknowledge that "kin," much like "story," is used in this context as an intersectional opportunity to share and build vocabulary between environmental humanities and Indigenous Studies. Donna Haraway used it in the title of the often cited *Staying with the Trouble: Making Kin in the Chthulucene* (Duke University Press, 2016), in which she defines kin as "a wild category that all people do their best to domesticate" and "something other/more than entities tied by ancestry or genealogy.... Kin is an assembling sort of word" (2, 102–3). For a deeper understanding of kinship, Haraway directs readers to TallBear's "Failed Settler Kinship, Truth and Reconciliation, and Science," noting that "making kin must be done with respect for historically situated, diverse kinships that should not be either generalized or appropriated in the interest of a too-quick common humanity, multispecies collective, or similar category. Kinships exclude as well as include, and they should do that" (Haraway 203, 207). Such an approach bolsters this book's argument against homogenizing

desert places or their human and more-than-human communities in favor of being better kin.
29. Kim TallBear, "Caretaking Relations, Not American Dreaming," *Kalfou* (Santa Barbara, CA) 6, no. 1 (2019): 38, https://doi.org/10.15367/kf.v6i1.228.
30. Kimmerer, *Braiding Sweetgrass*, 7.
31. Cajete, *Native Science*, 210.
32. Cajete, *Native Science*, 210.
33. Ofelia Zepeda, *Where Clouds Are Formed*, Sun Tracks; v. 63 (University of Arizona Press, 2008), 4.
34. Zepeda, *Where Clouds Are Formed*, 3.
35. Zepeda, *Where Clouds Are Formed*, 5.
36. Cajete, *Native Science*, 184.
37. Zepeda, *Where Clouds Are Formed*, 43.
38. Zepeda, *Where Clouds Are Formed*, 43.
39. Zepeda, *Where Clouds Are Formed*, 43.
40. Zepeda, *Where Clouds Are Formed*, 43.
41. Cajete, *Native Science*, 207.
42. Leslie Marmon Silko, *Yellow Woman and a Beauty of the Spirit* (Simon & Schuster, 2013), 33.
43. Silko, *Yellow Woman and a Beauty of the Spirit*, 53.
44. Voyles, *Wastelanding*, 7.
45. Silko, *Yellow Woman and a Beauty of the Spirit*, 70.
46. Leslie Marmon Silko, *Storyteller* (Penguin Publishing Group, 2012), 83.
47. Silko, *Yellow Woman and a Beauty of the Spirit*, 50.
48. Massey, *For Space*, 12. I first use Massey's definition of place in my chapter "Color, Place, and Memory in Leslie Marmon Silko's *Gardens in the Dunes*" for *Reading Aridity in Western American Literature* (2020).
49. In her Afterword to *Ocean Power: Poems from the Desert*, Sun Tracks; v. 32 (University of Arizona Press, 1995) titled "On the Tohono O'odham," Ofelia Zepeda uses "Desert People" as the English translation for Tohono O'odham (85). The *Encyclopedia of Native American History* provides the following information about the name: "By Upper Pimans, the word O'odham is a self-appointed term used to refer to their group as a whole and means 'we, the people.' The term Tohono means 'desert,' thus in Upper Piman, the name Tohono O'odham translates into

English as something similar to 'we, the people of the desert'" (Casey McAlduff, "Tohono O'odham," in *Encyclopedia of Native American History*, 2011, https://online-infobase-com.ezproxy1.lib.asu.edu/HRC/LearningCenter/Details/6?articleId=359168). Laguna Pueblo people are known in their native Keresan language as Ka'waika or Kawaik, meaning "lake people," and the word laguna is Spanish for lagoon and references a lake situated on Pueblo land (Donald T. Healy, "Pueblo of Laguna - New Mexico," in *Encyclopedia of Native American Flags*, 2021, https://online-infobase-com.ezproxy1.lib.asu.edu/HRC/Search/Details/6?articleId=558571&q=laguna%20pueblo). In "The First Water Is the Body," Natalie Diaz writes, "*Aha Makav* is the true name of our people, given to us by our Creator who / loosed the river from the earth and built it into our living bodies. / Translated into English, *'Aha Makav* means *the river runs through the / middle of our body, the same way it runs through the middle of our land.* / This is a poor translation, like all translations" (*Postcolonial Love Poem*, 46). Lorraine M. Sherer's translation, though outdated, is etymologically helpful: "The name Mojave [sometimes spelled Mohave] is composed of two Indian words, *aha*, water, and *macave*, along or beside. *Aha* denotes either singular or plural number. Mojaves translate the idiom 'along or beside the water,' or freely as 'people who live along the water (river)'" ("The Name Mojave, Mohave: A History of Its Origin and Meaning," *Southern California Quarterly* 49, no. 1 (March 1, 1967): 2, https://doi.org/10.2307/41170070).

50. Leanne Simpson, *Dancing on Our Turtle's Back: Stories of Nishnaabeg Re-Creation, Resurgence and a New Emergence* (Arbeiter Ring Pub., 2011), 21.

51. Philosopher Timothy Morton defines hyperobjects as "things that are massively distributed in time and space relative to humans" (*Hyperobjects: Philosophy and Ecology after the End of the World*, Posthumanities (University of Minnesota Press, 2013), 1, https://doi.org/10.5749/j.ctt4cggm7). Further, Morton argues that "one only sees pieces of a hyperobject at any one moment. Thinking them is intrinsically tricky" (4). Even with such an impossible task at hand, desert distortion and therefore storied deserts take on the challenge by trying to account for as many "pieces" of the desert hyperobject as possible. Enfolding possibility and multiplicity into one's understanding of deserts is a useful way of unfolding the hyperobjective

Desert, parsing it until maybe one day it is no more—creating infinitely many localized, dynamic, and storied deserts. As Morton attests, hyperobjects "are *nonlocal*; in other words, any 'local manifestation' of a hyperobject is not directly the hyperobject" (1). I argue then that localization and attention to specific desert communities and places is a practice against ecological and ethical harm resulting from the hyperobjective desert.

52. Osuna and Tynan, *Storied Deserts*, 7.
53. Natalie Diaz, *Postcolonial Love Poem: Poems* (Graywolf Press, 2020), 82.
54. Diaz, *Postcolonial Love Poem*, 82.
55. Diaz, *Postcolonial Love Poem*, 82.
56. Diaz, *Postcolonial Love Poem*, 82.
57. Diaz, *Postcolonial Love Poem*, 82.
58. Diaz, *Postcolonial Love Poem*, 82.
59. Diaz, *Postcolonial Love Poem*, 82–83.
60. Diaz, *Postcolonial Love Poem*, 83.
61. Diaz, *Postcolonial Love Poem*, 83.
62. Diaz, *Postcolonial Love Poem*, 83.
63. Diaz, *Postcolonial Love Poem*, 84. The full passage is: "You can't know the rattlesnake's power / if you've never felt its first name stretch and strike / in your mouth—like making lightning."
64. Candace Fujikane, *Mapping Abundance for a Planetary Future: Kanaka Maoli and Critical Settler Cartographies in Hawai'i* (Duke University Press, 2021), 3.
65. Fujikane, *Mapping Abundance for a Planetary Future*, 3.
66. Cajete, *Native Science*, 210.

CHAPTER 2

1. "The Treaty of Guadalupe Hidalgo," National Archives, August 15, 2016, https://www.archives.gov/education/lessons/guadalupe-hidalgo.
2. Tynan, *The Desert in Modern Literature and Philosophy*, 85.
3. Tynan, *The Desert in Modern Literature and Philosophy*, 194.
4. A previous name for parts of Texas. The Independent Republic of Fredonia was a short-lived but significant attempt by immigrant Americans in Mexican Texas to secede from Mexico.
5. Cormac McCarthy, *Blood Meridian, or, the Evening Redness in the West*, 1st Vintage International ed. (Vintage Books, 1992), 3, 5.

NOTES

6. McCarthy scholar John Sepich writes that the historical John Joel Glanton headed westward as "an emigrant seeking the gold of California who took a scalp-hunting job with Chihuahua in order to finance the rest of his trip" (22). Sepich, who spent years tracking down and compiling many of the archival materials and influential texts that McCarthy consulted to inform *Blood Meridian*, suggests that Glanton's "life story, as well as the conditions of the time in which he lived, is presented in McCarthy's novel with remarkable fidelity" (*Notes*, 5). For a detailed discussion of how McCarthy keeps or doesn't keep to the facts of Glanton's life, see the revised and expanded edition of Sepich's *Notes on* Blood Meridian (University of Texas Press, 2008).

7. Early discussions include Vereen M. Bell, "The Metaphysics of Violence: *Blood Meridian*," in *The Achievement of Cormac McCarthy* (Louisiana State University Press, 1988), 116–35; John Lewis Longley Jr., "The Nuclear Winter of Cormac McCarthy," *The Virginia Quarterly Review* 62, no. 4 (1986): 746–50. In the decades since, the discourse surrounding the novel's desert landscapes has become more dynamic, though still often engaging deserts as a space of/for violence. For examples, see Steven Shaviro, "'The Very Life of Darkness': A Reading of *Blood Meridian*," in *Perspectives on Cormac McCarthy*, rev. ed., ed. Edwin T. Arnold and Dianne C. Luce (University Press of Mississippi, 1999), 145–57; Liana Vrajitoru Andreasen, "*Blood Meridian* and the Spatial Metaphysics of the West," *Southwestern American Literature* 36, no. 3 (2011): 19–30; James Dorson, "Demystifying the Judge: Law and Mythical Violence in Cormac McCarthy's *Blood Meridian*," *Journal of Modern Literature* 36, no. 2 (2013): 105–21, https://doi.org/10.2979/jmodelite.36.2.105; Lee Clark Mitchell, "A Book 'Made Out of Books': The Humanizing Violence of Style in *Blood Meridian*," *Texas Studies in Literature and Language* 57, no. 3 (2015): 259–81, https://doi.org/10.7560/TSLL57301.

8. McCarthy, *Blood Meridian*, 204, 148, 63, 46, 246, 295, 147.

9. McCarthy, *Blood Meridian*, 96, 184.

10. Theoretical physicist and feminist philosopher Karen Barad's book *Meeting the Universe Halfway: Quantum Physics and the Entanglement of Matter and Meaning* (Duke University Press, 2007) takes up an extensive analysis of entanglements in a way that I speak to here. Barad loosely defines entanglements as "our connections and responsibilities to one another" while

more specifically asserting that they are "highly specific configurations and it is very hard work building apparatuses to study them, in part because they change with each intra-action" (xi, 74).

11. McCarthy, *Blood Meridian*, 29.
12. McCarthy, *Blood Meridian*, 29.
13. Andreasen, "Blood Meridian and the Spatial Metaphysics of the West," 25.
14. McCarthy, *Blood Meridian*, 139, 140.
15. McCarthy, *Blood Meridian*, 140.
16. Johann August Sutter, "a former Mexican government official, local *caudillo* (warlord), and Indian slave owner," hired James Marshall to build a sawmill on the American River on land belonging to the Maidu people (Edward D. Castillo, "Foreword," in *Exterminate Them! Written Accounts of the Murder, Rape, and Enslavement of Native Americans During the California Gold Rush* (Michigan State University Press, 1999), ix). Marshall employed Maidu, Nissenan, and other California Indian workers to help construct the sawmill, and it was a Maidu worker who first "uncovered gold," but as the Maidu "were already aware of the existence of gold" there was no way for them to know the colossal impact the discovery was going to have for all who lived in the region, but especially for Indigenous communities (Clifford E. Trafzer and Joel R. Hyer, *Exterminate Them!: Written Accounts of the Murder, Rape, and Slavery of Native Americans During the California Gold Rush* (Michigan State University Press, 1999), 15). After centuries of colonization, some of the land has made its way back to the region's Indigenous people. In 2019, the Maidu Summit Consortium, "a collective of Maidu tribes that has been working for nearly 20 years to acquire property for the native people," won a 2,325-acre portion of their land back as a result of Pacific Gas & Electric Co.'s bankruptcy (Kurtis Alexander, "Dixie Fire Burns Land Returned to Maidu," *San Francisco Chronicle*, August 21, 2021, sec. Main News, A9, Access World News). In 2021 the Dixie Fire, likely caused by the company, burned the newly acquired land, so the consortium's plan "to maintain it as an ecological and cultural reserve," restoring it and creating "what some Maidus called California's first tribal park," have been set back (Alexander, 9).
17. "The Discovery of Gold," Library of Congress, sec. California as I Saw It: First-Person Narratives of California's Early Years, 1849–1900, accessed

NOTES

February 11, 2023, https://www.loc.gov/collections/california-first-person-narratives/articles-and-essays/early-california-history/discovery-of-gold/.

18. Economic historians Karen Clay and Randall Jones state, "for the period 1848–1850, lower-bound estimates of overland migration are more than 101,000," while "for the period 1849–1850, arrivals by sea are conservatively estimated at 75,462": Karen Clay and Randall Jones, "Migrating to Riches? Evidence from the California Gold Rush," *The Journal of Economic History* 68, no. 4 (2008): 999–1000. They also note the boom in the number of miners in California, which hit 40,000 in December 1849 and "would peak at 100,000 in 1852" (999).

19. Andrew Shaler, "Indigenous Peoples and the California Gold Rush: Labour, Violence and Contention in the Formation of a Settler Colonial State," *Postcolonial Studies* 23, no. 1 (2020): 80, https://doi.org/10.1080/13688790.2020.1725221.

20. Damon B. Akins and William J. Bauer, *We Are the Land: A History of Native California* (University of California Press, 2021), 128.

21. McCarthy, *Blood Meridian*, 78.

22. McCarthy, *Blood Meridian*, 312.

23. McCarthy, *Blood Meridian*, 312.

24. McCarthy, *Blood Meridian*, 34.

25. McCarthy, *Blood Meridian*, 34.

26. Gloria Anzaldúa, *Borderlands / La Frontera: The New Mestiza*, 4th ed. (Aunt Lute Books, 2012), 25.

27. Anzaldúa, *Borderlands / La Frontera*, 25.

28. A recent example (2022) is an art exhibition curated by Gil Rocha called "The Border Is a Weapon/ Frontera es un Arma" (Ricky Yanas, "Dead Edges and Open Wounds: Considering 'The Border Is a Weapon/ Frontera Es Un Arma,' Curated by Gil Rocha," *Glasstire*, March 30, 2022, https://glasstire.com/2022/03/30/dead-edges-and-open-wounds-considering-the-border-is-a-weapon-frontera-es-un-arma-curated-by-gil-rocha/).

29. Stephen F. Austin, undertaking his late father's ambitions as an empresario, received permission from the Mexican government to bring 300 families to Texas to tend sugarcane and cotton. There were three stipulations that needed to be met: good character, Catholic, and abide by Mexican law. Mexico gave land and a seven-year tax exemption to those Americans

who developed the area (Ernesto Chávez, *The U.S. War with Mexico: A Brief History with Documents* (Bedford/St. Martin's, 2008), 5).
30. Chávez, *The U.S. War with Mexico*, 7.
31. Chávez, *The U.S. War with Mexico*, 8.
32. Chávez, *The U.S. War with Mexico*, 10.
33. Chávez, *The U.S. War with Mexico*, 14.
34. In February 2022, the DHS published an article detailing the potential of deploying Automated Ground Surveillance Vehicles (AGSVs) along the US side of the border that could "assist with enhancing the capabilities of CBP personnel, while simultaneously increasing their safety downrange" ("Feature Article: Robot Dogs Take Another Step Towards Deployment," U.S. Department of Homeland Security: Science and Technology, February 1, 2022, https://www.dhs.gov/science-and-technology/news/2022/02/01/feature-article-robot-dogs-take-another-step-towards-deployment).
35. Anzaldúa, *Borderlands / La Frontera*, 216.
36. Zapotec Indigenous scholar Lourdes Alberto writes, "the concept of Aztlán entered Chicano discourse with 'El plan espiritual de Aztlán,' drafted at the Denver Youth Conference in 1969. Although officially drafted by committee, Alurista is largely acknowledged as the primary author of 'El plan'" ("Nations, Nationalisms, and Indígenas: The 'Indian' in the Chicano Revolutionary Imaginary," *Critical Ethnic Studies* 2, no. 1 (2016): 121, https://doi.org/10.5749/jcritethnstud.2.1.0107). Alberto directs readers to the following pieces for more in-depth analysis: Daniel Cooper Alarcón, *The Aztec Palimpsest: Mexico in the Modern Imagination* (University of Arizona Press, 1997); Genaro M. Padilla, "Myth and Comparative Cultural Nationalism: The Ideological Uses of Aztlán," in *Aztlán: Essays On the Chicano Homeland*, ed. Rudolfo A. Anaya and Francisco A. Lomelí (University of New Mexico Press, 1989), 309–32; Rafael Pérez-Torres, "Refiguring Aztlán," *Aztlán* 22, no. 2 (1997): 13–41.
37. Alberto, "Nations, Nationalisms, and Indígenas," 112. For a brief overview of the rhetoric of mestizaje, see Eric Rodriguez and Everardo J. Cuevas's "Problematizing Mestizaje," *Composition Studies* 45, no. 2 (2017): 230–33.
38. María Josefina Saldaña-Portillo and Simón Ventura Trujillo, "Introduction: What Does Mestizaje Name?," *Aztlán* 46, no. 2 (2021): 149; Travis Franks, "'We Are Considered Undesirable Foreigners' in 'This Our Texas': Mexican American Settler Nativism in Caballero," *Melus* 43, no. 3 (2018):

87, https://doi.org/10.1093/melus/mly025.
39. Saldaña-Portillo and Trujillo, "What Does Mestizaje Name?", 122.
40. Saldaña-Portillo and Trujillo, "What Does Mestizaje Name?", 149.
41. Franks, "'We Are Considered Undesirable Foreigners' in 'This Our Texas,'" 87.
42. McCarthy, *Blood Meridian*, 79.
43. McCarthy, *Blood Meridian*, 155. The Gileños term might be used to refer to the village itself, as the people the Glanton gang were chased by and post-massacre are chasing are otherwise referred to as Apaches.
44. McCarthy, *Blood Meridian*, 155.
45. McCarthy, *Blood Meridian*, 159–60 (emphasis mine).
46. Margo Tamez, "Space, Position, and Imperialism in South Texas," *Chicana/Latina Studies* 7, no. 2 (2008): 118.
47. Jason De León, *The Land of Open Graves: Living and Dying on the Migrant Trail* (University of California Press, 2015), 69.
48. McCarthy, *Blood Meridian*, 165.
49. McCarthy, *Blood Meridian*, 185.
50. McCarthy, *Blood Meridian*, 168.
51. McCarthy, *Blood Meridian*, 169.
52. McCarthy, *Blood Meridian*, 170–71. In this scene, the Glanton Gang are referred to as Americans, but when they are north of the border they are often described as "Saxons" (McCarthy, 54). Christopher Douglas notes that the use of Saxon is a way to discuss "fighters" from the US War with Mexico in tribal instead of national terms ("The Flawed Design: American Imperialism in N. Scott Momaday's House Made of Dawn and Cormac McCarthy's *Blood Meridian*," *Critique - Bolingbroke Society* 45, no. 1 (2003): 6, https://doi.org/10.1080/00111610309595323).
53. McCarthy, *Blood Meridian*, 171.
54. Anzaldúa, *Borderlands / La Frontera*, 25.
55. Mitchell, "A Book 'Made Out of Books,'" 266.
56. Additional examples of traditional desert literature of this sort include: Mary Austin, *The Land of Little Rain* (Houghton, Mifflin, 1903); Aldo Leopold, *A Sand County Almanac: And Sketches Here and There* (Oxford University Press, 2020); Joseph Wood Krutch, *The Desert Year* (Sloane, 1952); Thomas Merton, ed., *The Wisdom of the Desert*, trans. Thomas Merton (New Directions, 1960). To use a contemporary label, each of

these texts could be considered a work of creative nonfiction; that is, they weave together the author's journey and personal observations with stories about desert lands and people. More such texts can be found in the anthology *The New Desert Reader: Descriptions of America's Arid Regions* (University of Utah Press, 2006), edited by Peter Wild with a focus on American deserts. For a delve into writing about deserts around the world, one can pick up its predecessor, *The Desert Reader: A Literary Companion* (University of New Mexico Press, 2003), edited by Gregory McNamee. In the realm of fiction, traditional texts include Zane Grey, *Riders of the Purple Sage* (Grosset & Dunlap, 1940 [1912]); Frank Herbert, *Dune* (Penguin, 2005 [1965]); Octavia E. Butler, *Parable of the Sower* (Four Walls Eight Windows, 1993).

57. Reyner Banham, *Scenes in America Deserta* (Gibbs M. Smith, Inc., 1982), 3.

58. Marcia Bjornerud, *Timefulness: How Thinking Like a Geologist Can Help Save the World* (Princeton University Press, 2020), 90.

59. Bjornerud, *Timefulness*, 89; Jemma Deer, *Radical Animism: Reading for the End of the World* (Bloomsbury Academic, 2022), 8.

60. In her commentary "Anthropocene, Capitalocene, Plantationocene, Chthulucene: Making Kin," Haraway traces the origins for the various "-cenes" listed in the title. She notes that the Capitalocene was conceptualized by Andreas Malm and Jason Moore independently of her own use of the term, and that their "collaborative webs thicken" as Moore's edited collection *Anthropocene or Capitalocene?: Nature, History, and the Crisis of Capitalism* (PM Press, 2016) brings Haraway, Moore, Malm, and others together around the word "that signifies capitalism as a way of organizing nature—as a multispecies, situated, capitalist world-ecology" (6). About the Plantationocene Haraway writes: "In a recorded conversation for *Ethnos* at the University of Aarhus in October, 2014, the participants collectively generated the name Plantationocene for the devastating transformation of diverse kinds of human-tended farms, pastures, and forests into extractive and enclosed plantations, relying on slave labor and other forms of exploited, alienated, and usually spatially transported labor" (162). The Chthulucene is her own contribution, "a name for an elsewhere and elsewhen that was, still is, and might yet be" based upon "tentacular thinking" and "making kin," ideas established in her popular book *Staying*

NOTES

with the Trouble (31). Symbiocene is a term from Glenn Albrecht, used recently by Serena Ferrando, which "focuses on nearness" and thus combats the distance the term Anthropocene places between human and nonhuman. Ferrando writes that Symbiocene "highlights the proximity of people to animal, vegetal, and mineral life without drawing boundaries between them, recognizing that they are equal agents in the same symbiotic system that is based on collaboration rather than competition" ("Gardening the Symbiocene: Andrea Zanzotto's and Daria Menicanti's Poetic Hospitability," *Ecozon@: European Journal of Literature, Culture and Environment*, March 1, 2024, https://ecozona.eu/article/view/4828. 120).

61. Donna Haraway, "Anthropocene, Capitalocene, Plantationocene, Chthulucene: Making Kin," *Environmental Humanities* 6, no. 1 (2015): 159–60, https://doi.org/10.1215/22011919-3615934.
62. Haraway, "Anthropocene, Capitalocene, Plantationocene, Chthulucene," 160.
63. Deer, *Radical Animism*, 10.
64. Deer, *Radical Animism*, 11.
65. Deer, *Radical Animism*, 8.
66. Bjornerud, *Timefulness*, 16.
67. Bjornerud, *Timefulness*, 162, 5.
68. Feminist theorists like Donna Haraway and Karen Barad have provided a rich discourse around "a praxis of care and response—response-ability—in ongoing multispecies worlding on a wounded terra" (Haraway, *Staying with the Trouble*, 105). With respect to this ever-present call to action, Barad writes that "We (but not only 'we humans') are always already responsible to the others with whom or which we are entangled, not through conscious intent but through the various ontological entanglements that materiality entails" (*Meeting the Universe Halfway*, 393).
69. Haraway, *Staying with the Trouble*, 116.
70. Bjornerud, *Timefulness*, 17.
71. "Petrified Wood - Petrified Forest National Park," U.S. National Park Service, March 16, 2018, https://www.nps.gov/pefo/learn/nature/petrified-wood.htm.
72. Barad explains that "the neologism 'intra-action' *signifies the mutual constitution of entangled agencies*. That is, in contrast to the usual 'interaction,' which assumes that there are separate individual agencies that precede

their interaction, the notion of intra-action recognizes that distinct agencies do not precede, but rather emerge through, their intra-action. It is important to note that the 'distinct' agencies are only distinct in a relational, not an absolute, sense, that is, *agencies are only distinct in relation to their mutual entanglement; they don't exist as individual elements*" (33).
73. Shaviro, "'The Very Life of Darkness': A Reading of *Blood Meridian*," 146–47.
74. McCarthy, *Blood Meridian*, 175, 186.
75. McCarthy, *Blood Meridian*, 111.
76. Deer, *Radical Animism*, 56.
77. McCarthy, *Blood Meridian*, 61–62.
78. McCarthy, *Blood Meridian*, 56.
79. McCarthy, *Blood Meridian*, 56–62.
80. Sepich, *Notes on* Blood Meridian, 164.
81. Deer, *Radical Animism*, 56.
82. Derek P. McCormack, "Remotely Sensing Affective Afterlives: The Spectral Geographies of Material Remains," *Annals of the Association of American Geographers* 100, no. 3 (2010): 642, https://doi.org/10.1080/00045601003795004.
83. John Wylie, "The Spectral Geographies of W.G. Sebald," *Cultural Geographies* 14, no. 2 (2007): 172, https://doi.org/10.1177/1474474007075353.
84. Wylie, "Spectral Geographies," 181.
85. This term first appears in French philosopher Jacques Derrida's *Specters of Marx: The State of the Debt, the Work of Mourning, and the New International*, trans. Peggy Kamuf (Routledge, 1994). It is also a play on the word ontology, which would sound the same in French and therefore reveal a double meaning. John Wylie writes of the relationship between the spectral and haunting in Derrida's work: "In Derrida's hands, spectrality, the revenant being of ghosts, becomes a *hauntology*, which at one and the same time displaces, and is the condition of received understandings of the constitution of space and time, presence and absence. The spectral is thus the very conjuration and unsettling of presence, place, the present, and the past" (172).
86. McCarthy, *Blood Meridian*, 246–47.
87. Shaviro, "'The Very Life of Darkness': A Reading of *Blood Meridian*," 152.
88. McCarthy, *Blood Meridian*, 48.

NOTES

89. McCarthy, *Blood Meridian*, 173.
90. McCarthy, *Blood Meridian*, 174.
91. Wylie, "Spectral Geographies," 185.
92. Mitchell, "A Book 'Made Out of Books,'" 264.
93. Shaviro, "'The Very Life of Darkness': A Reading of *Blood Meridian*," 155. These instances often revolve around the actions of the judge, the novel's villain and historian. For example, in a lengthy speech about the Ancestral Puebloans, the judge remarks, they "quit these parts ages since and of them there is no memory. They are rumors and ghosts in this land and they are much revered" (McCarthy, 146). However, his telling is itself a memory, even as it problematically feeds the "vanishing Indian" myth. McCarthy creates a double act of mis- and remembering, re-inscribing their story through the filter of the judge's perspective. The judge's need to sketch and then destroy found things like artifacts or tools into his own notebook, re-inscribing items as he sees fit, happens once as discussed at the beginning of this chapter and again when the Glanton Gang are at Hueco Tanks, a site now known to have provided people with shelter and water as long as 10,000 years ago, where the judge takes notices of the hundreds of "ancient paintings . . . tracing out the very ones which he required" into his notebook (173) Once he's copied the images, "with a piece of broken chert he scappled away one of the designs, leaving no trace of it only a raw place on the stone where it had been" (173).
94. Alberto, "Nations, Nationalisms, and Indígenas," 113.
95. "'Footprints of the Past' - Wupatki National Monument," U.S. National Park Service, January 18, 2023, https://www.nps.gov/wupa/index.htm.
96. Casey Capachi, "The Last of the Navajos to Live at Wupatki National Monument?", *The Washington Post*, March 26, 2014, https://www.washingtonpost.com/news/post-nation/wp/2014/03/26/the-last-of-the-navajos-to-live-at-wupatki-national-monument/.
97. Associated Press, "Navajo Family Fights to Stay on Monument Land in Northern Arizona," *The Guardian*, March 21, 2014, sec. World news, https://www.theguardian.com/world/2014/mar/21/navajo-family-fights-stay-monument-land-arizona.
98. Capachi, "The Last of the Navajos to Live at Wupatki National Monument?"
99. A leading scholar in desert aesthetics, John Beck explains that "the trope

of the desert as without form and void enables the proliferation of all other tropes; the desert becomes the place of infinite metaphorical multiplicity" (*Dirty Wars: Landscape, Power, and Waste in Western American Literature* (University of Nebraska Press, 2009), 63–64). For Beck, this means that the concept of "desert as vacancy" can produce ways of thinking about the desert as a chaotic unknown (64). McCarthy's imagery and language conjure scenes of the chaotic conditions of possibility in the desert as void, where anything is seemingly possible. In such instances, the desert operates as the large, open space, as "desert absolute . . . devoid of feature altogether," a "hallucinatory void" where "there was nothing to mark [the riders'] progress upon it" (295, 113). In such instances, Beck's "metaphorical multiplicity" fills the void with apparitions of the dust "blowing down the void like the smoke of distant armies," or the illusion of "primitive boats upturned upon that shoreless void" (105, 246).
100. Haraway, *Staying with the Trouble*, 203, 207.
101. Veronika Kratz, "Combatting Desertification and Narrating Environmental Crisis in the United Nations," in *Storied Deserts* (Routledge, 2024), 157.
102. Kratz, "Combatting Desertification," 157.
103. See John Sepich's concordance for the celestial encounters in *Blood Meridian*, which states "The landscape of McCarthy's Southwest is composed not only of deserts and mirage effects, but also of heavenly phenomena. The novel begins and ends on nights of meteor showers" (164). See also Tynan's discussion of the celestial: "A key recurring feature of McCarthy's deserts is their astronomical and sidereal character, their alignment with the heavenly bodies" (195).
104. Mitchell, "A Book 'Made Out of Books,'" 265–66.
105. Shaviro, "'The Very Life of Darkness': A Reading of *Blood Meridian*," 154.
106. McCarthy, *Blood Meridian*, 246, 63, 117.
107. This phrase is spoken by the judge in *Blood Meridian*, but I can't help but think that McCarthy is testifying to the power of his profession, his craft, and of story. Interestingly, activist and author Maya Angelou comes to the same conclusion: "words are things," she says, foretelling that "someday we'll be able to measure the power of words. I think they are things. I think they get on the walls, they get in your wallpaper, they get in your rugs, in your upholstery, in your clothes. And, finally, into you" ("Dr. Maya Angelou - Power of Words," 2013, https://www.youtube.com/

watch?v=8PXdacSqvcA).
108. McCarthy, *Blood Meridian*, 85.
109. Isabelle Stengers, "Gaia, the Urgency to Think (and Feel),"Keynote Address, Os Mil Nomes de Gaia do Antropoceno à Idade da Terra Colóquio Internacional, Casa de Rui Barbosa, Rio de Janeiro, Brazil, September 19, 2014, 1.
110. In addition to naming, I argue that McCarthy's use of Spanish words is an example of place-specific language. When the riders are south of the US-Mexico border there are more instances of Spanish words, and when they are in the north there are less. However, when they are in areas close to the border there is a mix. For example, at the end of their journey to Corralitos, which is close to the border, they stay "in the corral of a hacienda where all night men kept watchfires burning on the azoteas or roofs" (88). The use of both the English and Spanish word for roof reflects the bilingual, bicultural place. The author often uses language choice to mirror the cultural geography of borderlands areas, disrupting the idea of a culturally homogenous Desert Southwest and revealing desert abundance.
111. McCarthy, *Blood Meridian*, 32.
112. McCarthy, *Blood Meridian*, 214.
113. McCarthy, *Blood Meridian*, 215.
114. Shaviro, "'The Very Life of Darkness': A Reading of *Blood Meridian*," 153; McCarthy, *Blood Meridian*, 247.
115. Shaviro, "'The Very Life of Darkness': A Reading of *Blood Meridian*," 153.
116. Shaviro, "'The Very Life of Darkness': A Reading of *Blood Meridian*," 153.
117. Shaviro, "'The Very Life of Darkness': A Reading of *Blood Meridian*," 153–54.

CHAPTER 3

1. As discussed in chapter 1, Timothy Morton defines hyperobjects as "things that are massively distributed in time and space relative to humans" which "are *nonlocal*; in other words, any 'local manifestation' of a hyperobject is not directly the hyperobject" (*Hyperobjects,* 1). I argue then that localization and attention to specific desert communities and places is a practice against the ecological and ethical harms resulting from a perpetuation of the hyperobjective desert as abstraction or void.
2. In his chapter "Defining Post-Western Cinema: John Huston's *The Treasure*

NOTES

of the Sierra Madre (1948)," in *New Wests and Post-Wests: Literature and Film of the American West*, ed. Paul Varner (Cambridge Scholars Publishing, 2013), Neil Campbell explains, "post-Westerns emerged to explore 'western' themes in new contexts, casting fresh light on the provincial ideologies that gave rise to the fabled West in the first place" and "contribute to a critical regionalist rethinking of the Western's place in the assertion and reproduction of national ideology" (5–6). Though it's beyond the scope of the chapter to investigate the nuances of cinematic genres, I do consider and analyze *Sicario* as a post-Western film, where the additional spatial dimensions of North and South—performed by its verticality—complicate the traditional East-West dichotomy.

3. The next closest large city is Las Cruces, New Mexico, about an hour's drive north, which in the July 2021 US Census reported a population of 112,914. That figure pales in comparison to El Paso's 867,947 the same year, which itself is dwarfed by Juárez's 1.5 million people. El Paso–Juárez is the second largest metropolitan area along the US-Mexico border, after San Diego–Tijuana.

4. The film's striking cinematography of the landscape is intensified by its extraordinary sounds. Composer Jóhann Jóhannsson wrote the score for *Sicario*, though it is hardly what one might typically consider musical. As Jóhannsson explained in an interview, "I was working with a large, 55-piece orchestra, strings, brass, woodwind, but they serve more of a textural function—they're not really melodic. It's more textural, with a lot of extended techniques and spectral, textural writing" (Matt Grobar, "Encore: 'Sicario' Composer Jóhann Jóhannsson on Creating Propulsive Sound of Drug War Drama," *Deadline*, February 10, 2018). His key descriptors, "spectral" and "textural," are helpful ways of arresting the affective dimensions of sound into language. They attest to the layers of intensities that proliferate through the film, taking viewers above and below the desert environment, an aural dimension to verticality.

5. Joining the Rio Grande and stretches of highway to clearly mark the divide between El Paso and Juárez, the fence shown was erected in 2006, less than ten years before *Sicario* was filmed, as a result of the Secure Fence Act.

6. Colonias are unincorporated sections of a town or city with few to no amenities, often lacking electricity and running water.

7. *Sicario* (Lions Gate Entertainment, 2016), 25:42–47.
8. *Sicario*, 28:26–29:00.
9. Executive Order 9066, issued by President Franklin D. Roosevelt on February 19, 1942, as response to the bombing of Pearl Harbor, directly impacted over 120,000 people of Japanese ancestry, who "were evicted from the West Coast of the United States and held in relocation camps across the country"—two-thirds of whom were American citizens (Japanese-American Relocation, Poston Preservation). For further discussion, see Sandra C. Taylor, *Jewel of the Desert: Japanese American Internment at Topaz* (University of California Press, 1993); Wendy L. Ng, *Japanese American Internment During World War II: A History and Reference Guide* (Greenwood Publishing Group, 2002); Linda L. Ivey and Kevin W. Kaatz, *Citizen Internees: A Second Look at Race and Citizenship in Japanese American Internment Camps* (ABC-CLIO, LLC, 2017); Brian Masaru Hayashi, *Democratizing the Enemy: The Japanese American Internment* (Princeton University Press, 2010).
10. Beck, *Dirty Wars*, 5. Beck has a prolific amount of research on militarization of the American West with an emphasis on literature and deserts. See Beck, *Landscape as Weapon: Cultures of Exhaustion and Refusal* (Reaktion Books, 2021); John Beck and Ryan Bishop, *Technocrats of the Imagination: Art, Technology, and the Military-Industrial Avant-Garde* (Duke University Press, 2020).
11. *Sicario*, 38:32–38:36.
12. *Sicario*, 12:46–12:49.
13. *Sicario*, 11:45–11:57.
14. *Sicario*, 12:10–12:13.
15. *Sicario*, 12:18–12:24.
16. *Sicario*, 16:35–16:40.
17. Giorgio Agamben, *State of Exception* (University of Chicago Press, 2005), 4. In his book of the same name, Agamben repeatedly defines the state of exception in various iterations and political contexts. The arguments of this chapter take up the understanding that "the state of exception is neither external nor internal to the juridical order, and the problem of defining it concerns precisely a threshold, or a zone of indifference, where inside and outside do not exclude each other but rather blur with each other. The suspension of the norm does not mean its abolition, and the zone of

NOTES

anomie that it establishes is not (or at least claims not to be) unrelated to the juridical order" (23).

18. *Sicario*, 23:15–23:19.
19. *Sicario*, 23:19–23:22.
20. *Sicario*, 23:22–23:26.
21. *Sicario*, 37:32–37:40.
22. *Sicario*, 39:04–39:08.
23. John Beck, "Without Form and Void: The American Desert as Trope and Terrain," *Nepantla: Views from the South* 2, no. 1 (2001): 64.
24. *Sicario*, 57:43–57:47.
25. *Sicario*, 1:01:11–1:01:23.
26. *Sicario*, 1:01:25–1:01:26.
27. *Sicario*, 1:02:30–1:02:33.
28. *Sicario*, 1:03:18–1:03:53.
29. Melissa W. Wright, "Feminicidio, Narcoviolence, and Gentrification in Ciudad Juárez: The Feminist Fight," *Environment and Planning. D, Society & Space* 31, no. 5 (2013): 832, https://doi.org/10.1068/d17812.
30. *Sicario*, 1:34:58–1:35:22.
31. For more in-depth discussions of the scale and efficiency of the Medellín Cartel's cocaine operations in the twentieth century, see *Kings of Cocaine: Inside the Medellín Cartel - An Astonishing True Story of Murder, Money and International Corruption* (Garrett County Press, 2011) written by reporters Guy Gugliotta and Jeff Leen, and the 2006 documentary *Cocaine Cowboys*, directed by Billy Corben (Magnolia Pictures).
32. As discussed in chapter 2, Jason De León defines necroviolence as "violence performed and produced through the specific treatment of corpses that is perceived to be offensive, sacrilegious, or inhumane by the perpetrator, the victim (and her or his cultural group), or both . . . [it] is specifically about corporeal mistreatment and its generative capacity for violence" (69).
33. *Sicario*, 29:10–29:24.
34. Though this component doesn't make it into the film, the Mexican War on Drugs, launched by former President Felipe Calderón in 2007, saw a marked increase in abuse of law on the part of Mexican government and state officials. The abuse includes violence against state citizens in the form of rape, torture, and disappearances and has

NOTES

led to the disappearances of over 100,000 people as of 2022 (Vanessa Buschschlüter, "Mexico Disappearances Reach Record High of 100,000 Amid Impunity," BBC News, May 17, 2022, https://www.bbc.com/news/world-latin-america-61477704). For a more detailed discussion of the Mexican government exploiting the state of exception into the rule, see historian Alexander Aviña, "Killing Machine: How Mexican and US States of Exception Turned Revolutionaries and Migrants into Bare Life, 1969–1996," in *On Othering: Processes and Politics of Unpeace*, ed. Yasmin Saikia and Chad Haines (Athabasca University Press, 2024).

35. *Sicario*, 31:38–31:47.
36. *Sicario*, 1:19:08–1:19:15.
37. *Sicario*, 1:10:22–1:10:26.
38. *Sicario*, 1:12:06–1:12:30.
39. Maximiliano Hernández, *Sicario*'s Maximiliano Hernández, interview by Angela María Ortíz S., 2015, 2:10–2:26, https://www.sefijaonline.com/wp-content/uploads/2015/12/Maximiliano-Herna%CC%81ndez.mp3.
40. *Sicario*, 46:34–46:39.
41. The man angrily asks Matt: "How's the auditor gonna react to an $8,000 check to fuckin' Domino's Pizza?" (46:40–46).
42. *Sicario*, 47:04–47:44.
43. *Sicario*, 56:35–56:38.
44. *Sicario*, 56:42–57:07. The migrants speak to Alejandro in Spanish, and the excerpt here is using the English subtitles provided in the film.
45. *Sicario*, 57:10–57:20.
46. De León, *Land of Open Graves*, 30.
47. De León, *Land of Open Graves*, 30.
48. Quoted in WNYC Studios Radiolab, "Border Trilogy Part 2: Hold the Line," 20:23-20:26, accessed February 11, 2023, https://www.radiolab.org/episodes/border-trilogy-part-2-hold-line.
49. Quoted in Radiolab, 20:36–20:49.
50. De León, *Land of Open Graves*, 31.
51. Radiolab, "Border Trilogy Part 2," 26:39–26:52.
52. Radiolab, "Border Trilogy Part 2," 43:46–43:50.
53. De León, *Land of Open Graves*, 27, 68.
54. Hernández, Sicario's Maximiliano Hernández, 10:51–11:08.

NOTES

CHAPTER 4

1. Elvia R. Arriola, "Accountability for Murder in the Maquiladoras: Linking Corporate Indifference to Gender Violence at the U.S.-Mexico Border," in *Making a Killing: Femicide, Free Trade, and La Frontera*, ed. Alicia Gaspar de Alba and Georgina Guzmán (University of Texas Press, 2010), 25; Edmé Domínguez et al., "Women Workers in the Maquiladoras and the Debate on Global Labor Standards," *Feminist Economics* 16, no. 4 (2010): 187, https://doi.org/10.1080/13545701.2010.530603; Deborah M. Weissman, "The Political Economy of Violence: Toward an Understanding of the Gender-Based Murders of Ciudad Juarez," *North Carolina Journal of International Law* 30, no. 4 (March 11, 2005): 7–8; Melissa W. Wright, "The Dialectics of Still Life: Murder, Women, and Maquiladoras," *Public Culture* 11, no. 3 (1999): 461, https://doi.org/10.1215/08992363-11-3-453.
2. Arriola, "Accountability," 40.
3. "Border Patrol History," U.S. Customs and Border Protection, July 21, 2020, https://www.cbp.gov/border-security/along-us-borders/history.
4. Pedro Rios, "For 25 Years, Operation Gatekeeper Has Made Life Worse for Border Communities," *The Washington Post*, October 1, 2019, https://www.washingtonpost.com/outlook/2019/10/01/years-operation-gatekeeper-has-made-life-worse-border-communities/.
5. William J. Krouse, "CRS Report for Congress: U.S. Border Patrol Operations," Congressional Research Service, November 10, 1997, 3–4, The Library of Congress.
6. Krouse, "CRS Report for Congress," 5–6; Mark Binelli, "Taking Freedom: 'Build That Wall!': A Local History," *Pacific Standard*, May 4, 2018, https://psmag.com/social-justice/build-that-wall-a-local-history.
7. Victor M. Ortiz, "The Unbearable Ambiguity of the Border," *Social Justice* 28, no. 2 (84) (Summer 2001): 100.
8. Julian Lim, *Porous Borders: Multiracial Migrations and the Law in the U.S.-Mexico Borderlands* (University of North Carolina Press, 2017), 11.
9. Luis Alberto Urrea, *The Devil's Highway: A True Story* (Paw Prints, 2005), 48 (emphasis added).
10. Blurred lines abound, as even the group's name is up for debate. Urrea explains that in Southern Arizona there are only two Border Patrol sectors, so "the confusion comes easy. . . . Walkers are identified by sector,

not station, so the Wellton crew was erased from the headlines" because they "just happened to have died in the Yuma sector" as opposed to the Tucson one (Urrea, *The Devil's Highway*, 18, 33). They are the Wellton 26 or the Yuma 14, depending on whom you ask. To explain the discrepancy between the numbers, though there were fourteen fatalities, Wellton Border Patrol Officer Friendly tells Urrea there were twenty-six bodies, and "all of them are victims, even the live ones. And they're mine" (33). Regardless of which sector claims ownership, for most of the book the walkers are north of the US-Mexico border, trekking the Devil's Highway.

11. Urrea, *The Devil's Highway*, 103. Giving the US-Mexico Border its familiar shape, the Gadsden Purchase is a treaty signed by James Gadsden, US minister to Mexico, in December of 1853 and ratified in 1854. The agreement, also known as the Treaty of La Mesilla, was for the US to "pay Mexico $10 million for a 29,670 square mile portion of Mexico that later became part of Arizona and New Mexico" ("Milestones: 1830–1860: Gadsden Purchase, 1853–1854," Department of State: Office of the Historian, accessed February 16, 2023, https://history.state.gov/milestones/1830-1860/gadsden-purchase). As part of the political motivation to sign, the treaty was "prompted in part by advocates of a southern transcontinental railroad, for which the most practical route would pass through the acquired territory" ("Gadsden Purchase," in *Britannica Academic*, accessed February 16, 2023, https://academic-eb-com.ezproxy1.lib.asu.edu/levels/collegiate/article/Gadsden-Purchase/35784). A significant and persistent consequence of the agreement is that the newly defined US-Mexico border cut through Tohono O'odham lands, "making some tribal members 'Americans' and others 'Mexicans,' though neither government granted them full citizenship" (Andrae M. Marak and Laura Tuennerman, *At the Border of Empires: The Tohono O'odham, Gender, and Assimilation, 1880–1934* (University of Arizona Press, 2013), 14). While initially the border "remain[ed] porous," the creation of Border Patrol and its increased surveillance and enforcement has resulted in cultural and geopolitical divides upon Indigenous communities on both sides (Marak and Tuennerman, 14). As Jason De León puts it, "no community along the southern border, however, has been as negatively affected by border crossings, migrant fatalities, or Border Patrol presence as the Tohono O'odham" (*Land of Open Graves*, 302).

NOTES

12. Urrea, *The Devil's Highway*, 55.
13. The name of this route, according to Byrd Howell Granger, "was justly applied because many who followed it suffered the tortures of the damned from heat and thirst. The route meandered from water hole to water hole, and it was always problematic whether such holes would be holding water. Further, at times shifting sands made portions of the trail impassable so that far too often travellers perished before finding their way or water to sustain them" (111–12).
14. Urrea, *The Devil's Highway*, 28.
15. Urrea, *The Devil's Highway*, 29.
16. Urrea, *The Devil's Highway*, 112.
17. Urrea, *The Devil's Highway*, 113.
18. Urrea, *The Devil's Highway*, 113.
19. Urrea, *The Devil's Highway*, 134.
20. Urrea, *The Devil's Highway*, 138.
21. Urrea, *The Devil's Highway*, 138.
22. Urrea, *The Devil's Highway*, 39.
23. Urrea, *The Devil's Highway*, 108.
24. Urrea, *The Devil's Highway*, 136.
25. Urrea, *The Devil's Highway*, 137.
26. Urrea, *The Devil's Highway*, 108.
27. Urrea, *The Devil's Highway*, 135.
28. Urrea, *The Devil's Highway*, 15.
29. De León, *Land of Open Graves*, 66.
30. De León, *Land of Open Graves*, 68.
31. For more extensive scholarship about Ivon's positionality as a lesbian protagonist, see Irene Mata's "Writing on the Walls: Deciphering Violence and Industrialization in Alicia Gaspar de Alba's *Desert Blood*," *MELUS* 35, no. 3 (September 2010): 15-40. For an insightful analysis of the act and attitudes around adoption in the novel, see Tereza Jiroutová Kynčlová's "Woman Killing and Adoption in Alicia Gaspar de Alba's *Desert Blood: The Juárez Murders* (2005)," *Ex-Centric Narratives: Journal of Anglophone Literature, Culture and Media*, no. 3 (2019): 83, https://doi.org/10.26262/exna.v0i3.7550.
32. Alicia Camacho Schmidt pushes back against understanding gendered violence in Juárez "as a regressive cultural manifestation of masculine

aggression," and instead suggests, "it is perhaps better understood as a *rational* expression of the contradictions arising from the gendered codes of neo-liberal governance and development. The combined processes of economic restructuring and political transition have had the perverse effect of increasing the state's stake in the denationalization of poor women's citizenship precisely at the moment of their emergence as new political and economic actors. The global economies that convert subaltern women into commodities interrupt women's purchase on the most basic right to personal security. The *feminicidio* represents an assault on this bodily agency in the extreme" (Alicia Schmidt Camacho, "Ciudadana X: Gender Violence and the Denationalization of Women's Rights in Ciudad Juárez, Mexico," *CR: The New Centennial Review* 5, no. 1 (2005): 267, https://doi.org/10.1353/ncr.2005.0030). Citing a range of scholarship concerning gendered violence—Arvin, Tuck, & Morrill, 2013; Dougherty & Calafell, 2019; Lugones, 2007, 2010; Mack, Bershon, Laiche, & Navarro, 2018; Perry, 2018; Veronelli, 2016—Ashley Noel Mack and Tiara R. Na'puti propose an engagement in "a decolonial feminist orientation [that] understands gendered violence, such as sexual assault, as part of colonial violence and attends to the combined processes of racialization, gender dichotomization, and heterosexualism in modernity" (Ashley Noel Mack and Tiara R. Na'puti, "'Our Bodies Are Not *Terra Nullius*': Building a Decolonial Feminist Resistance to Gendered Violence," *Women's Studies in Communication* 42, no. 3 (July 3, 2019): 348, https://doi.org/10.1080/07491409.2019.1637803). See also Rosa-Linda Fregoso and Cynthia Bejarano, *Terrorizing Women: Feminicide in the Americas* (Duke University Press, 2010).

33. Steven S. Volk and Marian E. Schlotterbeck, "Gender, Order, and Femicide: Reading the Popular Culture of Murder in Ciudad Juárez," in *Making a Killing: Femicide, Free Trade, and La Frontera*, ed. Alicia Gaspar de Alba and Georgina Guzmán (University of Texas Press, 2010), 129.
34. Alicia Gaspar de Alba, *Desert Blood: The Juárez Murders* (Arte Publico Press, 2005), 22.
35. Etymologically, the word stems from the infinitive, *rastrear*, meaning to track, trail, drag, or trace ("Rastreo," in *A Comprehensive Etymological Dictionary of the Spanish Language with Families of Words Based on Indo-European Roots* (Xlibris, 2014)).

NOTES

36. Gaspar de Alba, *Desert Blood*, 239–40.
37. Gaspar de Alba, *Desert Blood*, 240.
38. Gaspar de Alba, *Desert Blood*, 241.
39. Gaspar de Alba, *Desert Blood*, 111.
40. Gaspar de Alba, *Desert Blood*, 137.
41. Gaspar de Alba, *Desert Blood*, 23.
42. Gaspar de Alba, *Desert Blood*, 255.
43. Gaspar de Alba, *Desert Blood*, 168, 263.
44. Gaspar de Alba, *Desert Blood*, 165, 166.
45. Gaspar de Alba, *Desert Blood*, 326.
46. Urrea, *The Devil's Highway*, 106.
47. Urrea, *The Devil's Highway*, 89.
48. Urrea, *The Devil's Highway*, 90.
49. Urrea, *The Devil's Highway*, 122. Also, see Maurice Merleau-Ponty's *The Visible and the Invisible: Followed by Working Notes* (Northwestern University Press, 1968), especially 248–56, for a discussion about "flesh of the world."
50. Urrea, *The Devil's Highway*, 123. Urrea refers to "Desolation" in the following passage about the Devil's Highway itself: "In many ancient religious texts, fallen angels were bound in chains and buried beneath a desert known only as Desolation. This could be the place" (4).
51. Urrea, *The Devil's Highway*, 124.
52. Urrea, *The Devil's Highway*, 125.
53. Urrea, *The Devil's Highway*, 128.
54. Urrea, *The Devil's Highway*, 120.
55. Urrea, *The Devil's Highway*, 117.
56. Urrea, *The Devil's Highway*, 19.
57. Urrea, *The Devil's Highway*, 117.
58. Urrea, *The Devil's Highway*, 117.
59. Urrea, *The Devil's Highway*, 117.
60. Urrea, *The Devil's Highway*, 66.
61. Urrea, *The Devil's Highway*, 66.
62. Urrea, *The Devil's Highway*, 4.
63. Urrea, *The Devil's Highway*, 157.
64. Urrea, *The Devil's Highway*, 37.
65. De León, *Land of Open Graves*, 73.

66. De León, *Land of Open Graves*, 75–81.
67. De León, *Land of Open Graves*, 81.
68. Urrea, *The Devil's Highway*, 37–38.
69. Urrea, *The Devil's Highway*, 220.
70. McCarthy, *Blood Meridian*, 159.
71. Urrea, *The Devil's Highway*, 20.
72. Urrea, *The Devil's Highway*, 207.
73. For more in-depth research that explores the connections between gendered violence and economic globalization with specific attention to the feminicidios and maquiladoras in Juárez, see Maria Cristina Morales and Cynthia Bejarano, "Transnational Sexual and Gendered Violence: An Application of Border Sexual Conquest at a Mexico-US Border," *Global Networks (Oxford)* 9, no. 3 (2009): 420–39, https://doi.org/10.1111/j.1471-0374.2009.00261.x; Weissman, "Political Economy of Violence."
74. Leslie Salzinger, *Genders in Production: Making Workers in Mexico's Global Factories* (University of California Press, 2003), 29.
75. Wright, "The Dialectics of Still Life," 461.
76. Mary-Kay Bachour, "Disrupting the Myth of Maquila Disposability: Sites of Reproduction and Resistance in Juárez," *Women's Studies International Forum* 48 (2015): 181, https://doi.org/10.1016/j.wsif.2014.11.010.
77. See Bachour's "Disrupting the Myth of Maquila Disposability," which warns against scholarship that "consume[s] and reproduce[s] the image of the maquiladora worker as one who passively accepts the violence she is subjected to on a daily basis" and instead addresses the importance of engaging various "resistance efforts against the economic exploitation of the maquila body," including that "many women and families have created groups in protest against the increased forms of sexual violence faced by women on the Mexican-U.S. border" (183, 182). Additionally, Edmé Domínguez et al. provide helpful insights into ongoing debates—integration thesis versus exploitation thesis—about women's labor in maquiladoras globally: "According to the integration theses, women workers with industrial, export-based jobs in the formal sector would become winners in the long run as their salaries would increase and their working conditions improve following a rapid growth of export-oriented production. The exploitation theses emphasized the negative conditions in these jobs and the fact that the competition between low-wage production zones would

lead to the deterioration of, instead of the improvement of, salaries and working conditions for these women workers" ("Women Workers in the Maquiladoras and the Debate on Global Labor Standards," 189).

78. Elsa is dying, and Ivon and Ximena visit her and meet her son. When they ask about how she got pregnant, especially knowing that the maquilas fire pregnant employees to avoid paying for maternity leave, Elsa is clear that she doesn't know how she conceived her child. She describes two of the tests that the factory doctor made her undergo: the first was a "pelvic exam" in which they "took something out of [her] to make sure [she] wasn't pregnant" and the second was a week later, during which the doctor "put something else inside [her] . . . sharp, almost like a needle" (Gaspar de Alba, *Desert Blood*, 91). Ivon and Ximena eventually realize that she was artificially inseminated by a doctor experimenting with making contraceptives (91–92).

79. Kynčlová, "Woman Killing and Adoption."

80. Gaspar de Alba, *Desert Blood*, 254. *Desert Blood* calls these migrants "*gente humilde* . . . humble people from the interior that have been lured to this border by the promise of jobs" (167). Before Irene ever goes missing, her cousin Ximena is explaining the work they do with Contra el Silencio to search for missing women in the desert. She tells Irene they are called "*muchachas del sur* because so many of them come from small towns and villages in the south. Their families never even find out they're missing. Or worse: dead" (24). The bodies of *muchachas del sur* are somehow even more subject to erasure by proximity to the Border.

81. Salzinger, *Genders in Production*, 188. For a detailed analysis and examples of pregnancy discrimination against maquila workers at the end of the twentieth century, consult Elvia R. Arriola's "Voices from the Barbed Wires of Despair: Women in the Maquiladoras, Latina Critical Legal Theory, and Gender at the U.S.-Mexico Border," *DePaul Law Review* 49, no. 3 (March 1, 2000): 729, 783–88.

82. Gaspar de Alba, *Desert Blood*, 318, 323.

83. Wright, "The Dialectics of Still Life," 456.

84. Gaspar de Alba, *Desert Blood*, 179.

85. Gaspar de Alba, *Desert Blood*, 179.

86. Gaspar de Alba, *Desert Blood*, 279.

87. Gaspar de Alba, *Desert Blood*, 25.

88. Gaspar de Alba, *Desert Blood*, v.
89. Gaspar de Alba, *Desert Blood*, 251, 252.
90. Gaspar de Alba, *Desert Blood*, 171, 221.
91. Gaspar de Alba, *Desert Blood*, 286.
92. Gaspar de Alba, *Desert Blood*, v.
93. Marianne Sullivan, *Tainted Earth: Smelters, Public Health, and the Environment*, 1st ed. (Rutgers University Press, 2014), 58.
94. John Burnett, "A Toxic Century: Mining Giant Must Clean Up Mess," NPR, February 4, 2010, sec. Environment, https://www.npr.org/2010/02/04/122779177/a-toxic-century-mining-giant-must-clean-up-mess.
95. Sullivan's work on the environmental health crises posed by smelting operations in the American West singles out ASARCO's presence in El Paso as particularly hazardous and informative. In *Tainted Earth: Smelters, Public Health, and the Environment*, she explains that the scientific investigations carried out there in the 1970s were responsible for broadening general understanding of the effects of lead poisoning and prolonged exposure to lead, including the finding that lead exposure is possible through air pollution, where previously it was thought that only direct exposure to contaminated soil could cause harm. Ultimately, she writes, "for environmental and public health scientists as well as regulators, El Paso was a wakeup call that established a clear link between community health and industrial emissions—it furthered a growing interest in subclinical lead poisoning and set a high standard for scientific rigor in community environmental health investigations" (71).
96. Gaspar de Alba, *Desert Blood*, 240.
97. Sullivan, *Tainted Earth*, 58.
98. See chapter 2 for further definition of spectral as used in this book.
99. De León, *Land of Open Graves*, 69.
100. Philosopher Quentin Meillassoux explains a specter as "A dead person who has not been properly mourned, who haunts us, bothers us, refusing to pass over to the 'other side,' where the dearly-departed can accompany us at a distance sufficient for us to live our own lives without forgetting them" ("Spectral Dilemma," trans. Robin Mackay, *Collapse: Philosophical Research and Development* 4 (May 2008): 261).
101. De León, *Land of Open Graves*, 71. See Pauline Boss, "Ambiguous Loss Theory: Challenges for Scholars and Practitioners," *Family Relations* 56,

NOTES

no. 2 (2007): 105–11, https://doi.org/10.1111/j.1741-3729.2007.00444.x.
102. Urrea, *The Devil's Highway*, 36.
103. Gaspar de Alba, *Desert Blood*, 77.
104. Gaspar de Alba, *Desert Blood*, 77.
105. Urrea, *The Devil's Highway*, 97.
106. Urrea, *The Devil's Highway*, 204.
107. Gaspar de Alba, *Desert Blood*, 21, 141.
108. Gaspar de Alba, *Desert Blood*, 155.
109. Gaspar de Alba, *Desert Blood*, 295.
110. Gaspar de Alba, *Desert Blood*, 295.
111. Burnett, "A Toxic Century."
112. "ASARCO filed for Chapter 11 protection in 2005, then emerged from bankruptcy in 2009 by signing one of the largest environmental settlements in U.S. history: $1.79 billion to clean and restore more than 80 locations around the country. . . . The demolition cost about $2 million and was organized and paid for by the Texas Custodial Trust, which was established as part of Asarco's bankruptcy settlement agreement and was funded with $52 million to address contamination on the property" (Erika Orden, "El Paso Says Goodbye to Landmark," Recasting the Smelter, April 14, 2013, https://www.RecastingtheSmelter.com/?p=4149).
113. Burnett, "A Toxic Century."

CHAPTER 5

1. Christine Y. Kim and Nancy Meyer, "James Turrell: A Life in Art," in *James Turrell: A Retrospective* (Los Angeles County Museum of Art, 2013), 43.
2. "Skyspaces," James Turrell, accessed February 11, 2023, https://jamesturrell.com/work/picture-plane/.
3. Alexa Hazel, "Roden Crater," *The Point Magazine*, December 19, 2021, https://thepointmag.com/criticism/roden-crater/.
4. Craig E. Adcock and James Turrell, *James Turrell: The Art of Light and Space* (University of California Press, 1990), xx.
5. Adcock and Turrell, *James Turrell*, xx.
6. Michael Govan, "Inner Light: The Radical Reality of James Turrell," in *James Turrell: A Retrospective* (Los Angeles County Museum of Art, 2013), 23.

NOTES

7. Govan, "Inner Light," 26.
8. Michael Govan, "Spaces Inhabited by Consciousness," in *James Turrell: A Retrospective* (Los Angeles County Museum of Art, 2013), 209.
9. Maurice Merleau-Ponty, *Phenomenology of Perception*, trans. Daniel A. Landes (Routledge, 2013), 71.
10. Mark C. Taylor, *Refiguring the Spiritual: Beuys, Barney, Turrell, Goldsworthy* (Columbia University Press, 2012), 104.
11. Kathleen Stewart, "Atmospheric Attunements," *Environment and Planning. D, Society & Space* 29, no. 3 (2011): 452, https://doi.org/10.1068/d9109.
12. Gernot Böhme, "The Phenomenology of Light," in *James Turrell: Geometrie des Lichts / Geometry of Light*, ed. Ursula Sinnreich (Hatje Cantz, 2009), 69.
13. Böhme, "The Phenomenology of Light," 69.
14. Stewart, "Atmospheric Attunements," 452.
15. Böhme, "The Phenomenology of Light," 73.
16. Adcock and Turrell, *James Turrell*, 2.
17. Adcock and Turrell, *James Turrell*, 172.
18. Stewart, "Atmospheric Attunements," 449.
19. Quoted in Richard Andrews et al., *James Turrell: Sensing Space* (Henry Art Gallery, University of Washington, 1992), 50.
20. E. C. Krupp, "Bothering to Look," in *James Turrell: A Retrospective* (Los Angeles County Museum of Art, 2013), 239.
21. Jay Cheshes, "James Turrell's New Masterpiece in the Desert," *WSJ Magazine*, January 14, 2019, https://www.wsj.com/articles/james-turrells-new-masterpiece-in-the-desert-11547480071.
22. Cheshes, "James Turrell's New Masterpiece in the Desert."
23. "About," *Roden Crater* (blog), 2023, https://rodencrater.com/about/.
24. Gilles Deleuze and Félix Guattari, *A Thousand Plateaus: Capitalism and Schizophrenia*, trans. Brian Massumi (University of Minnesota Press, 1987), 253.
25. Andrews et al., *James Turrell*, 16.
26. Voyles, *Wastelanding*, 10.
27. Adcock and Turrell, *James Turrell*, 154.
28. Cheshes, "James Turrell's New Masterpiece in the Desert."
29. Cheshes, "James Turrell's New Masterpiece in the Desert."

NOTES

30. "About," *Roden Crater* (blog), 2023, https://rodencrater.com/about/.
31. Andrews et al., *James Turrell*, 16.
32. Chris Michno, "Notes from the Turrell Project," *The Other Side: Alternative Reading for Alternative People*, February 11, 1992, 8.
33. Michno, "Notes from the Turrell Project," 9.
34. *James Turrell: Passageways*, 1995, 20:17–52.
35. "James Turrell's Roden Crater Leaves Lasting Impact on Students in Herberger Institute Field Labs," *Medium*, April 5, 2019, https://medium.com/herberger-institute/james-turrells-roden-crater-leaves-lasting-impact-on-students-in-herberger-institute-field-labs-663b79418d74.
36. Quoted in Mary Beth Faller, "Letting in the Light: ASU, Artist James Turrell to Partner on Masterwork in the Desert," *ASU News*, January 14, 2019, https://news.asu.edu/20190114-creativity-asu-artist-james-turrell-partner-masterwork-roden-crater.
37. Edward Abbey, *Desert Solitaire: A Season in the Wilderness*, 9th ed. (1968; repr., Ballantine Books, 1981), 6.
38. Edward Abbey, *Confessions of a Barbarian: Selections from the Journals of Edward Abbey, 1951–1989*, 1st ed., ed. David Petersen (Little, Brown, 1994). In this collection of Abbey's writings, he not once but twice asks "Am I a racist?," where the first of such prompts is followed by "I guess I am. I certainly do not wish to live in a society dominated by blacks, or Mexicans, or Orientals. Look at Africa, at Mexico, at Asia" (307). The second time he pontificates about his own notion of what makes a superior race, which "if such a thing were plausible, would be harmlessness," a standard by which, he argues, Indigenous peoples of Australia, Africa, and "maybe the Hopis of Arizona" would live up to "(But even there, the reason may lie simply in their lack of power and technology)" (336–37).
39. Raj Patel, "The Misanthropocene?," *Earth Island Journal* 28, no. 1 (2013): 21.
40. Haraway, *Staying with the Trouble*, 101.
41. "Rafa Esparza at OMCA," 2024, https://www.youtube.com/watch?v=EkkCmLN_2IM; *Artist Lecture Series: Rafa Esparza*, 2018, 45:48–45:53, https://www.youtube.com/watch?v=PRqiJ84WTJ0.
42. *Artist Lecture Series*, 45:48–45:53.
43. "Rafa Esparza at OMCA."
44. Travis Diehl, "Land Rites," *Frieze*, March 20, 2017, https://www.frieze.

NOTES

com/article/land-rites.

45. Alicia Inez Guzmán, "Rafa Esparza's 'Brown Matter' Part I: When the Building Blocks of Home Inhabit the Whitney | Tierra Firme," *Tierra Firme* (blog), June 1, 2017, http://tierrafirmeprojects.com/rafa-esparzas-brown-matter-part-i-when-the-building-blocks-of-home-inhabit-the-whitney.
46. *Artist Lecture Series*, 1:06:40.
47. Rafa Esparza, Rafa Esparza Talks About "Tierra. Sangre. Oro." at Ballroom Marfa, interview by Kate Green, Artforum, November 21, 2017, https://www.artforum.com/interviews/rafa-esparza-talks-about-tierra-sangre-oro-at-ballroom-marfa-72422.
48. Carmen Hermo, "Through Collaborative Work, Centering Queer, Brown Folks, Rafa Esparza Looks to Destabilize Artistic Authority," ARTnews.com, January 14, 2020, https://www.artnews.com/art-news/artists/rafa-esparza-artist-shaping-art-2020s-1202675032/.
49. Diehl, "Land Rites."
50. "Whitney Biennial 2017: Rafa Esparza," 2017, https://www.youtube.com/watch?v=CfiKE8CuuN4.
51. Alicia Inez Guzmán, "Rafa Esparza," *Tierra Firme* (blog), accessed February 11, 2023, http://tierrafirmeprojects.com/rafa-esparza.
52. Guzmán, "Rafa Esparza's 'Brown Matter' Part I."
53. Guzmán, "Rafa Esparza's 'Brown Matter' Part I."
54. Esparza, Rafa Esparza Talks About "Tierra. Sangre. Oro." at Ballroom Marfa.
55. *Whitney Biennial 2017*.
56. "Rafa Esparza at OMCA."
57. *Artist Lecture Series*.
58. Laura Copelin, "Tierra. Sangre. Oro.," *Terremoto*, September 27, 2014, https://terremoto.mx/en/online/tierra-sangre-oro/.
59. Copelin, "Tierra. Sangre. Oro."
60. Copelin, "Tierra. Sangre. Oro."
61. Copelin, "Tierra. Sangre. Oro."
62. Esparza, Rafa Esparza Talks About "Tierra. Sangre. Oro." at Ballroom Marfa.
63. Esparza, Rafa Esparza Talks About "Tierra. Sangre. Oro." at Ballroom Marfa.

NOTES

64. Esparza, Rafa Esparza Talks About "Tierra. Sangre. Oro." at Ballroom Marfa.
65. "Rafa Esparza at OMCA."
66. *Artist Lecture Series*, 1:19:10.
67. "Rafa Esparza: Staring at the Sun," MASS MoCA, November 15, 2018, https://massmoca.org/rafa-esparza/.
68. Carolina A. Miranda, "Two Artists—from L.A. and Tijuana—Present Their Visions of the Border at MASS MoCA," *Los Angeles Times*, November 29, 2019, sec. Entertainment & Arts, https://www.latimes.com/entertainment-arts/story/2019-11-29/u-s-mexico-border-art-rafa-esparza-marcos-ramirez-erre-mass-moca.
69. Miranda, "Two Artists—from L.A. and Tijuana—Present Their Visions of the Border at MASS MoCA."
70. Miranda, "Two Artists—from L.A. and Tijuana—Present Their Visions of the Border at MASS MoCA."
71. Gwyneth Shanks, "Adobe, Dust, and Water: Rafa Esparza and Rebeca Hernandez's Building: A Simulacrum of Power," *X-TRA Contemporary Art Journal* 20, no. 2 (Winter 2018), https://www.x-traonline.org/article/adobe-dust-and-water-rafa-esparza-and-rebeca-hernandezs-building-a-simulacrum-of-power/.
72. Diehl, "Land Rites."
73. Cajete, *Native Science*, 210.
74. Shanks, "Adobe, Dust, and Water."

BEYOND

1. "The Archeology of Buffalo Soldiers and Apaches in the Southwest (U.S. National Park Service)," accessed December 18, 2024, https://www.nps.gov/articles/archeology-of-buffalo-soldiers-and-apaches-in-the-southwest.htm.

BIBLIOGRAPHY

Abbey, Edward. *Confessions of a Barbarian: Selections from the Journals of Edward Abbey, 1951–1989*, 1st ed. Edited by David Petersen. Little, Brown, 1994.

———. *Desert Solitaire: A Season in the Wilderness*, 9th ed. 1968. Reprint, Ballantine Books, 1981.

Ach, Jada, and Gary Reger, eds. *Reading Aridity in Western American Literature*. Lexington Books, 2020.

Adcock, Craig E., and James Turrell. *James Turrell: The Art of Light and Space*. University of California Press, 1990.

Agamben, Giorgio. *State of Exception*. University of Chicago Press, 2005.

Akins, Damon B., and William J. Bauer. *We Are the Land: A History of Native California*. University of California Press, 2021.

Alberto, Lourdes. "Nations, Nationalisms, and Indígenas: The 'Indian' in the Chicano Revolutionary Imaginary." *Critical Ethnic Studies* 2, no. 1 (2016): 107–27. https://doi.org/10.5749/jcritethnstud.2.1.0107.

Alexander, Kurtis. "Dixie Fire Burns Land Returned to Maidu." *San Francisco Chronicle* (CA), August 21, 2021, sec. Main News. Access World News.

Andreasen, Liana Vrajitoru. "*Blood Meridian* and the Spatial Metaphysics of the West." *Southwestern American Literature* 36, no. 3 (2011): 19–30.

Andrews, Richard, James Turrell, Chris Bruce, and Henry Art Gallery. *James Turrell: Sensing Space*. Henry Art Gallery, University of Washington, 1992.

Anzaldúa, Gloria. *Borderlands / La Frontera: The New Mestiza*, 4th ed. Aunt Lute Books, 2012.

Arriola, Elvia. "Voices from the Barbed Wires of Despair: Women in the

Maquiladoras, Latina Critical Legal Theory, and Gender at the U.S.-Mexico Border." *DePaul Law Review* 49, no. 3 (March 1, 2000): 729.

Arriola, Elvia R. "Accountability for Murder in the Maquiladoras: Linking Corporate Indifference to Gender Violence at the U.S.-Mexico Border." In *Making a Killing: Femicide, Free Trade, and La Frontera*, edited by Alicia Gaspar de Alba and Georgina Guzmán, 25–61. University of Texas Press, 2010.

Asscher, Carine, dir. *James Turrell: Passageways* (film). C. A. Productions / Centre de Georges Pompidou, 1995.

Associated Press. "Navajo Family Fights to Stay on Monument Land in Northern Arizona." *The Guardian*, March 21, 2014, sec. World news. https://www.theguardian.com/world/2014/mar/21/navajo-family-fights-stay-monument-land-arizona.

Austin, Mary. *The Land of Little Rain*. Houghton Mifflin, 1903.

Aviña, Alexander. "Killing Machine: How Mexican and US States of Exception Turned Revolutionaries and Migrants into Bare Life, 1969–1996." In *On Othering: Processes and Politics of Unpeace*, edited by Yasmin Saikia and Chad Haines, 177–98. Athabasca University Press, 2024. https://doi.org/10.15215/aupress/9781771993869.009.

Bachour, Mary-Kay. "Disrupting the Myth of Maquila Disposability: Sites of Reproduction and Resistance in Juárez." *Women's Studies International Forum* 48 (2015): 174–84. https://doi.org/10.1016/j.wsif.2014.11.010.

Banham, Reyner. *Scenes in America Deserta*. Gibbs M. Smith, Incorporated, 1982.

Barad, Karen. *Meeting the Universe Halfway: Quantum Physics and the Entanglement of Matter and Meaning*. Duke University Press, 2007.

Beck, John. *Dirty Wars: Landscape, Power, and Waste in Western American Literature*. University of Nebraska Press, 2009.

———. *Landscape as Weapon: Cultures of Exhaustion and Refusal*. Reaktion Books, 2021.

———. "Without Form and Void: The American Desert as Trope and Terrain." *Nepantla: Views from the South* 2, no. 1 (2001): 63–83.

Beck, John, and Ryan Bishop. *Technocrats of the Imagination: Art, Technology, and the Military-Industrial Avant-Garde*. Duke University Press, 2020.

Bell, Vereen M. "The Metaphysics of Violence: *Blood Meridian*." In *The Achievement of Cormac McCarthy*, 116–35. Louisiana State University

Press, 1988.

Bennett, Jane. *Vibrant Matter: A Political Ecology of Things*. A John Hope Franklin Center Book. Duke University Press, 2010. https://doi.org/10.1515/9780822391623.

Binelli, Mark. "Taking Freedom: 'Build That Wall!': A Local History." *Pacific Standard*, May 4, 2018. https://psmag.com/social-justice/build-that-wall-a-local-history.

Bjornerud, Marcia. *Timefulness: How Thinking Like a Geologist Can Help Save the World*. Princeton University Press, 2020.

Böhme, Gernot. "The Phenomenology of Light." In *James Turrell: Geometrie des Lichts / Geometry of Light*, edited by Ursula Sinnreich, 69–78. Hatje Cantz, 2009.

Boss, Pauline. "Ambiguous Loss Theory: Challenges for Scholars and Practitioners." *Family Relations* 56, no. 2 (2007): 105–11. https://doi.org/10.1111/j.1741-3729.2007.00444.x.

Buell, Lawrence. "Foreword." In *Prismatic Ecology: Ecotheory Beyond Green*, edited by Jeffrey Jerome Cohen, ix–xii. University of Minnesota Press, 2013. https://doi.org/10.5749/j.ctt5hjk31.3.

Burnett, John. "A Toxic Century: Mining Giant Must Clean Up Mess." NPR, February 4, 2010, sec. Environment. https://www.npr.org/2010/02/04/122779177/a-toxic-century-mining-giant-must-clean-up-mess.

Buschschlüter, Vanessa. "Mexico Disappearances Reach Record High of 100,000 Amid Impunity." BBC News, May 17, 2022. https://www.bbc.com/news/world-latin-america-61477704.

Butler, Octavia E. *Parable of the Sower*. Four Walls Eight Windows, 1993.

Cajete, Gregory. *Native Science: Natural Laws of Interdependence*, 1st ed. Clear Light Publishers, 2000.

Campbell, Neil. "Defining Post-Western Cinema: John Huston's *The Treasure of the Sierra Madre* (1948)." In *New Wests and Post-Wests: Literature and Film of the American West*, edited by Paul Varner. Cambridge Scholars Publishing, 2013. http://ebookcentral.proquest.com/lib/asulib-ebooks/detail.action?docID=1477555.

Capachi, Casey. "The Last of the Navajos to Live at Wupatki National Monument?" *The Washington Post*, March 26, 2014. https://www.washingtonpost.com/news/post-nation/wp/2014/03/26/the-last-of-the-navajos-to-live-at-wupatki-national-monument/.

BIBLIOGRAPHY

Casey, Edward. *The Fate of Place: A Philosophical History*. University of California Press, 1996.

Casey, Edward S. *Getting Back into Place: Toward a Renewed Understanding of the Place-World*. Indiana University Press, 1993.

Castillo, Edward D. "Foreword." In *Exterminate Them: Written Accounts of the Murder, Rape, and Enslavement of Native Americans During the California Gold Rush*, edited by Clifford E. Trafzer and Joel R. Hyer, ix–xi. Michigan State University Press, 1999.

Chávez, Ernesto. *The U.S. War with Mexico: A Brief History with Documents*. Bedford/St. Martin's, 2008.

Cheshes, Jay. "James Turrell's New Masterpiece in the Desert." *WSJ Magazine*, January 14, 2019. https://www.wsj.com/articles/james-turrells-new-masterpiece-in-the-desert-11547480071.

Clay, Karen, and Randall Jones. "Migrating to Riches? Evidence from the California Gold Rush." *The Journal of Economic History* 68, no. 4 (2008): 997–1027.

Cohen, Jeffrey Jerome. *Stone: An Ecology of the Inhuman*. University of Minnesota Press, 2015.

Cooper Alarcón, Daniel. *The Aztec Palimpsest: Mexico in the Modern Imagination*. University of Arizona Press, 1997.

Copelin, Laura. "Tierra. Sangre. Oro." *Terremoto*, September 27, 2014. https://terremoto.mx/en/online/tierra-sangre-oro/.

Corben, Billy, dir. *Cocaine Cowboys* (film). Magnolia Pictures, 2006.

De León, Jason. *The Land of Open Graves: Living and Dying on the Migrant Trail*. University of California Press, 2015.

Deer, Jemma. *Radical Animism: Reading for the End of the World*. Bloomsbury Academic, 2022.

Deleuze, Gilles, and Félix Guattari. *A Thousand Plateaus: Capitalism and Schizophrenia*. Translated by Brian Massumi. University of Minnesota Press, 1987.

Department of State: Office of the Historian. "Milestones: 1830–1860: Gadsden Purchase, 1853–1854." Accessed February 16, 2023. https://history.state.gov/milestones/1830-1860/gadsden-purchase.

Derrida, Jacques. *Specters of Marx: The State of the Debt, the Work of Mourning, and the New International*. Translated by Peggy Kamuf. Routledge, 1994.

Diaz, Natalie. *Postcolonial Love Poem: Poems*. Graywolf Press, 2020.

Diehl, Travis. "Land Rites." *Frieze*, March 20, 2017. https://www.frieze.com/article/land-rites.

Domínguez, Edmé, Rosalba Icaza, Cirila Quintero, Silvia López, and Åsa Stenman. "Women Workers in the Maquiladoras and the Debate on Global Labor Standards." *Feminist Economics* 16, no. 4 (2010): 185–209. https://doi.org/10.1080/13545701.2010.530603.

Dorson, James. "Demystifying the Judge: Law and Mythical Violence in Cormac McCarthy's *Blood Meridian*." *Journal of Modern Literature* 36, no. 2 (2013): 105–21. https://doi.org/10.2979/jmodelite.36.2.105.

Douglas, Christopher. "The Flawed Design: American Imperialism in N. Scott Momaday's *House Made of Dawn* and Cormac McCarthy's *Blood Meridian*." *Critique - Bolingbroke Society* 45, no. 1 (2003): 3–24. https://doi.org/10.1080/00111610309595323.

Ellingson, Ter. *The Myth of the Noble Savage*. University of California Press, 2001.

Esparza, Rafa. "Rafa Esparza Talks About 'Tierra. Sangre. Oro.' at Ballroom Marfa." Interview by Kate Green. Artforum, November 21, 2017. https://www.artforum.com/interviews/rafa-esparza-talks-about-tierra-sangre-oro-at-ballroom-marfa-72422.

Faller, Mary Beth. "Letting in the Light: ASU, Artist James Turrell to Partner on Masterwork in the Desert." ASU News, January 14, 2019. https://news.asu.edu/20190114-creativity-asu-artist-james-turrell-partner-masterwork-roden-crater.

Ferrando, Serena. "Gardening the Symbiocene: Andrea Zanzotto's and Daria Menicanti's Poetic Hospitality." *Ecozon@: European Journal of Literature, Culture and Environment*, March 1, 2024. https://ecozona.eu/article/view/4828.

Franks, Travis. "'We Are Considered Undesirable Foreigners' in 'This Our Texas': Mexican American Settler Nativism in Caballero." *MELUS* 43, no. 3 (2018): 86–102. https://doi.org/10.1093/melus/mly025.

Fregoso, Rosa-Linda, and Cynthia Bejarano. *Terrorizing Women: Feminicide in the Americas*. Duke University Press, 2010.

Fujikane, Candace. *Mapping Abundance for a Planetary Future: Kanaka Maoli and Critical Settler Cartographies in Hawai'i*. Duke University Press, 2021.

"Gadsden Purchase." In *Britannica Academic*. Accessed February 16, 2023. https://academic-eb-com.ezproxy1.lib.asu.edu/levels/collegiate/article/

Gadsden-Purchase/35784.

Gaspar de Alba, Alicia. *Desert Blood: The Juárez Murders*. Arte Publico Press, 2005.

Govan, Michael. "Inner Light: The Radical Reality of James Turrell." In *James Turrell: A Retrospective*, 13–35. Los Angeles: Los Angeles County Museum of Art, 2013.

———. "Spaces Inhabited by Consciousness." In *James Turrell: A Retrospective*, 207–12. Los Angeles County Museum of Art, 2013.

Govan, Michael, and Christine Y. Kim, eds. *James Turrell: A Retrospective*. Los Angeles County Museum of Art, 2013.

Grey, Zane. *Riders of the Purple Sage*. Grosset & Dunlap, 1940.

Grobar, Matt. "Encore: 'Sicario' Composer Jóhann Jóhannsson on Creating Propulsive Sound of Drug War Drama." *Deadline*, February 10, 2018.

Grusin, Richard A. *The Nonhuman Turn*. University of Minnesota Press, 2015.

Gugliotta, Guy, and Jeff Leen. *Kings of Cocaine: Inside the Medellín Cartel - An Astonishing True Story of Murder, Money and International Corruption*. Garrett County Press, 2011.

Guzmán, Alicia Inez. "Rafa Esparza." *Tierra Firme* (blog). Accessed February 11, 2023. http://tierrafirmeprojects.com/rafa-esparza.

———. "Rafa Esparza's 'Brown Matter' Part I: When the Building Blocks of Home Inhabit the Whitney | Tierra Firme." *Tierra Firme* (blog), June 1, 2017. http://tierrafirmeprojects.com/rafa-esparzas-brown-matter-part-i-when-the-building-blocks-of-home-inhabit-the-whitney.

Haraway, Donna. "Anthropocene, Capitalocene, Plantationocene, Chthulucene: Making Kin." *Environmental Humanities* 6, no. 1 (2015): 159–65. https://doi.org/10.1215/22011919-3615934.

Haraway, Donna J. *Staying with the Trouble: Making Kin in the Chthulucene*. Duke University Press, 2016.

Hayashi, Brian Masaru. *Democratizing the Enemy: The Japanese American Internment*. Princeton University Press, 2010.

Hazel, Alexa. "Roden Crater." *The Point Magazine*, December 19, 2021. https://thepointmag.com/criticism/roden-crater/.

Healy, Donald T. "Pueblo of Laguna - New Mexico." In *Encyclopedia of Native American Flags*, 2021. https://online-infobase-com.ezproxy1.lib.asu.edu/HRC/Search/Details/6?articleId=558571&q=laguna%20pueblo.

Herbert, Frank. *Dune*. Penguin, 2005 [1965].

BIBLIOGRAPHY

Hermo, Carmen. "Through Collaborative Work, Centering Queer, Brown Folks, Rafa Esparza Looks to Destabilize Artistic Authority." ARTnews.com, January 14, 2020. https://www.artnews.com/art-news/artists/rafa-esparza-artist-shaping-art-2020s-1202675032/.

Hernández, Maximiliano. "*Sicario*'s Maximiliano Hernández." Interview by Angela María Ortíz S., 2015. https://www.sefijaonline.com/wp-content/uploads/2015/12/Maximiliano-Herna%CC%81ndez.mp3.

Iovino, Serenella, and Serpil Oppermann. *Material Ecocriticism*. University Press, 2014.

———. "Material Ecocriticism: Materiality, Agency, and Models of Narrativity." *Ecozon@* 3, no. 1 (2012): 75–91. https://doi.org/10.37536/ECOZONA.2012.3.1.452.

Ivey, Linda L., and Kevin W. Kaatz. *Citizen Internees: A Second Look at Race and Citizenship in Japanese American Internment Camps*. ABC-CLIO, LLC, 2017.

Ivry, Sara. "Historian J.T. Roane Explores Black Ecologies." *JSTOR Daily*, February 14, 2024. https://daily.jstor.org/historian-j-t-roane-explores-black-ecologies/.

Jiroutová Kynčlová, Tereza. "Woman Killing and Adoption in Alicia Gaspar de Alba's *Desert Blood: The Juárez Murders* (2005)." *Ex-Centric Narratives: Journal of Anglophone Literature, Culture and Media*, no. 3 (2019): 76–92. https://doi.org/10.26262/exna.v0i3.7550.

Jones, Josh. "Hear the Only Instrumental Ever Banned from the Radio: Link Wray's Seductive, Raunchy Song, 'Rumble' (1958) | Open Culture," April 18, 2017. https://www.openculture.com/2017/04/the-only-instrumental-every-banned-from-the-radio-link-wrays-rumble-1958.html.

Kawagley, A. Oscar. *A Yupiaq Worldview: A Pathway to Ecology and Spirit*, 2nd ed. Long Waveland Press, 2006.

Kim, Christine Y., and Nancy Meyer. "James Turrell: A Life in Art." In *James Turrell: A Retrospective*, 37–48. Los Angeles County Museum of Art, 2013.

Kimmerer, Robin. *Braiding Sweetgrass: Indigenous Wisdom, Scientific Knowledge and the Teachings of Plants*. Milkweed Editions, 2013.

Kohn, Eduardo. *How Forests Think: Toward an Anthropology Beyond the Human*. University of California Press, 2013.

Kratz, Veronika. "Combatting Desertification and Narrating Environmental Crisis in the United Nations." In *Storied Deserts*. Routledge, 2024.

BIBLIOGRAPHY

Krouse, William J. "CRS Report for Congress: U.S. Border Patrol Operations." Congressional Research Service, November 10, 1997. The Library of Congress.

Krupp, E. C. "Bothering to Look." In *James Turrell: A Retrospective*, 236–47. Los Angeles County Museum of Art, 2013.

Krutch, Joseph Wood. *The Desert Year*. Sloane, 1952.

LeMenager, Stephanie, and Teresa Shewry. "Green." In *Keywords for Environmental Studies*, edited by Joni Adamson, William A. Gleason, and David N. Pellow, 128–30. New York University Press, 2016.

Leopold, Aldo. *A Sand County Almanac: And Sketches Here and There*. Oxford University Press, 2020.

Library of Congress. "The Discovery of Gold," sec. California as I Saw It: First-Person Narratives of California's Early Years, 1849–1900. Accessed February 11, 2023. https://www.loc.gov/collections/california-first-person-narratives/articles-and-essays/early-california-history/discovery-of-gold/.

Lim, Julian. *Porous Borders: Multiracial Migrations and the Law in the U.S.-Mexico Borderlands*. University of North Carolina Press, 2017.

Longley, John Lewis, Jr. "The Nuclear Winter of Cormac McCarthy." *The Virginia Quarterly Review* 62, no. 4 (1986): 746–50.

Mack, Ashley Noel, and Tiara R. Na'puti. "'Our Bodies Are Not *Terra Nullius*': Building a Decolonial Feminist Resistance to Gendered Violence." *Women's Studies in Communication* 42, no. 3 (July 3, 2019): 347–70. https://doi.org/10.1080/07491409.2019.1637803.

Marak, Andrae M., and Laura Tuennerman. *At the Border of Empires: The Tohono O'odham, Gender, and Assimilation, 1880–1934*. University of Arizona Press, 2013.

MASS MoCA. "Rafa Esparza: Staring at the Sun," November 15, 2018. https://massmoca.org/rafa-esparza/.

Massey, Doreen. *For Space*. SAGE, 2005.

Mata, Irene. "Writing on the Walls: Deciphering Violence and Industrialization in Alicia Gaspar de Alba's *Desert Blood*." *MELUS* 35, no. 3 (September 2010): 15-40.

Maya Angelou. "Dr. Maya Angelou - Power of Words." Lencha Sanchez. March 5, 2013. Video, 1:26. https://www.youtube.com/watch?v=8PXdacSqvcA.

McAlduff, Casey. "Tohono O'odham." In *Encyclopedia of Native American History*, vol. 3, 2011. https://online-infobase-com.ezproxy1.lib.asu.edu/HRC/LearningCenter/Details/6?articleId=359168.
McCarthy, Cormac. *Blood Meridian, or, the Evening Redness in the West*, 1st Vintage International ed. Vintage Books, 1992.
McCormack, Derek P. "Remotely Sensing Affective Afterlives: The Spectral Geographies of Material Remains." *Annals of the Association of American Geographers* 100, no. 3 (2010): 640–54. https://doi.org/10.1080/00045601003795004.
McNamee, Gregory. *The Desert Reader: A Literary Companion*. University of New Mexico Press, 2003.
Medium. "James Turrell's Roden Crater Leaves Lasting Impact on Students in Herberger Institute Field Labs." April 5, 2019. https://medium.com/herberger-institute/james-turrells-roden-crater-leaves-lasting-impact-on-students-in-herberger-institute-field-labs-663b79418d74.
Meillassoux, Quentin. "Spectral Dilemma." Translated by Robin Mackay. *Collapse: Philosophical Research and Development* 4 (May 2008): 261–76.
Mentz, Steve. "Brown." In *Prismatic Ecology: Ecotheory Beyond Green*, edited by Jeffrey Jerome Cohen, 193–212. University of Minnesota Press, 2013. https://doi.org/10.5749/j.ctt5hjk31.3.
———. *Ocean*. Bloomsbury Publishing USA, 2020.
Merleau-Ponty, Maurice. *Phenomenology of Perception*. Translated by Daniel A. Landes. Routledge, 2013.
———. *The Visible and the Invisible: Followed by Working Notes*. Northwestern University Press, 1968.
Merton, Thomas, ed. *The Wisdom of the Desert*. Translated by Thomas Merton. New Directions, 1960.
Michno, Chris. "Notes from the Turrell Project." *The Other Side: Alternative Reading for Alternative People*, February 11, 1992.
Miranda, Carolina A. "Two Artists—from L.A. and Tijuana—Present Their Visions of the Border at MASS MoCA." *Los Angeles Times*, November 29, 2019, sec. Entertainment & Arts. https://www.latimes.com/entertainment-arts/story/2019-11-29/u-s-mexico-border-art-rafa-esparza-marcos-ramirez-erre-mass-moca.
Mitchell, Lee Clark. "A Book 'Made Out of Books': The Humanizing Violence of Style in *Blood Meridian*." *Texas Studies in Literature and*

Language 57, no. 3 (2015): 259–81. https://doi.org/10.7560/TSLL57301.

Moore, Jason W. *Anthropocene or Capitalocene?: Nature, History, and the Crisis of Capitalism*. PM Press, 2016.

Morales, Maria Cristina, and Cynthia Bejarano. "Transnational Sexual and Gendered Violence: An Application of Border Sexual Conquest at a Mexico-US Border." *Global Networks* (Oxford) 9, no. 3 (2009): 420–39. https://doi.org/10.1111/j.1471-0374.2009.00261.x.

Morton, Timothy. *Being Ecological*. The MIT Press, 2018.

———. *Hyperobjects: Philosophy and Ecology after the End of the World*. Posthumanities. University of Minnesota Press, 2013. https://doi.org/10.5749/j.ctt4cggm7.

National Archives. "The Treaty of Guadalupe Hidalgo," August 15, 2016. https://www.archives.gov/education/lessons/guadalupe-hidalgo.

Ng, Wendy L. *Japanese American Internment During World War II: A History and Reference Guide*. Greenwood Publishing Group, 2002.

Nixon, Rob. *Slow Violence and the Environmentalism of the Poor*. Harvard University Press, 2011.

O'Brien, Suzanne Crawford. "Civilization Is Poison to the Indian: Missionization, Authenticity, and the Myth of the Vanishing Indian." In *Coming Full Circle*, 71–99. University of Nebraska Press, 2013.

Orden, Erika. "El Paso Says Goodbye to Landmark." *Recasting the Smelter*, April 14, 2013. https://www.RecastingtheSmelter.com/?p=4149.

Ortiz, Victor M. "The Unbearable Ambiguity of the Border." *Social Justice* 28, no. 2 (84) (Summer 2001): 96–112.

Osuna, Celina. "Color, Place, and Memory in Silko's *Gardens in the Dunes*." In *Reading Aridity in Western American Literature*, edited by Jada Ach and Gary Reger, 223–42. Lexington Books, 2020.

Osuna, Celina, and Aidan Tynan, eds. *Storied Deserts*, 1st ed. Routledge, 2024.

Padilla, Genaro M. "Myth and Comparative Cultural Nationalism: The Ideological Uses of Aztlán." In *Aztlán: Essays on the Chicano Homeland*, edited by Rudolfo A. Anaya and Francisco A. Lomelí, 309–32. University of New Mexico Press, 1989.

Patel, Raj. "The Misanthropocene?" *Earth Island Journal* 28, no. 1 (2013): 21.

Pérez-Torres, Rafael. "Refiguring Aztlán." *Aztlán* 22, no. 2 (1997): 13–41.

Peters-Little, Frances. "'Nobles and Savages' on the Television." *Aboriginal History* 27 (2003): 16–38.

BIBLIOGRAPHY

Radiolab, WNYC Studios. "Border Trilogy Part 2: Hold the Line." Accessed February 11, 2023. https://www.radiolab.org/episodes/border-trilogy-part-2-hold-line.

Rafa Esparza. "Artist Lecture Series: Rafa Esparza." LACC Visual & Media Arts. June 27, 2018. Video, 1:46:34. https://www.youtube.com/watch?v=PRqiJ84WTJ0.

Rafa Esparza. "Rafa Esparza at OMCA." Oakland Museum of California (OMCA). September 26, 2024. Video, 6:52. https://www.youtube.com/watch?v=EkkCmLN_2IM.

Rafa Esparza. "Whitney Biennial 2017: Rafa Esparza." Whitney Museum of American Art. June 5, 2017. Video, 3:09. https://www.youtube.com/watch?v=CfiKE8CuuN4.

"Rastreo." In *A Comprehensive Etymological Dictionary of the Spanish Language with Families of Words Based on Indo-European Roots*, vol. II (H–Z and Appendix): 44. Xlibris, 2014.

Rawls, James J. *Indians of California: The Changing Image*, 1st ed. University of Oklahoma Press, 1984.

Rios, Pedro. "For 25 Years, Operation Gatekeeper Has Made Life Worse for Border Communities." *The Washington Post*, October 1, 2019. https://www.washingtonpost.com/outlook/2019/10/01/years-operation-gatekeeper-has-made-life-worse-border-communities/.

Roane, J. T., and Justin Hosbey. "Mapping Black Ecologies." *Current Research in Digital History* 2 (2019). https://doi.org/10.31835/crdh.2019.05.

Roden Crater. "About," 2023. https://rodencrater.com/about/.

Rodriguez, Eric, and Everardo J. Cuevas. "Problematizing Mestizaje." *Composition Studies* 45, no. 2 (2017): 230–33.

Rowland, M. J. "Return of the 'Noble Savage': Misrepresenting the Past, Present and Future." *Australian Aboriginal Studies* (Canberra), no. 2 (2004): 2–14. https://doi.org/10.3316/ielapa.449221711277109.

Saldaña-Portillo, María Josefina, and Simón Ventura Trujillo. "Introduction: What Does Mestizaje Name?" *Aztlán* 46, no. 2 (2021): 149–59.

Salzinger, Leslie. *Genders in Production: Making Workers in Mexico's Global Factories*. University of California Press, 2003.

Schmidt Camacho, Alicia. "Ciudadana X: Gender Violence and the Denationalization of Women's Rights in Ciudad Juárez, Mexico." *CR* 5, no. 1 (2005): 255–92. https://doi.org/10.1353/ncr.2005.0030.

Senate of California. "Journals of the Legislature of the State of California at Its Second Session: Held at the City of San Jose," 1851.

Sepich, John. *Notes on* Blood Meridian, rev. and expanded ed., 1st University of Texas Press ed. Southwestern Writers Collection Series. University of Texas Press, 2008.

Shaler, Andrew. "Indigenous Peoples and the California Gold Rush: Labour, Violence and Contention in the Formation of a Settler Colonial State." *Postcolonial Studies* 23, no. 1 (2020): 79–98. https://doi.org/10.1080/13688790.2020.1725221.

Shanks, Gwyneth. "Adobe, Dust, and Water: Rafa Esparza and Rebeca Hernandez's Building: A Simulacrum of Power." *X-TRA Contemporary Art Journal* 20, no. 2 (Winter 2018). https://www.x-traonline.org/article/adobe-dust-and-water-rafa-esparza-and-rebeca-hernandezs-building-a-simulacrum-of-power/.

Shaviro, Steven. "'The Very Life of Darkness': A Reading of *Blood Meridian*." In *Perspectives on Cormac McCarthy*, edited by Edwin T. Arnold and Dianne C. Luce, rev. ed., 145–57. Southern Quarterly Series. University Press of Mississippi, 1999.

Sherer, Lorraine M. "The Name Mojave, Mohave: A History of Its Origin and Meaning." *Southern California Quarterly* 49, no. 1 (March 1, 1967): 1–36. https://doi.org/10.2307/41170070.

Silko, Leslie Marmon. *Storyteller*. Penguin Publishing Group, 2012.

———. *Yellow Woman and a Beauty of the Spirit*. Simon & Schuster, 2013.

Simpson, Leanne. *Dancing on Our Turtle's Back: Stories of Nishnaabeg Re-Creation, Resurgence and a New Emergence*. Arbeiter Ring Pub., 2011.

Slovic, Scott. *Getting Over the Color Green: Contemporary Environmental Literature of the Southwest*. University of Arizona Press, 2001.

Stengers, Isabelle. *Cosmopolitics*. Posthumanities 9. University of Minnesota Press, 2010.

———. "Gaia, the Urgency to Think (and Feel)." Keynote Address presented at the Os Mil Nomes de Gaia do Antropoceno à Idade da Terra Colóquio Internacional, Casa de Rui Barbosa, Rio de Janeiro, Brazil, September 19, 2014.

Stewart, Kathleen. "Atmospheric Attunements." *Environment and Planning. D, Society & Space* 29, no. 3 (2011): 445–53. https://doi.org/10.1068/d9109.

Sullivan, Marianne. *Tainted Earth: Smelters, Public Health, and the*

Environment, 1st ed. Rutgers University Press, 2014.

Szabo, Szerena, and Jane Webster. "Perceived Greenwashing: The Effects of Green Marketing on Environmental and Product Perceptions." *Journal of Business Ethics* 171, no. 4 (2021): 719–39. https://doi.org/10.1007/s10551-020-04461-0.

TallBear, Kim. "Caretaking Relations, Not American Dreaming." *Kalfou* 6, no. 1 (2019): 24–41. https://doi.org/10.15367/kf.v6i1.228.

Tamez, Margo. "Space, Position, and Imperialism in South Texas." *Chicana/Latina Studies* 7, no. 2 (2008): 112–21.

Taylor, Mark C. *Refiguring the Spiritual: Beuys, Barney, Turrell, Goldsworthy*. Columbia University Press, 2012.

Taylor, Sandra C. *Jewel of the Desert: Japanese American Internment at Topaz*. University of California Press, 1993.

Trafzer, Clifford E., and Joel R. Hyer. *Exterminate Them!: Written Accounts of the Murder, Rape, and Slavery of Native Americans During the California Gold Rush*. Michigan State University Press, 1999.

Tsing, Anna Lowenhaupt. *The Mushroom at the End of the World: On the Possibility of Life in Capitalist Ruins*. Edition Unstated. Princeton University Press, 2015.

Turrell, James. "Skyscapes." Accessed February 11, 2023. https://jamesturrell.com/work/picture-plane.

Tynan, Aidan. *The Desert in Modern Literature and Philosophy: Wasteland Aesthetics*. Crosscurrents. Edinburgh University Press, 2020. https://doi.org/10.1515/9781474443371.

Urrea, Luis Alberto. *The Devil's Highway: A True Story*. Paw Prints, 2005.

U.S. Customs and Border Protection. "Border Patrol History," July 21, 2020. https://www.cbp.gov/border-security/along-us-borders/history.

U.S. Department of Homeland Security: Science and Technology. "Feature Article: Robot Dogs Take Another Step Towards Deployment," February 1, 2022. https://www.dhs.gov/science-and-technology/news/2022/02/01/feature-article-robot-dogs-take-another-step-towards-deployment.

U.S. National Park Service. "The Archeology of Buffalo Soldiers and Apaches in the Southwest." Accessed December 18, 2024. https://www.nps.gov/articles/archeology-of-buffalo-soldiers-and-apaches-in-the-southwest.htm.

———. "'Footprints of the Past' - Wupatki National Monument," January 18, 2023. https://www.nps.gov/wupa/index.htm.

———. "Petrified Wood - Petrified Forest National Park," March 16, 2018. https://www.nps.gov/pefo/learn/nature/petrified-wood.htm.

Valaskakis, Gail Guthrie. *Indian Country: Essays on Contemporary Native Culture*. Indigenous Studies. Wilfrid Laurier University Press, 2005.

Villeneuve, Denis, dir. *Sicario* (film). Lions Gate Entertainment, 2016.

Vizenor, Gerald. "Aesthetics of Survivance: Literary Theory and Practice." In *Survivance: Narratives of Native Presence*, 1–23. University of Nebraska Press, 2008. http://ebookcentral.proquest.com/lib/asulib-ebooks/detail.action?docID=452198.

Volk, Steven S., and Marian E. Schlotterbeck. "Gender, Order, and Femicide: Reading the Popular Culture of Murder in Ciudad Juárez." In *Making a Killing: Femicide, Free Trade, and La Frontera*, edited by Alicia Gaspar de Alba and Georgina Guzmán, 121–53. University of Texas Press, 2010.

Voyles, Traci Brynne. *Wastelanding: Legacies of Uranium Mining in Navajo Country*, 1st ed. University of Minnesota Press, 2015.

Wald, Sarah D., David J. Vazquez, Priscilla Solis Ybarra, Sarah Jaquette Ray, and Laura Pulido. *Latinx Environmentalisms: Place, Justice, and the Decolonial*. Temple University Press, 2019.

Weil, Kari. *Thinking Animals: Why Animal Studies Now?* Columbia University Press, 2012. https://doi.org/10.7312/weil14808.

Weissman, Deborah M. "The Political Economy of Violence: Toward an Understanding of the Gender-Based Murders of Ciudad Juarez." *North Carolina Journal of International Law* 30, no. 4 (March 11, 2005): 795-868.

Wild, Peter. *The New Desert Reader: Descriptions of America's Arid Regions*. University of Utah Press, 2006.

Wright, Melissa W. "Feminicidio, Narcoviolence, and Gentrification in Ciudad Juárez: The Feminist Fight." *Environment and Planning. D, Society & Space* 31, no. 5 (2013): 830–45. https://doi.org/10.1068/d17812.

———. "The Dialectics of Still Life: Murder, Women, and Maquiladoras." *Public Culture* 11, no. 3 (1999): 453–73. https://doi.org/10.1215/08992363-11-3-453.

Wylie, John. "The Spectral Geographies of W. G. Sebald." *Cultural Geographies* 14, no. 2 (2007): 171–88. https://doi.org/10.1177/1474474007075353.

Yanas, Ricky. "Dead Edges and Open Wounds: Considering 'The Border Is a Weapon/ Frontera Es Un Arma,' Curated by Gil Rocha." *Glasstire*, March 30, 2022. https://glasstire.com/2022/03/30/dead-edge

s-and-open-wounds-considering-the-border-is-a-weapon-frontera-es-un-arma-curated-by-gil-rocha/.

Zepeda, Ofelia. *Ocean Power: Poems From the Desert*. Sun Tracks, vol. 32. University of Arizona Press, 1995.

———. *Where Clouds Are Formed*. Sun Tracks, vol. 63. University of Arizona Press, 2008.

INDEX

Note: Entry numbers in italics refer to images.

Abbey, Edward, 9, 15, 55, 144–45
abstraction, 7, 9, 24, 66–67, 119
abundance, 6, 9, 19, 38, 147, 160–61
    desert, 41, 54–55, 64–68, 76, 83,
        99, 118, 127, 131, 139–40, 150,
        158, 162, 164
    of desert places, 10, 14, 38, 83, 101,
        107, 160, 162
Ach, Jada, 18, 163
acquisition, 40, 80, 141, 156
adobe, 13, 132, 145–54, 156–58. *See also*
    Pueblo Revival homes
aesthetics, 6, 12, 25, 82, 109, 128, 135,
    147, 156, 161
    Brown, 150
    desert, 7, 12, 76, 98, 131, 133, 150,
        158, 160, 162
    vertical, 83, 98, 162
    wasteland, 6–7, 24–25, 158
    Wild West, 67
affect, 7, 13, 24–25, 27, 67, 110, 132–
    33, 135, 137
Agamben, Giorgio, 85, 97
Age of Discovery, 40
agriculture, 56
Alaimo, Stacy, 15
Alberto, Lourdes, 63

algorithms, 8
ALTAR Centro de Investigación, 19
ambiguous loss, 127
America (Baudrillard), 55
American Industrial Revolution, 42
American literature, 6, 52–53
American Oasis (Paoletta), 163
American Smelting and Refining
    Company, 125–29
American West, 22, 42, 44, 73, 80,
    133, 140, 163
Americanist literature, 14
Andreasen, Liana, 43
Andrews, Richard, 139–40, 142
androcentrism, 122
animals, 8, 21, 25, 32, 33, 36, 48, 61, 64, 67,
    117, 119–20, 137
    bears, 105
    cattle, 61
    coatimundi, 8
    coyotes, 66, 120
    horses, 54, 61, 76, 112
    lizards, 67
    mules, 45, 61
    owls, 66–67
    snakes
        rattlesnakes, 36–37, 118

INDEX

sandvipers, 67
scorpions, 113, 118
spiders, 68, 144
   tarantulas, 67, 118
vultures, 144
   turkey vultures, 120
wolves, 66, 105
annexation, 49
Anthropocene, 7, 22, 41, 56–58, 69, 145
anthropocentrism, 65, 69
anti-Westerns, 42
Anzaldúa, Gloria, 47–48, 50, 54, 62
apertures, 132, 136–37, 139, 143, 146
apocalyptic literature and film, 68, 145
Arabian Sands (Thesiger), 55
archival work, 156
Argote, Carmen, 149
Arid Empire: The Entangled Fates of Arizona and Arabia (Koch), 163
Arid Lands, The: History, Power, Knowledge (Davis), 163
Arizona/New Mexico Plateau, 11, 32
Arriola, Elvia R., 102
artificial intelligence, 8
Asscher, Carine, 142
assemblages, 10–11, 61
   human, 25, 140
   human-as-humus, 56, 145
   inhuman, 56, 145
   more-than-human, 11, 25, 56, 69, 140, 145
   nonhuman, 68–69, 140
   other-than-human, 56, 145
Asteroid City (film), 19
atmospheric attunements, 135–38
aviation, 133
Aztlán, 50

Ballroom Marfa, 150
Banham, Reyner, 9, 55
Barbie (film), 19
Baudrillard, Jean, 55

Beck, John, 80, 86
Being Ecological (Morton), 10
being-with, 28, 131, 139–40, 148, 158
being-without, 131, 158
Big Lebowski, The (film), 71
biodiversity, 22, 32
biopolitics, 47, 99, 101, 123
Bjornerud, Marcia, 56–58, 61
Black Ecologies, 17
Blade Runner: 2049 (film), 71
Blood Meridian, or the Evening Redness in the West (McCarthy), 41–43, 45–47, 51, 53–54, 61, 69
   desert abundance in, 65–67
   desert world-building in, 66
   elemental immediacy in, 59
   naming in, 66–67, 110
   racial passing in, 120
   scholarship on, 11, 41–42, 54, 59, 66
   Sicario and, 83
   spectral in, 61
blue environmentalism, 15
blue humanities, 15–16
bodies, 8, 10, 12, 16, 31, 36, 38, 46, 59, 61, 71, 80–81, 84, 89, 98, 101, 103–4, 106, 109, 111–112, 115–16, 118–25, 127, 129, 136, 147, 155–56
Böhme, Gernot, 135–36
borderlands ecology, 106, 150, 152, 158–61, 163
Borderlands/La Frontera (Anzaldúa), 48
borders
   Border Highway, 72, 77, 113, 125
   crossings, 95, 102, 106, 110
   fence, 72, 77, 159
   national, 41, 47, 103, 114
   natural, 113
   policies, 12
      Prevention Through Deterrence, 12, 96–98, 103, 111, 120
   regions, 90, 104
   US-Mexico, 11–12, 43, 48–49, 71, 76,

INDEX

81–82, 85, 96–98, 101–2, 104–7, 111, 129, 140, 161
US-Mexico borderlands, 17, 27, 40–41, 47, 50, 52, 54–55, 61, 64, 72, 83–84, 87–88, 97, 102–3, 106, 121–22, 127, 147, 150, 156
Bosque Redondo, 63
Boss, Pauline, 127
Bowtie (industrial land), 145
bracero workers, 151, *152*
Braiding Sweetgrass (Kimmerer), 26, 28
brickmaking, 145, 147. *See also* adobe
bridges, 72, 77, 80–81, 85–86, 89–90, 113, 159
   Bridge of the Americas/Puente internacional Cordova de las Américas, 76
brown ecology, 16
Brown Humanities/Ecologies, 17. *See also* brown ecology
brown logic, 16
brown matter, 13, 149, 151, 158
Buell, Lawrence, 14
Buffalo Soldiers, 162
Building: A Simulacrum of Power (Esparza artwork), 145
Burnett, John, 129
Burnett, Peter Hardeman, 22, 47
Bush, George, Jr., 72
Bustamante, Nao, 149

Cabeza de Vaca, Álvar Núñez, 40
Cajete, Gregory, 21, 26, 32, 38
Calavera, La. *See* Smelter Town
California Gold Rush, 22–23, 44–45
California State Parks, 145
Camino del Diablo, El. *See* Devil's Highway
Cánovas, Sandro, 149
capitalism, 38, 122
   global, 122
   supercapitalism, 13
Capitalocene, 56

Carson, Rachel, 15
cartels, 88, 95–96, 114, 121. *See also under* violence
   drug tunnels, 87, 90, 94
   Medellín Cartel, 89
   mules for, 88, 92, 95
   in *Sicario*, 12, 71–72, 82, 84–86, 88–93, 95, 98
   Sonora Cartel, 89
cartography, 28
CBP. *See under* US federal agencies
CDC. *See under* US federal agencies
celestial, the, 13, 66, 68, 132–33, 135–38, 144
celestial vaulting, 133, 141
centering, 16, 32, 48, 101, 133, 140
   decentering, 57, 69, 101, 131, 133, 140
   (*see also* human, the: decentering the human)
   recentering, 57, 69, 101, 133, 140
Cha, San, *153*
Chávez, Ernesto 49
Cheshes, Jay, 141
Chicano movement, 50
Chinese migrant workers, 162
Chthulucene, 56, 58
cinematography, 12, 71, 73, 76, 82, 98
cities, 27, 59, 76–77, 84, 103, 114, 121, 141
   El Paso, 4, 72, 77, 80, 84–85, 93, 96, 102–3, 111, 114–15, 125–26
   El Paso–Juárez area, 12, 72, 76–77, 84–85, 88, 103, 111, 113–14, 125–26, 128, 129
   Juárez, 12, 72, 76–77, 80–81, 84–85, 87–88, 90, 96, 102–3, 112–13, 115, 121–23, 125, 159
   Phoenix, 4, 71, 90
   Tucson, 29, 31, 103
citizenship, 85, 97, 113–14
Clark, William, 42
cleanliness, 155
climate change, 11–13, 17, 22, 38, 56, 69

221

INDEX

anthropogenic, 11, 56, 101
  climate crises, 13, 18, 25, 55, 58
Clinton, Bill, 96
Clockshop (nonprofit org.), 145
close reading, 11, 37, 42, 59, 65, 69, 83, 150
  ecocritical, 11, 25
  practice of, 36–37, 65, 106, 143
Coatlicue (Aztec diety), 149
cognitive imperialism, 35
Cohen, Jeffrey Jerome, 10
collective memory, 44–45, 95
  individual and collective memories, 13, 127
colleges and universities
  Arizona State University, 138, 141–43
  Navajo Technical University, 142
  Pitzer College, 142
  University of Strathclyde, 4
  Yale University, 19
colonialism, 8, 13, 19, 22, 41, 50, 65, 147, 160. *See also* colonization; violence: colonial
  nuclear, 19
  settler, 23–24, 32, 42, 44, 131
colonias, 80, 112
colonization, 7, 40, 50, 147, 158
  American, 45
  decolonization, 148
  European, 21–22, 49
  Mexican, 49–50
  settler colonizers, 32–33, 40, 53, 65
  Spanish, 40, 44, 50
community-building, 13
Confederate States of America, 48
Configurations (journal), 15
conquistadors, 22, 40, 48
contemporary literature, 11, 18, 24, 52
corporal histories, 46
corruption, 89–91, 98
Cortés, Hernán, 40
Cortez, Beatriz, 147, 149
cowboys, 82, 105

critical theory, 10, 26, 30, 161
Crutzen, Paul, 56
Cuk Ṣon. *See* Tucson
cultural erasure, 6, 8, 15, 17, 44, 160
cultural geography, 9, 11, 72
cultures, 7, 10, 17, 24, 35, 42, 55, 63–64, 114, 144, 148, 163

Dalla Costa, Wanda, 142
Dark Winds (film), 19
Davis, Diana K., 163
DDT, 151
Deakins, Roger, 71, 76, 82
deanthropocentrizing the desert, 68
deep time, 57–58, 61, 69
Deer, Jemma, 57–58, 60
dehumanizing the desert, 68
De León, Jason, 52, 96–97, 111, 120, 127
Deleuze, Gilles, 7, 10, 25, 138
de Oñate, Juan, 40
deserts
  agency, 10, 161, 163
  apocalypse, 145
  Chihuahuan Desert, 11, 76, 96, 103, 112, 114, 121–22, 127, 129–30, 152
  entanglements, 11, 82, 103
  existences, 19
  futures, 162
  hauntology, 12, 127, 120, 162
  lawlessness, 88
  Mojave Desert, 11, 36, 55
  Painted Desert, 132, 127
  placemaking, 13, 131–32, 148, 156, 158, 163
  Sonoran Desert, 11–12, 31–32, 36, 93, 95, 103, 106–7, 109, 120, 127, 129–30, 152
  thinking, 9
  utopia, 145
  vastness, 9, 109, 119, 121, 124
  as void, 6
  in world literature, 6

222

INDEX

Desert Black (Meché), 163
Desert Blood (Gaspar de Alba), 12, 101, 103–4, 111–14, 121–29
Desert Futures Collective, 19
Desert Imaginations (El Guabli), 163
Desert in Modern Literature and Philosophy, The (Tynan), 18, 24
Desert Reader, The: A Literary Companion (McNamee), 14
Desert Reader, The (Wild), 14
Desert Solitaire (Abbey), 9, 55, 144
desertification, 65
  anti-desertification, 65
Deserts Are Not Empty (Henni), 19, 163
Desertscapes in the Global South and Beyond (Shekhawat, Alex, and Rangarajan), 19
Devil's Highway, 106–8, 115, 127
  book (Urrea), 12, 95, 101, 103–12, 115–17, 120, 124, 126–29
diaspora, 50
  African, 17
Diaz, Natalie, 11, 27–28, 35–37
Diehl, Travis, 156
Dirty Wars (Beck), 80
disease, 40, 45, 155, 162
  cancer, 129, 162
  plague, 45
    heliotropic plague, 45
  tuberculosis, 129
  tumors, 129
distortion, 10, 34, 57, 101, 116, 131, 133, 160
  desert, 4, 7, 9–10, 19, 25–29, 32, 34–35, 38, 41–42, 46, 55, 57–58, 61, 64–66, 69, 72, 76, 99, 101, 104–5, 109, 111, 113–14, 129, 131–33, 136, 140, 145, 150–51, 158, 160–62, 164
  of bodies, 36
  of distortion, 10
  in music, 27
  in poetry, 27

spatiotemporal, 48
double discrimination, 52
downwinder communities, 162
drags, 107
drug mules. *See under* cartels
drug trade, 89
drugs
  cocaine, 88, 118
  diet pills, 118
  ephedra, 118
  fat-burners, 118
Dune (film), 19, 145
dwelling, 12, 27, 137

Earth (planet), 6, 18, 56–57, 59, 136–37, 141, 158, 161
Earthrise (photo), 57–58
Eastwood, Clint, 73
ecocriticism 11, 13, 14, 25–26, 41, 64, 66
  material ecocriticism, 25–26
ecological crisis, 10, 13, 18
1883 (TV series), 71
elemental desert, 63, 82, 109, 118, 124
elemental immediacy, 11, 41, 59, 60, 61, 64, 67, 113, 117, 119, 136
El Guabli, Brahim, 163
El Paso Strong, 160
embodiment, 4, 50, 65, 101, 116, 122, 133–34, 140, 160
  embodied experiences, 13, 127, 134, 136, 143, 148
  embodied practices, 3, 155
  embodied relationships with land, 11
  embodiment of distortion, 57, 116, 133, 136
emergence, 29, 32, 39, 41, 59–60, 103, 106, 147
emergency, 10, 85, 97
environment, 17, 68, 120, 128, 150
  environmental futures, 28, 38, 164
  environmental humanities, 10, 13, 15, 25–26

INDEX

environmental racism, 8
erotics of landscape, 66
eruption, 12, 27, 59–60, 64
esparza, rafa, 13, 131–32, 145–51, 153, 155–56, 158
Esparza, Ramón, 145–46
Estrucuyu, 33–34
Executive Order 9066, 162
exoticism, 6, 24, 33, 55, 65
exploitation
    of authority, 86, 101, 115, 121
    of desert places, 83, 86, 127
    of environmental resources, 33
    of female workers, 102, 122–23
    of Indigenous people, 24
    of labor, 102, 122, 127, 160–62
    of land, 8
    of US-Mexico border area, 84, 102
extermination, 22–23, 47
extra-corporal histories, 46

factories. *See maquiladoras*
Fahler, Timo, 149
familiarity, 30, 65, 68
    familiarization, 65, 101, 134, 140
        defamiliarization, 72, 83, 98, 101, 109, 119, 134, 140, 147–48
        refamiliarization, 140, 148
Fargo (film), 71
fauna, 8, 66, 118. *See also* animals
FBI. *See under* US federal agencies
felt experience, 4, 19, 134
felt intensities 10, 28, 119, 138
femicide. See *feminicidios*
feminicidios, 12, 111, 114, 121, 123–24, 126
fertility, 13
Figure / Ground: Beyond the White Field (artwork by esparza), 147–51
filibusters, 42–43, 47, 59, 62
Flagstaff, Arizona, 4, 132, 142
flora, 8, 31, 66, 118. *See also* plants
Flores, Marco Antonio, 155

folklore, 26
Ford, John, 15, 67, 73
Fort Huachuca, 162
Forty Niners, 44–45
freedom, 35, 109
Frontier Thesis, 105
Fujikane, Candace, 38
Furiosa: A Mad Max Saga (film), 19
futures, 17–18, 22, 28, 35, 37–38, 55, 61, 64, 69, 101, 122, 140, 144, 146, 148, 156, 162, 164
futurity, 17, 32, 160

Gadsden Purchase, 49, 105
gallery spaces, 146–48, 151
    John Eckel Foundation Gallery, 147
"Ganzfelds" (Turrell), 132, 135
García, María, 149
Gardens in the Dunes (Silko), 16, 34
Gaspar de Alba, Alicia, 12, 101, 103, 111–13, 115, 121–22, 124–29
genocide, 22–23, 47
geology, 9, 58, 137
    geologic formations, 8, 34, 141
        Arches National Park, 8
        Chaco Canyon, 142
        Monument Valley, 8, 73
    geologic processes, 56, 58
    geologic time, 11, 35, 41, 55–57, 59, 64, 82, 137
Getting Over the Color Green (Slovic), 14
Glanton Gang, 42, 44, 51, 53–54, 62
global warming. *See* climate change
going green, 13
    green exceptionalism, 16
    green exclusivism, 16
    green marketing, 14
    greenwashing, 14
Gómez, Myrriah, 19
Govan, Michael, 133
Griffith Observatory, 137
Guattari, Félix, 7, 10, 25, 138

INDEX

Guggenheim Fellowship, 132, 140
guías, 107–9, 118–19
Gulf of Mexico, 49–50
Guzmán, Alicia Inez, 148

haecceity, 138–39, 143
Haraway, Donna, 56, 58, 65, 145
heat. *See under* weather and natural phenomena
heat death (hyperthermia), 116–17
helicopters, 12, 76–77, 80, 83, 103–4
Hell or High Water (film), 71
Henni, Samia, 163
Hernández, Maximilliano, 90, 93, 98
Hernández, Sebastián, 153–54, *154*
Hero Brothers, 33
Hidalgo Processing Center, 151
hierarchy of power, 12, 83, 86, 88–90, 93–94, 96–98, 107, 114, 122, 126
High Desert (film), 19
historical erasure, 43, 120, 144
histories, 6–7, 10, 17–19, 24, 32–33, 35, 39, 42–47, 54–55, 58, 61, 64, 122, 144, 146–47, 156, 162–63
history, 26, 39, 42–43, 52, 147
   colonial, 65
   cultural, 15
   Desert Southwest, 156
   History (capital H), 39–44, 55
   human, 57
   Mexican, 54
   migrant, 95
   US, 45
   US-Mexico borderlands, 156
   Western, 63
homesickness, 6, 72
horizon, the, 4, 8, 12, 54, 59, 76–77, 82, 128, 138, 140
horizontality, 12, 54, 73, 76–77, 80, 82–83, 85, 94–95, 98, 101, 104, 106–9, 111–12, 115–16, 119, 122, 127, 129–30
   horizontal storytelling, 111

Hosbey, Justin, 17
human agency, 25, 57
   inhuman, 26
   more-than-human, 26
   nonhuman, 11, 25–26, 41, 54, 59, 64, 67, 144
   other than human, 22, 26
human exceptionalism, 57
human rights, 97
human, the, 19, 28, 30, 65, 68, 118, 143
   decentering the human, 64–65, 68–69
   decentralizing the human, 144
hyperobject, 12, 129
   hyperobjective desert, 35, 73
hyperthermia. *See* heat death

ICE. *See under* US federal agencies
illegal immigration, 49, 94, 97, 102, 106–7
imagination, 8, 18, 35, 59, 65, 105
   cultural, 65
   human, 6
   environmental, 8
   national, 15, 109
indigeneity
   false portrayals of Indigenous people, 23
   vanishing Indian myth, 23, 63–64, 140
Indigenous cosmologies, 11, 26, 35
Indigenous creation stories, 23, 32
Indigenous creativity, 24
Indigenous economies of abundance, 38
Indigenous epistemologies, 11
Indigenous groups
   Akimel O'odham, 11, 27
   Aztec, 40, 105, 149
   Comanche, 162
   Diné, 63–64, 141, 162
   Gila River Indian Tribe. *See* Akimel O'odham
   Hopi, 141–42

225

INDEX

Kiowa, 162
Laguna Pueblo, 11, 27, 32, 34–35
Lipan Apache, 52, 162
Maidu, 44
Maya, 105, 149
Mescalero Apache, 162
Mojave, 11, 27, 35. *See also* languages: Mojave language
Navajo. *See* Diné
Tohono O'odham, 11, 27, 30–31, 35. *See also* languages: O'odham language
Warm Springs Apache, 162
Indigenous histories, 24
Indigenous joy, 24
Indigenous logic, 21, 38, 156
Indigenous stories, 26
Indigenous Studies, 10–11, 26, 38, 63
kidnapping of Indigenous youth, 23
industrialization, 102. *See also* American Industrial Revolution
hyper-industrialization, 22
injustice, 53, 129
    environmental, 8, 22, 69, 126, 140
instability, 66
interconnectedness, 4, 36, 68
intergenerational temporalities, 61
intergenerational trauma, 24
internment camps, 63, 80, 162
interstate highways, 55
Invention of the American Desert, The (Massey and Nisbet), 19, 163
Iovino, Serenella, 25, 32

Jiménez, Joe, 147
Jiroutová Kynčlová, Tereza, 122
justice, 12, 20, 35, 72, 84–85, 87, 114
    environmental, 17
    vigilante, 43, 106

Kimmerer, Robin Wall, 26, 28
Kingdom of France, 48

Kingdom of Spain, 48
kinship, 17, 28, 37, 68, 145
Koch, Natalie, 163
Kochininako (Yellow-Woman), 33
Kratz, Veronika, 65
Krupp, Ed, 137–38, 143

land ethic, 15
Land of Open Graves, The (De León), 120
land stewardship, 18
landscapes, 6–8, 15, 18, 22, 24, 30, 32, 42, 45–46, 51, 55, 59–62, 64–65, 67–68, 77, 98, 108–9, 113, 127, 131, 140, 145, 151. *See also* erotics of landscape; storied landscapes
language, 4, 7, 27–28, 31, 37, 64–66, 68, 102, 161
    material language, 68
languages, 10, 31, 38, 42, 53, 117
    English, 31, 34
    Mojave, 36–37
    O'odham, 31
    Spanish, 105
Larsen, Nella, 52
    Latinx Studies, 10
law enforcement, 12, 72, 84, 86, 91. *See also* US federal agencies: Border Patrol
legality, 64, 98
LeMenager, Stephanie, 13
Leone, Sergio, 67, 73
Leopold, Aldo, 15
Lewis, Meriwether, 42
Lim, Julian, 104
literary theory, 10
lithic, the, 10, 58
local intimacies, 164
    Lomas de Poleo, 113, 125
Los Alamos, 80
Los Angeles Times, 155
Lynch, Tom, 14

Macías, Dorian Ulises López, 147

INDEX

Mad Max: Fury Road (film), 67
magnetism of the north, 104
Manhattan Project, 19
Manifest Destiny, 44–45, 105
maquiladoras, 12, 102, 111–12, 114–15, 121–23, 125, 127–28
Marfa, Texas, 149–50
Marshall, James, 44
MASS MoCA, 151
Massey, Doreen, 9, 34
Massey, Lyle, 163
materialist turn, 25
matsutake mushrooms, 10
McCarthy, Cormac, 11, 24, 41–46, 52–53, 60, 62, 66–67
McNamee, Gregory, 14
Meché, Brittany, 163
Medellín, Colombia, 88–89
Meissner, Doris, 97
Mentz, Steve, 15–16
Merleau-Ponty, Maurice, 134
mestizaje, 17, 50
method, 6, 55, 65, 146
methodology, 35, 39, 158, 164
Mexican Cession, 11, 40
Mexican Texas, 48–49
Michno, Chris, 142
Migra, La, 110, 117
migration, 96, 102
    anti-immigrant rhetoric, 160
    mass migration, 45
    migrant deaths, 12, 96, 103
    migrants, 12, 44, 50, 84, 93–98, 102, 106–7, 109–11, 118, 120–22, 124, 127, 129, 151, 162
militarization, 7, 81, 88, 127
military, 49–50, 80, 82, 88
militias, 22
mind/body binary, 7
mining, 19, 38, 56, 140
    uranium mining, 7
mirage, 29, 60

Misanthropocene, 145
Mitchell, Lee Clark, 54, 62, 66
modernist literature, 24
modernity, 25, 63
modern literature. *See* contemporary literature
Montana, Star, 149
moon, 62, 66–67, 135, 149
    moonlight, 136
morality, 85, 88, 98, 142, 155
Morton, Timothy, 10
mountains, 7–8, 15–16, 30–31, 44–45, 54, 58, 60, 66–67, 72–73, 77, 82, 85, 108, 110–11, 117, 137, 140
    Black Mountains, 31
    Franklin Mountains, 113
    Growler Mountains, 108–9, 116–17
    Mount Cristo Rey, 113, 125
    Rocky Mountains, 140
    Santa Catalina Mountains, 30–31
    Sierra Nevada, 162
multiplicity, 7, 9, 14–15, 23, 30, 32, 34, 37–38, 41, 50, 56, 58, 65, 69, 80, 83, 99, 106–7, 111, 131, 140, 162

Nabhan, Gary, 163
Nadel, Leonard, 151
NAFTA, 12, 96, 102, 121, 126
namelessness, 66, 110
naming, 31, 56–57, 64, 66–67
narcotrafficking, 72
narcoviolence, 86, 88, 93, 95, 97–98. *See also* narcotrafficking
narrative, 9, 11, 22–25, 27, 33–35, 39, 44–46, 49–51, 53–54, 65, 107, 122, 145, 151, 162–63. *See also* sites of narrativity
National Defense Areas, 50
national security, 85, 97, 103
natural resources. *See also* mining; oil drilling
    air, 29, 47, 59, 116, 125, 128, 132, 138

INDEX

ash, 136
basalt, 136
cinder, 136, 139, 143
coal, 56
earth, 38, 59, 138, 141, 146–50, 153, 155–56, 158
    extraction of, 11, 22, 56, 160, 162
limestone, 113, 136
marble, 136–37
metals
    antimony, 126
    cadmium, 126
    copper, 125–26
    gold, 22, 44–45, 105
    lead, 126, 129
    silver, 22
    uranium, 162
    zinc, 124, 126
oil, 56
quartz, 144
rocks, 34, 56, 60, 68, 109, 113, 117, 137
    dirt, 4, 16, 59, 81, 117, 147–48, 155
    dust, 4, 64, 106, 148, 155
    sand, 7, 16, 18, 59–60, 62, 65–67, 104, 107, 109, 113, 116–17
    soil, 117, 125, 146–47, 149
    water, 7, 25, 35, 38, 42, 47–48, 56, 59–60, 66, 95, 107, 112, 116–17, 119, 138, 146
nature, 13–15, 96, 120, 132, 135
    culture and, 7, 15, 68, 82
    nature writing, 6, 9
Nature of Desert Nature, The (Nabhan), 163
nearness, 104, 111, 115. *See also* proximity
necroviolence, 52–53, 89, 120, 127
neo-Westerns, 73
Nevada Test Site, 80
New Desert Reader, The (Wild), 14
new materialisms, 10
1923 (TV series), 71
1917 (TV series), 71
Nisbet, James, 163

noble savages trope, 23
No Country for Old Men (film), 71
non-naming, 67
Nope (film), 19
Norteño people, 105
North Star, 133
NPR, 129
nuclear bombing, 7, 141
    nuclear bomb testing, 11, 19, 80, 162
Nuclear Nuevo México (Gómez), 19

Object Lessons series, 15
ocean, 15
    Pacific, 49, 141
oil drilling, 7
O'Keeffe, Georgia, 15
Operation Blockade. *See* Operation Hold the Line
Operation Gatekeeper, 96, 102
Operation Hold the Line 96, 102
Operation Safeguard, 96, 103
Operation Rio Grande, 103
Oppenheimer (film), 19
Oppermann, Serpil, 25, 32
optical democracy, 68–69
oral history, 33
oral storytelling, 18
oral tradition, 144
Ore-Giron, Eamon, 147, 149
orientation, 21, 28, 31, 34, 36, 42, 55, 58, 110, 113, 137
    disorientation, 3–4, 28–29, 42, 55, 57–58, 64, 66, 69, 73, 76, 98, 105, 110, 113, 116, 119, 132, 137, 140, 161
    reorientation, 28–29, 34, 42, 45, 55, 57–58, 64, 66, 69, 76–77, 105, 113, 119, 137, 140, 150, 161
Original Instructions, 28
Ortiz, Victor, 104
Other Side, The (newspaper), 142
outlaws, 46, 105

INDEX

"Ozymandias," 55–56

palimpsests, 7, 11, 41, 50, 61, 66
Paoletta, Kyle, 163
Parable of the Sower (Butler), 145
Passageways (Turrell), 142
Passing (Larsen), 52
Patel, Raj, 145
Pearl Harbor, 80
pennies, 124–25
Perceptual Cells, 132
performativity, 150
personhood, 30
Petrified Forest, 58
phenomenology, 9, 12, 35, 57, 116, 133–34, 139
   desert, 13, 135–39, 143, 145, 158, 162
   of light, 135–36
   nonhuman, 30
Phenomenology of Perception (Merleau-Ponty), 134
place through time, 41, 44–45, 55
"Place Where Clouds Are Formed, The," 29, 31–32
Plantationocene, 56
plants, 21, 32, 64, 67, 117, 137, 139
   cactuses, 7, 30
      saguaro, 6, 8, 30–31, 118
   creosote, 8, 116
   cottonwood trees, 36
   Joshua trees, 8
   juniper trees, 144
   ocotillo, 8
plasticity, 34
poetry 27, 65
   Indigenous women poets, 11, 26–28, 33, 36–37, 55
Policía Federal, 80
politics, 162
   border politics, 49, 98
   geopolitics, 12, 38, 47, 82, 99, 102, 112, 160

identity politics, 52
necropolitics, 53, 127
Polk, James K., 44
polleros. See *guías*
pollos. See walkers
pollution, 8, 38, 125, 127, 129
polyphony, 7
polytemporal perception, 41, 55
population density, 80, 149, 160
Porras-Kim, Gala, 147
portraiture, 149, 151, 153, 155
possibility, 7, 10, 19, 24, 27, 30–32, 34, 36–37, 41, 43, 50, 55, 68, 99, 107, 111, 113, 131, 134, 140, 145, 160, 162, 164
postapocalyptic literature and film, 7
Postcolonial Love Poem (Diaz), 35
posthumanism, 11
postmodern literature, 24
post-Westerns, 73
prepositions, 4, 10, 13, 34, 161
Prismatic Ecologies: Ecotheory Beyond Green (Cohen), 16
"Proclamation," 31–32
proximity, 54, 84, 96, 123, 128, 136
Pueblo Revival homes, 146

queerness, 13, 145–46, 151, 156
Quitobaquito Hills, 116

racial "passing," 52, 120
radiation exposure, 162
radical animism, 57–58, 65
   book (Deer), 57
Radiolab (podcast), 97
rainbow, 23–24
rastreos, 112, 114, 124–25
rattlesnakes, 35–37, 118
Reading Aridity in Western American Literature (Ach and Reger), 18
Red Dead Redemption (video game), 67
Reger, Gary, 18, 163
re-inscribing, 63

INDEX

relationality, 10, 21, 41, 50, 161
relationship-building, 13, 65, 146
rendition, 151
Reno, Janet, 96
Republic of Mexico, 39–40, 48–49
Republic of Texas, 48–49
"Revisiting Mestizaje Twenty Years Later," 50
Reyes, Silvestre, 96
rivers
    Colorado River, 36, 38
    Los Angeles River, 146
    Nueces River, 49
    Rio Grande, 40, 49, 113–14, 128
    Salt River, 38
Roane, J. T., 17
Roden Crater, 5, *134*
Roden Crater Project, 13, 132, 138, 142
Rodriguez, Ruben, 149
Roosevelt, Franklin D., 162
"Rumble" (song), 27

Saldaña-Portillo, María Josefina, 50
sand dunes, 8, 36
Sand, Water, Salt (Ach), 163
Santa Anna, Antonio López de, 49
scalping, 23, 42, 45, 47, 51–53
Scenes in America Deserta (Banham), 9
seascape, 15
Secure Fence Act of 2006, 103
Sekaquaptewa, Gene, 142
Shanks, Gwyneth, 155–56
Shaviro, Steven, 59, 62, 66, 68–69
Shelley, Percy Bysshe, 55–56
Sheridan, Taylor, 71
Shewry, Teresa, 13
Sicario, 12, 71–72, *73–75*, 76–77, *78–79*, 80–84, *81*, *83*, 86, 88–94, *92*, *94*, 97–99, 104, 114, 134
signcutters, 107–8
"Significance of the Frontier in American History, The," 105

Silko, Leslie Marmon, 11, 16, 27–28, 32–34, 37
Simpson, Leanne, 35
sites of narrativity, 11, 25
sky myopia, 133
Skyspaces, 132
    "Air Apparent," 139
    "Night Raiment 2024," 141
    "Skyspace," 141
    "Skyspace Espíritu de Luz," 141
    "Ta Khut Skyspace," 141
Skystone Foundation, 141
Slovic, Scott, 14–15
slow violence, 23–24
smell
    of adobe, 148, 157–58
    of brown, 16
    of creosote, 72
    of death, 127–29
    of diesel, 128
    of sewer, 128
Smelter Town, 125, 129
Smith, Stella Peshlakai, 63–64
"Snake-Light," 35–36
Sonora State Police, 90, 92
sound
    of breathing, 29
    of desert places, 67
    of freight trains, 159
    of gunshots, 54
    of helicopters, 77
    of planets, 138
    of rock and roll, 27
    in *Sicario*, 77, 80
    of wolves, 66
Southern Pacific Railroad, 162
Southwest, 18, 22, 41, 44, 52, 56, 140, 147
    American, 49, 55, 109, 162
    Desert, 8, 14, 18, 22, 25, 40–41, 48, 64, 127, 129, 132, 140, 146, 152, 156, 160
    Southwest Borderlands, 43, 76, 103

INDEX

Southwest in American Literature and Art (Teague), 14
space of exception, 97–98, 101
Spanish missions, 40
Spanish Texas, 48
spatiotemporality, 11, 31, 48, 61, 119, 137
Stagecoach (film), 73
Staring at the Sun, 147, 150–51, *157*
state of exception, 85–86, 97
State of the Union, 44
Stengers, Isabelle, 66
stewardship, 12, 17. *See also* land stewardship
Stewart, Kathleen, 131, 135–37
storied deserts, 10–11, 29, 32, 34–38, 41–42, 54, 61, 77, 95, 99, 107, 112, 122, 127, 150, 159, 162
Storied Deserts: Reimagining Global Arid Lands (Osuna and Tynan), 18, 162
storied landscapes, 45, 57
storied matter, 18, 25–26, 32, 36, 149
Storyteller (Silko), 33
suburban sprawl, 77
Sullivan, Marianne, 125
surveillance, 7, 48, 81, 83, 127
    technology, 12, 72, 76, 103
        aerial footage, 12, 73, 76–77, 80–82, 98
        drones, 12, 72, 82
        infrared cameras, 72, 83, 98
        night vision, 82, 98, 103
        satellites, 12, 72, 76–77, 80, 82, 95
survival, 101, 106, 108, 118–19
    survivability, 17
    survivance, 24
sustainability, 12–13, 26
Sutter, John, 44
Symbiocene, 56

TallBear, Kim, 28
Tamez, Margo, 52
Teague, David W., 14

temporal uncertainty, 46
terrestrial, the, 85, 132–33, 135–38
Thesiger, Wilfred, 55
    spectral connections with land, 13
    spectral deserts, 63–64, 127
    spectral geographies, 61, 64
    spectral writing, 62
    spectrality, 61–64, 127
Thousand Plateaus, A (Deleuze and Guattari), 7, 138
tierra, 147
Tierra. Sangre. Oro. (art exhibition), 147, 149–51
time through place, 41, 55, 61, 64
timefulness, 58, 61, 65
topography, 59, 73
Transcontinental Railroad, 162
trauma, 13, 127, 151
    intergenerational, 24, 48, 129
travel writing, 24, 55, 109
Treaty of Guadalupe Hidalgo, 11, 39–40, 43
Trujillo, Simón Ventura, 50
Tsing, Anna, 10
Turner, Frederick Jackson, 105
Turrell, James, 13, 131–43, 145–46, 148, 156, 158
Twin Brothers, 33
Tynan, Aidan, 18, 24–25, 42, 162

uncertain times. *See* temporal uncertainty
United Nations, 65
unsettling, 10, 21, 42, 61, 66, 161
urbanization, 56
Urrea, Luis Alberto, 12, 95, 101, 103–11, 115–20, 126–28
US federal agencies, 12, 72, 84, 88–89, 93–94. *See also* La Migra
    Air Force, 76, 87
    Army, 82, 162
    Border Patrol, 77, 94–96, 102–3, 106–7, 111, 113, 115–16,

INDEX

120–21, 124, 126
Centers for Disease Control and Protection, 129
Customs and Border Protection, 94
Department of Defense, 71, 85
Federal Bureau of Investigation, 71, 86, 93, 98
Immigration and Customs Enforcement, 93–94
Immigration and Naturalization Service, 97
National Park Service, 55, 63
US South, 17

Valaskakis, Gail Guthrie, 23–24
Vázquez de Coronado, Francisco, 40
Veracruz, Mexico, 12, 109
verbs, 161
    verbal communication, 146
    verbal storytelling, 26
verticality, 12, 72–73, 76–77, 80, 82–83, 85, 98, 104, 111, 113, 116, 129, 162. *See also* aesthetics: vertical aesthetics
    vertical axis of power, 84
    vertical hierarchy of power, 77, 89–90, 93, 95, 98, 107, 134
    vertical storytelling, 99
vigilante justice, 43, 106
vigilantes. *See* outlaws
Villeneuve, Denis, 12, 19, 71, 82
violence, 42–43, 52–54, 62, 86–90, 98, 101, 111, 126–27, 129–30, 160. *See also feminicidios*, narcoviolence, necroviolence
    cartel, 71, 114, 121
    colonial, 13, 23–24, 45, 48, 51, 53, 62, 64, 127, 140
    domestic, 123
    economy of, 51
    gang, 27, 53–54, 62
    gendered, 12–13, 102, 111, 114, 120–24, 127, 140
    human, 62, 127
    immediate, 23–24
    nonhuman, 127
    political, 27
    racialized, 13, 51, 53, 120, 127, 140, 151–52, 160
    sexual, 111, 123
    state, 128
    systemic, 64, 101
vitality, 14
volcanoes, 4, 61, 133, 136–38, 141, 143
    Roden Crater, 4, *5*, 9, 133, *134*, 135–39, 141–45, 156, 158
    Sunset Crater Volcano National Monument, 143
Voyles, Traci Brynne, 8, 33, 140

walkers, 95, 104, 106–11, 116–19, 128
wars
    American Revolution, 42
    US Civil War, 46
    French and Indian War, 42
    US War with Mexico, 22, 39–41, 47–49
    War on Drugs, 81, 89, 93
    World War II, 80, 162
Washington Post, The, 63
waste disposal, 11
wasteland, 8, 22, 24, 32–33, 35, 42, 145, 160–61. *See also* aesthetics: wasteland aesthetics; wilderness
wastelanding, 8, 140
Water Knife, The (Abbey), 145
… we are the mountain (artwork by esparza), 154–55
weather and natural phenomena, 6, 133. *See also* atmospheric attunements; climate change; heat death
    aridity, 6, 15, 17–19, 22, 25, 30, 55, 57, 59, 65, 118–19, 127, 131, 160, 164
    atmosphere, 3, 17, 29, 42, 56, 59–60, 67, 72, 80, 98, 128, 131, 133,

INDEX

135–37, 139, 143, 145, 147–48, 158, 160
biosphere, 56
climate, 11, 58, 139, 146–48
clouds, 5, 29–30, 67, 72, 82, 139
cold, 4, 6, 11, 57, 67, 116, 133, 139, 151
condensation, 29
daylight, 139
droughts, 11
dust devils, 59–60
eclipses, 133
equinoxes, 133
erosion, 56
flash floods, 12, 60
forest fires, 12
haboobs, 7
heat, 6–7, 9–11, 29–30, 35, 41, 57, 59–60, 84, 108–10, 113, 115–19, 124, 133, 139
humidity, 146
hydrosphere, 56
light, 3–4, 9–10, 17, 23–24, 29–30, 41, 57, 59–60, 68–69, 82, 109, 113, 115, 117–19, 132–33, 135–38, 143, 158
   moonlight 135
   starlight 29, 136
   sunlight, 115, 117–18, 136
lightning, 12, 37, 60, 68
lithosphere, 56
monsoons, 8, 72, 82
moon 62, 66, 57, 135, 149
natural disasters, 11
rain, 30, 42, 59, 67, 72, 139
shadow, 4, 73, 77, 82, 132, 135, 138
snow, 67, 151
sun, 4, 6–7, 60, 62, 67, 117, 135, 137, 139, 146, 149, 160
   sunrise, 133, 137–38, 142
   sunset, 7, 82, 133
stars, 29, 64, 67–68, 110, 136, 143, 139
wind, 4, 12, 30, 36, 41, 59–60, 62, 67, 82, 124, 139

Wellton 26, 105–9, 111, 115–16, 118–20, 127
Westworld (film), 67, 76
Where Clouds Are Formed (Zepeda), 29
whiteness
   of institutional spaces, 147
   of mainstream environmentalism, 15
whitewashing, 24
Whitney Biennial, 147–48
Wild, Peter, 14
Wild West trope, 12, 88. *See also* aesthetics: Wild West aesthetics
wilderness, 6, 15, 25, 46–47, 67. *See also* wasteland
Wild, Weird, West: Essays on Arid America (Reger), 163
Wind River (film), 71
wonder, 19–20, 32, 37, 66
world-building 64, 66
Wray, Link, 27
Wright, Melissa, 122
Wupatki National Monument, 63–64, 142
Wylie, John, 61–62

xenophobia, 160
Xerophilia: Ecocritical Explorations in Southwestern Literature (Lynch), 14

Yash'ka, 34
Yellowstone (TV series), 71
Yuma 14. *See* Wellton 26

Zepeda, Ofelia, 11, 27–32, 34, 36–37

ABOUT THE AUTHOR

Celina Osuna is a scholar and an artist. She is an assistant professor of English at the University of Texas at El Paso, and her research, with an emphasis on Indigenous and Latinx Environmentalisms, explores aesthetics of desert places in literature, art, and film and their impacts on cultural imagination and geopolitical relationships to land. She is co-editor of *Storied Deserts: Reimagining Global Arid Lands* (2024).
(AUTHOR PHOTO BY FARSH FARROKHNIA)

www.ingramcontent.com/pod-product-compliance
Lightning Source LLC
Chambersburg PA
CBHW030540230426
43665CB00010B/966